PrimeFaces Beginner's Guide

Get your JSF-based projects up and running with this
easy-to-implement guide on PrimeFaces

K. Siva Prasad Reddy

[PACKT] open source*
PUBLISHING   community experience distilled

BIRMINGHAM - MUMBAI

PrimeFaces Beginner's Guide

First published: November 2013

Production Reference: 1181113

Published by Packt Publishing Ltd.
Livery Place
35 Livery Street
Birmingham B3 2PB, UK.

ISBN 978-1-78328-069-8

www.packtpub.com

Cover Image by Prashant Timappa Shetty (sparkling.spectrum.123@gmail.com)

Credits

Author

K. Siva Prasad Reddy

Reviewers

Thomas Andraschko

Mauricio Fenoglio

Sudheer Jonna

Nilesh Namdeo Mali

Acquisition Editor

Joanne Fitzpatrick

Lead Technical Editor

Ritika Dewani

Technical Editors

Gauri Dasgupta

Jalasha D'costa

Dipika Gaonkar

Siddhi Rane

Project Coordinator

Kranti Berde

Proofreaders

Julie Jackson

Joanna McMahon

Indexer

Tejal R. Soni

Graphics

Sheetal Aute

Production Coordinator

Nilesh R. Mohite

Cover Work

Nilesh R. Mohite

About the Author

K. Siva Prasad Reddy is a Senior Software Engineer living in Hyderabad, India, and having more than seven years of experience in developing enterprise applications with Java and JavaEE technologies. Siva is a Sun Certified Java Programmer and has a lot of experience in server-side technologies such as Java, JavaEE, Spring, Hibernate, MyBatis, JSF, PrimeFaces, and WebServices (SOAP/REST). Siva is also the author of *Java Persistence with MyBatis 3*, *Packt Publishing*.

Siva normally shares the knowledge he has acquired on his blog at www.sivalabs.in. If you want to find out more about his work, you can follow him on Twitter (@sivalabs) and GitHub (https://github.com/sivaprasadreddy).

I would like to thank my wife Neha, for all the support she gave me at every step of the process; without her this wouldn't have been possible.

Also, thanks to my parents and sister for their moral support in completing this dream.

About the Reviewers

Thomas Andraschko was born in 1989 in Bavaria, Germany. He has over seven years of expertise in software development, wherein his first JSF experience was in 2008 with Apache MyFaces 1.2 and Apache MyFaces Trinidad.

Over the years, he has managed various projects, with other technologies as well, such as JSP, Servlets, Spring MVC, .NET WinForms, and even Ninject and ASP.NET.

Thomas is the founder of PrimeFaces Extensions, an Apache OpenWebBeans committer since 2012, and a PrimeFaces core developer and committer since 2013.

Thomas normally shares his knowledge on his blog at http://tandraschko.blogspot.de.

Thomas is currently employed at the Institut für Vorsorge und Finanzplanung GmbH as Software Architect.

This is the first time he has been involved in the publication of a book.

> I would like to thank my friends Çağatay Çivici and Oleg Varaksin for their work on PrimeFaces and PrimeFaces Extensions, and their great teamwork in the last few years.
>
> Also, a big thanks to all other PrimeFaces Extensions team members, the Apache MyFaces community, and the Apache OpenWebBeans community.

Mauricio Fenoglio is a Senior Software Engineer and Architect living in Montevideo, Uruguay. He is a Computer Engineering graduate who studied Informatics at The University of the Republic.

He has over five years of experience developing enterprise web applications, especially using JEE.

He is also an active contributor to the open source project PrimeFaces Extensions. He enjoys using JSF, PrimeFaces, and the most up-to-date web technologies.

When he isn't coding, he likes to hang out with his girlfriend and practice kitesurfing at the nearest beach.

This is the first time he has been involved in the publication of a book as a reviewer.

Sudheer Jonna was born in Andhra Pradesh, India, in 1987. Currently, he is working as a software developer in Chennai, India. He has completed his Master's degree in Computer Applications from JNTU University. His main occupation in the last three years has been building web applications based on Struts, JSF, Spring, jQuery, and JPA—all relating to the banking and financial securities domain.

He is an experienced JSF expert and has been working with the component library of PrimeFaces since 2011. He is also a well-known, recognized member of the PrimeFaces community and project member of the PrimeFaces Extensions project—additional JSF 2 components for PrimeFaces.

Besides these mentioned technologies, he writes technical articles, online training, book reviews (for Packt Publishing), provides suggestions through forums and blogs, and involves himself in optimizing performance in web applications during his free time. He is interested in the R&D of various popular J2EE frameworks and many other technologies.

Sudheer can be contacted on his Gmail account, `sudheer.jonna@gmail.com`, where he also shares his knowledge.

Nilesh Namdeo Mali has completed his B.E. in Computer Engineering from Pune University. He has more than five years of experience in software development, especially in J2EE, JSF, and PrimeFaces. He is also committer to the PrimeFaces Extensions open source project.

I would like to thank my family for supporting me.

www.PacktPub.com

Support files, eBooks, discount offers and more

You might want to visit www.PacktPub.com for support files and downloads related to your book.

Did you know that Packt offers eBook versions of every book published, with PDF and ePub files available? You can upgrade to the eBook version at www.PacktPub.com and as a print book customer, you are entitled to a discount on the eBook copy. Get in touch with us at service@packtpub.com for more details.

At www.PacktPub.com, you can also read a collection of free technical articles, sign up for a range of free newsletters and receive exclusive discounts and offers on Packt books and eBooks.

http://PacktLib.PacktPub.com

Do you need instant solutions to your IT questions? PacktLib is Packt's online digital book library. Here, you can access, read and search across Packt's entire library of books.

Why Subscribe?

- ◆ Fully searchable across every book published by Packt
- ◆ Copy and paste, print and bookmark content
- ◆ On demand and accessible via web browser

Free Access for Packt account holders

If you have an account with Packt at www.PacktPub.com, you can use this to access PacktLib today and view nine entirely free books. Simply use your login credentials for immediate access.

Table of Contents

Preface

PrimeFaces is a leading open source user interface (UI) component library for Java Server Faces (JSF)-based web applications. PrimeFaces provides more than 100 UI components with a rich look and feel and theming support. At the time of writing this book, the latest version of PrimeFaces is 4.0, which works well with JSF 2.x.

PrimeFaces Beginner's Guide will take you through the process of installing, configuring, and using PrimeFaces in your JSF-based web applications. Usage of PrimeFaces components are explained through simple and practical examples with step-by-step instructions. By the end of the book, you will have a hands-on experience on how to use PrimeFaces effectively.

What this book covers

Chapter 1, Introduction to PrimeFaces, introduces PrimeFaces, along with details on how to install and configure it by creating a simple Hello World application. This chapter also provides an overview of various PrimeFaces features, such as AJAX support, Partial Page Rendering (PPR), and explains Poll and Remote Command components, which come in very handy at times.

Chapter 2, Introducing Sample Application TechBuzz, provides an overview of the sample application TechBuzz, which we are going to build incrementally throughout the book, and explains what PrimeFaces components will be used for various requirements. This chapter also provides an overall picture on setting up the development environment with all the required software, such as JDK, IDE, database, and so on.

Chapter 3, Using PrimeFaces Common Utility Components, introduces various commonly used utility components provided by PrimeFaces, such as Growl, Tooltip, BlockUI, NotificationBar, and so on. This chapter also explains new features introduced in PrimeFaces 4.0, such as Fragment, Sticky, Search Expression Framework, and Dialog Framework.

Chapter 4, Introducing PrimeFaces Client Side Validation Framework, covers PrimeFaces Client Side Validations (CSV) Framework in detail, explaining how to configure and enable client-side validations, integrating the CSV framework with the Bean Validation API, and extending the CSV framework to support custom JSF Validators/-Converters and custom Bean Validation Annotations.

Chapter 5, Introducing Text Input Components, covers various input text components such as InputText, InputTextArea, Password, InputMask, Inplace Editor, and Rich Text Editor. This chapter also explains the AutoComplete component in detail, explaining how to use it with POJO support, multiple item selection, and so on.

Chapter 6, Working with Selection Input Components, covers several PrimeFaces selection components, including SelectOneMenu, SelectManyMenu, SelectOneRadio, SelectManyCheckbox, PickList, MultiSelectListbox, and so on.

Chapter 7, Introducing Advanced Input Components, explains how to work with advanced input components, such as Calendar, Rating, Spinner, and Slider. Readers will also learn about uploading and downloading files using FileUpload and FileDownload components. This chapter also explains how to prevent span and bots using CAPTCHA validation.

Chapter 8, Working with Data Components, covers various data components, such as DataList, DataGrid, and explains DataTable features in depth, including pagination, sorting, filtering, row/cell editing, and so on. Readers will also learn about exporting DataTable data to Excel, PDF, and XML using the DataExporter component.

Chapter 9, Introducing Advanced Data Visualization Components, introduces advanced data visualization components, such as Carousel, TagCloud, and Schedule. Readers will also learn about displaying data in a Tree structure using Tree and TreeTable components.

Chapter 10, Working with Layout Components, explains how to create simple and complex layouts using Panel, PanelGrid, AccordionPanel, TabView, and Layout components, and describes various customization options. This chapter also covers creating workflow-style forms using the Wizard component and Portal-like Layouts using the Dashboard component.

Chapter 11, Introducing Navigation Components, explains creating different styles of menus using various navigation components, such as Menu, SlideMenu, TieredMenu, Menubar, MegaMenu, TabMenu, and Breadcrumb.

Chapter 12, Drawing Charts, covers how to visualize data in a graphical format using a variety of chart formats, such as Line, Bar, Pie, and Donut charts. This chapter also introduces how to render charts created by the JFreeChart API.

Chapter 13, Using PrimeFaces Themes, introduces how to use built-in themes provided by PrimeFaces and how to create custom themes using the online ThemeRoller tool. Readers will also learn about how to dynamically change themes using the ThemeSwitcher component. This chapter also gives a brief overview of various PrimeFaces sibling projects, such as PrimeFaces Extensions, PrimeUI, PrimeFaces Mobile, and PrimeFaces Push.

What you need for this book

You will need the following software to follow the examples:

- ◆ Java JDK 1.5+ (http://www.oracle.com/technetwork/java/javase/downloads/index.html)
- ◆ PrimeFaces latest version (http://www.primefaces.org/downloads.html)
- ◆ MySQL (http://www.mysql.com/) or any other relational database that has a JDBC driver
- ◆ Eclipse (http://www.eclipse.org) or any of your favorite Java IDE
- ◆ Apache Maven build tool (http://maven.apache.org/)
- ◆ Browser tools: as we are going to learn a lot more about UI design using the PrimeFaces component, it would be really helpful to have tools such as the FireBug plugin for Firefox or Chrome Developer Tools for the Google Chrome browser

Who this book is for

This book is for you if you would like to learn and use PrimeFaces for your JSF-based applications, and if you are looking for a practical guide with an easy-to–follow, step-by-step approach along with plenty of examples. Prerequisites required for this book are basic JSF and jQuery skills.

Conventions

In this book, you will find several headings appearing frequently.

To give clear instructions of how to complete a procedure or task, we use:

Time for action – heading

1. Action 1
2. Action 2
3. Action 3

Instructions often need some extra explanation so that they make sense, so they are followed with:

What just happened?

This heading explains the working of tasks or instructions that you have just completed.

You will also find a number of styles of text that distinguish between different kinds of information. Here are some examples of these styles, and an explanation of their meaning.

Code words in text, database table names, folder names, filenames, file extensions, pathnames, dummy URLs, user input, and Twitter handles are shown as follows: "We can disable AJAX submit by setting attribute `ajax="false"`."

A block of code is set as follows:

```
<h:panelGrid columns="2">
  <p:outputLabel value="UserName"/>
  <p:inputText value="#{userController.userName}"/>
  <p:outputLabel value="Password"/>
  <p:password value="#{userController.password}"/>
  <p:commandButton action="#{userController.login}" value="Login" />
</h:panelGrid>
```

When we wish to draw your attention to a particular part of a code block, the relevant lines or items are set in bold:

```
<h:panelGrid columns="2">
  <p:outputLabel value="UserName"/>
  <p:inputText value="#{userController.userName}"/>
  <p:outputLabel value="Password"/>
  <p:password value="#{userController.password}"/>
  <p:commandButton action="#{userController.login}" value="Login" />
</h:panelGrid>
```

Any command-line input or output is written as follows:

```
cd /ProgramData/Propeople
rm -r Drush
git clone --branch master http://git.drupal.org/project/drush.git
```

New terms and **important words** are shown in bold. Words that you see on the screen, in menus or dialog boxes for example, appear in the text like this: "On the **Select Destination Location** screen, click on **Next** to accept the default destination."

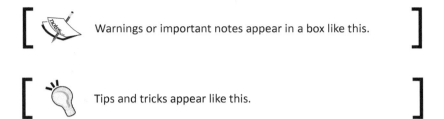

> Warnings or important notes appear in a box like this.

> Tips and tricks appear like this.

Reader feedback

Feedback from our readers is always welcome. Let us know what you think about this book—what you liked or may have disliked. Reader feedback is important for us to develop titles that you really get the most out of.

To send us general feedback, simply send an e-mail to feedback@packtpub.com, and mention the book title through the subject of your message.

If there is a topic that you have expertise in and you are interested in either writing or contributing to a book, see our author guide on www.packtpub.com/authors.

Customer support

Now that you are the proud owner of a Packt book, we have a number of things to help you to get the most from your purchase.

Downloading the example code

You can download the example code files for all Packt books you have purchased from your account at http://www.packtpub.com. If you purchased this book elsewhere, you can visit http://www.packtpub.com/support and register to have the files e-mailed directly to you.

Errata

Although we have taken every care to ensure the accuracy of our content, mistakes do happen. If you find a mistake in one of our books—maybe a mistake in the text or the code—we would be grateful if you would report this to us. By doing so, you can save other readers from frustration and help us improve subsequent versions of this book. If you find any errata, please report them by visiting http://www.packtpub.com/submit-errata, selecting your book, clicking on the **errata submission form** link, and entering the details of your errata. Once your errata are verified, your submission will be accepted and the errata will be uploaded to our website, or added to any list of existing errata, under the Errata section of that title.

Piracy

Piracy of copyright material on the Internet is an ongoing problem across all media. At Packt, we take the protection of our copyright and licenses very seriously. If you come across any illegal copies of our works, in any form, on the Internet, please provide us with the location address or website name immediately so that we can pursue a remedy.

Please contact us at copyright@packtpub.com with a link to the suspected pirated material.

We appreciate your help in protecting our authors, and our ability to bring you valuable content.

Questions

You can contact us at questions@packtpub.com if you are having a problem with any aspect of the book, and we will do our best to address it.

1

Introduction to PrimeFaces

Java Server Faces (JSF) is a component-oriented framework for building web application using Java. JSF makes it easy to build web application by automating common tasks such as populating input parameter values into Java Beans by parsing input parameters, performing validations, and rendering or updating views. But building web application with rich User Interfaces (UI) still remains a challenge as Java developers may or may not be good at building fancy UI components using HTML, JavaScript directly. As JSF is a component-based framework, it allows building custom UI components with rich look and feel and can be reusable in any project.

The good news is that there are many open source and proprietary frameworks providing readymade reusable UI components, which can be used in any JSF-based applications. Among the several UI component libraries available today, PrimeFaces is an outstanding UI component library in terms of features and ease of use.

In this chapter, we will cover:

- ◆ Introducing the features of PrimeFaces
- ◆ Installing and configuring PrimeFaces
- ◆ Creating a HelloWorld application using PrimeFaces
- ◆ Creating simple forms using PrimeFaces
- ◆ Performing form validations
- ◆ Performing client-side validations
- ◆ Understanding partial page rendering (PPR)

- Updating view using AJAX
- Updating view using AJAX listeners
- Performing tasks periodically using the poll component
- Invoking server-side methods from JavaScript using RemoteCommand

In this chapter, we will see what features make PrimeFaces an outstanding library, how to install and configure PrimeFaces and start using some of its basic components.

PrimeFaces is an open source JSF component library with 100+ rich UI components support. It has built-in AJAX support based on standard JSF 2.0 AJAX APIs.

Introducing the features of PrimeFaces

PrimeFaces provides the following set of features, which makes it powerful UI component library yet easy to use:

- More than 100 rich UI components
- Built-in AJAX support
- Zero configurations
- Does not require any third-party library dependencies for most of the components
- Integrated with ThemeRoller
- 30+ readily available themes
- Supports IE8+, Chrome, Firefox, Safari, and Opera browsers

Installing and configuring PrimeFaces

The PrimeFaces library comes as a single jar file and doesn't have any mandatory third-party library dependencies. So to use PrimeFaces, it is sufficient to add PrimeFaces jar along with a JSF implementation library such as Oracle's Mojarra or Apache's MyFaces.

However, based on the PrimeFaces features that you want to use, you may need to add some third-party libraries. The following table describes library dependency needed for a particular feature:

Dependency	Type	Version	Description
JSF runtime	2.0, 2.1, or 2.2	Required	Apache MyFaces or Oracle Mojarra
itext	2.1.7	Optional	DataExporter (PDF)
apache poi	3.7	Optional	DataExporter (Excel)

Dependency	Type	Version	Description
rome	1.0	Optional	FeedReader
commons-fileupload	1.2.1	Optional	FileUpload
commons-io	1.4	Optional	FileUpload

The preceding table contains the third-party library versions, which are tested and known to be working fine with PrimeFaces-4.0 version. Other versions might also work fine but they are not officially tested.

If you are using a servlet container such as Apache Tomcat, then you need to add JSF implementation library dependencies such as Oracle's Mojarra or Apache MyFaces. If you are using any JavaEE application servers such as, JBoss AS, Glassfish, WebLogic, and so on; then there is no need to add JSF implementation libraries explicitly as they come in-built with application server. Some application servers may not have latest JSF implementation libraries. So, check whether your application server has JSF 2.0 or 2.1 or 2.2 implementation libraries or not. Consult your application server specific documentation to see how to override server libraries with latest versions.

In this book, we will be using **PrimeFaces-4.0**, which is latest version at the time of writing along with Oracle's **Mojarra-2.2.3** JSF implementation.

Time for action – installing and configuring PrimeFaces

Perform the following steps to install and configure PrimeFaces to your web application:

1. Configure JSF FacesServlet in `web.xml`:

```
<servlet>
  <servlet-name>Faces Servlet</servlet-name>
  <servlet-class>javax.faces.webapp.FacesServlet</servlet-class>
  <load-on-startup>1</load-on-startup>
</servlet>
<servlet-mapping>
  <servlet-name>Faces Servlet</servlet-name>
  <url-pattern>*.jsf</url-pattern>
</servlet-mapping>
```

Downloading the example code

You can download the example code files for all Packt books you have purchased from your account at http://www.packtpub.com. If you purchased this book elsewhere, you can visit http://www.packtpub.com/support and register to have the files e-mailed directly to you.

2. If you are not using **Maven**, then you can download PrimeFaces-4.0.jar from http://www.primefaces.org/downloads.html and add it to classpath.

3. If you are using Maven, then add PrimeFaces maven repository to the repository list, and add PrimeFaces-4.0 dependency in pom.xml.

```xml
<repository>
  <id>prime-repo</id>
  <name>Prime Repo</name>
  <url>http://repository.primefaces.org</url>
</repository>

<dependency>
  <groupId>org.primefaces</groupId>
  <artifactId>primefaces</artifactId>
  <version>4.0</version>
</dependency>

<dependency>
  <groupId>com.sun.faces</groupId>
  <artifactId>jsf-api</artifactId>
  <version>2.2.3</version>
</dependency>

<dependency>
  <groupId>com.sun.faces</groupId>
  <artifactId>jsf-impl</artifactId>
  <version>2.2.3</version>
</dependency>
```

What just happened?

We have configured PrimeFaces repository and primefaces-4.0.jar dependency in our maven pom.xml, so that the PrimeFaces library is available to the web application classpath. We have configured FacesServlet and mapped to the URL pattern *.jsf, other popular URL patterns used are /faces/*, *.faces, and *.xhtml.

The PrimeFaces libraries from 4.0 version will be available in Maven Central, so you need not configure the PrimeFaces repository. But if you want to use snapshot versions, you need to configure the PrimeFaces repository in pom.xml.

Creating a HelloWorld application using PrimeFaces

In previous section, we have configured and installed PrimeFaces. To start using PrimeFaces components, all we need to do is adding the namespace xmlns:p=http://primefaces. org/ui to JSF pages.

Let us create a simple JSF page using PrimeFaces to see whether we have successfully installed and configured PrimeFaces.

Time for action – creating a HelloWorld program using PrimeFaces

Let us create a helloworld.xhtml file with the PrimeFaces namespace configuration, and use the PrimeFaces editor component to display a rich HTML editor. Perform the following steps:

1. To start using PrimeFaces components all we need to do is add the namespace xmlns:p=http://primefaces.org/ui in JSF facelets page.

```
<!DOCTYPE html>
<html xmlns="http://www.w3.org/1999/xhtml"
      xmlns:h="http://java.sun.com/jsf/html"
      xmlns:f="http://java.sun.com/jsf/core"
      xmlns:ui="http://java.sun.com/jsf/facelets"
      xmlns:p="http://primefaces.org/ui">
<f:view contentType="text/html">
<h:head>
  <title>First PrimeFaces Page</title>
</h:head>
<body>
  <h:form>
    <p:editor value="Hello World, PrimeFaces
      Rocks!!"/>
  </h:form>
</body>
</f:view>
</html>
```

2. Run the application and point your browser to `http://localhost:8080/chapter01/helloworld.jsf`. We can see the rich text editor as follows:

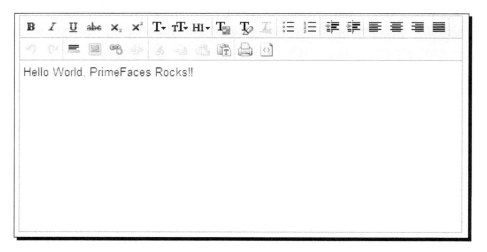

What just happened?

We have tested PrimeFaces configuration by using PrimeFaces editor component `<p:editor/>`. As we have configured PrimeFaces properly, we are able to see rich HTML editor.

◆ Make sure you have the `<h:head>` tag in your facelets page to avoid "PrimeFaces not found" JavaScript error.

◆ To make PrimeFaces work properly on webkit layout engine-based browsers such as, Chrome/Safari, enforce `contentType` to text/html using `<f:view contentType="text/html">`.

Creating simple forms using PrimeFaces

PrimeFaces provides various input elements such as `inputText`, `password`, `inputTextarea`, `commandButton`, `commandLink`, and so on, which are extensions to the standard JSF components providing additional features and theming support.

To get a feel of how to use PrimeFaces components, let us create a simple user registration form using PrimeFaces components.

Time for action – creating a user registration form

Let's start using PrimeFaces components by creating a simple user registration form, steps for the same are as follows:

1. Create a `User.java` **POJO (Plain Old Java Object)**:

```
public class User
{
  private Integer id;
  private String userName;
  private String password;
  private String firstName;
  private String lastName;
  private String email;
  private String phone;
  //setters & getters
}
```

2. Create a JSF managed bean `UserController.java`, using the following code:

```
@ManagedBean
@RequestScoped
public class UserController
{
  private User registrationUser;

  public UserController() {
    this.registrationUser = new User();
  }

  public User getRegistrationUser() {
    return registrationUser;
  }
  public void setRegistrationUser(User registrationUser) {
    this.registrationUser = registrationUser;
  }

  public String register()
  {
    System.out.println("Register User :"+
      this.registrationUser);
    String msg = "User Registered Successfully";
    FacesContext.getCurrentInstance().addMessage(null, new
      FacesMessage(FacesMessage.SEVERITY_INFO, msg, msg));
```

```
        FacesContext.getCurrentInstance().getExternalContext()
          .getFlash().setKeepMessages(true);
        return "registration.jsf?faces-redirect=true";
    }

}
```

3. Create a `registration.xhtml` page to build the user registration form using PrimeFaces components as follows:

```
<!DOCTYPE html>
<html xmlns="http://www.w3.org/1999/xhtml"
      xmlns:h="http://java.sun.com/jsf/html"
      xmlns:f="http://java.sun.com/jsf/core"
      xmlns:ui="http://java.sun.com/jsf/facelets"
      xmlns:p="http://primefaces.org/ui">

<h:head>
  <title>Registration</title>
</h:head>
<body>
  <h:form id="registrationForm">
    <p:panel header="Registration Form" style="width: 500px;">
<p:messages/>
    <h:panelGrid columns="2">
      <p:outputLabel value="UserName:"/>
      <p:inputText id="userName" value="#{userController.
registrationUser.userName}" label="UserName" />

      <p:outputLabel value="Password:"/>
      <p:password id="password" value="#{userController.
registrationUser.password}" label="Password"/>

      <p:outputLabel value="FirstName:"/>
      <p:inputText id="firstName" value="#{userController.
registrationUser.firstName}" label="FirstName"/>

      <p:outputLabel value="LastName:"/>
      <p:inputText id="lastName" value="#{userController.
registrationUser.lastName}"/>

      <p:outputLabel value="Email:"/>
      <p:inputText id="email" value="#{userController.
registrationUser.email}"/>
```

```
        <p:outputLabel value=""/>
        <p:commandButton action="#{userController.register}"
value="Register" update="registrationForm"/>

    </h:panelGrid>
    </p:panel>
  </h:form>
</body>
</html>
```

4. Run the application and point your browser to `http://localhost:8080/chapter01/registration.jsf`. Then you can see the following screenshot, **Registration Form**:

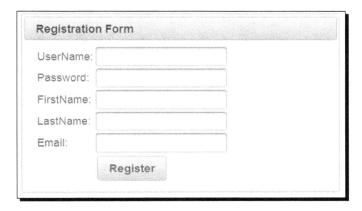

What just happened?

We have created a sample user registration form using PrimeFaces UI components `<p:inputText/>`, `<p:password/>`, `<p:commandButton/>`, and so on. We are looking for input components with rich look and feel because we used PrimeFaces components, which are extensions to the standard JSF UI components with theming support.

Performing form validations

Validating user submitted data is very common and a crucial part of any web application. JSF itself provides support for UI component validation and PrimeFaces enhances it with additional features.

In the previous section, we have created a sample user registration form but we did not validate the form for any mandatory fields. Let us enhance the registration form with the validations for mandatory fields.

Assume we have the following validation rules for the registration form:

◆ `UserName` should not be blank.

◆ `Password` should not be blank and should be at least four characters.

◆ `FirstName` should not be blank.

Time for action – validating the user registration form

We can use JSF validations for performing the earlier mentioned validations on the registration form. We can also perform validations using PrimeFaces AJAX-based validations by hooking up with JavaScript events, for this perform the following steps:

1. Update `registrationWithVal.xhtml` to build a user registration form along with validation support using the following code:

```
<!DOCTYPE html>
<html xmlns="http://www.w3.org/1999/xhtml"
      xmlns:h="http://java.sun.com/jsf/html"
      xmlns:f="http://java.sun.com/jsf/core"
      xmlns:ui="http://java.sun.com/jsf/facelets"
      xmlns:p="http://primefaces.org/ui">

<h:head>
  <title>Registration</title>
</h:head>
<body>
  <h:form id="registrationForm">
    <p:panel header="Registration Form" style="width: 800px;">
    <p:messages />
    <h:panelGrid columns="3">
      <p:outputLabel value="UserName:*"/>
      <p:inputText id="userName" value="#{userController.
registrationUser.userName}"
          required="true" label="UserName" >
        <p:ajax event="keyup"  update="userNameMsg"/>
      </p:inputText>
      <p:message id="userNameMsg" for="userName"/>
```

```
        <p:outputLabel value="Password:*"/>
        <p:password id="password" value="#{userController.
registrationUser.password}"
            required="true" label="Password">
        <f:validateLength minimum="4"/>
        <p:ajax update="passwordMsg" event="keyup"/>
        </p:password>
        <p:message id="passwordMsg" for="password"/>

        <p:outputLabel value="FirstName:*"/>
        <p:inputText id="firstName" value="#{userController.
registrationUser.firstName}"
            required="true" label="FirstName">

        </p:inputText>
        <p:message id="firstNameMsg" for="firstName"/>

        <p:outputLabel value="LastName:"/>
        <p:inputText id="lastName" value="#{userController.
registrationUser.lastName}"/>
        <p:message id="lastNameMsg" for="lastName"/>

        <p:outputLabel value="Email:"/>
        <p:inputText id="email" value="#{userController.
registrationUser.email}"/>
        <p:message id="emailMsg" for="email"/>

        <p:outputLabel value=""/>
        <p:commandButton action="#{userController.register}"
value="Register" update="registrationForm"/>
        <p:outputLabel value=""/>


    </h:panelGrid>
    </p:panel>
  </h:form>
</body>
</html>
```

2. Run the application and point your browser to `http://localhost:8080/chapter1/registrationWithVal.jsf`. Leave `UserName` and `FirstName` blank and enter `password` with less than four characters and submit the form. Then **Registration Form** will be redisplayed with errors as shown in the following screenshot:

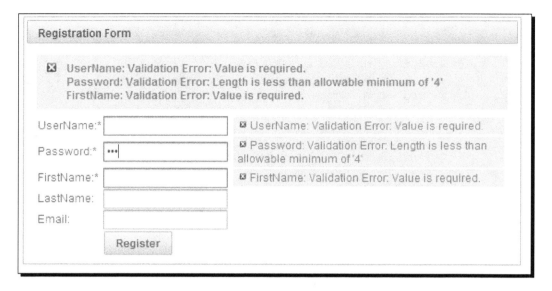

What just happened?

We have used input validations such as required, minimum length, and so on. We have used PrimeFaces AJAX-based validations using `<p:ajax>` on the `keyup` JavaScript event. So as you type in the `password`, it will get validated and update the validation message immediately. You can also use `<p:ajax>` with other JavaScript events such as `keydown`, `keypress`, `mouseover`, and so on.

> Beware of registering AJAX event listeners for JavaScript events such as `keyup`, `keydown`, and so on; as it may increase processing overhead and degrade performance. So use this feature cautiously.

Performing client-side validations

PrimeFaces also supports hooking up client-side JavaScript event handlers (`onclick`, `onblur`, `onchange`, and so on) for many of its UI Components. We can use this feature to perform client-side validations and reduce the server validation roundtrips.

Time for action – client-side e-mail validation

In our **Registration Form**, we can do some basic e-mail format validation on client side itself thereby reducing the server roundtrip. We can create a JavaScript function to validate e-mail using Regex, and then hook it up with the `onchange` event on e-mail input field. Perform the following steps for the same:

1. Write a JavaScript function to validate e-mail address:

```
function validateEmail()
{
  var emailReg = /^([\w-\.]+@([\w-]+\.)+[\w-]{2,4})?$/;
  var email = $.trim($("#userForm\\:email").val());
  if(email ==''){
    $("#userForm\\:emailMsg").text("");
    $("#userForm\\:emailMsg").attr("class", "");
    return;
  }
  if( emailReg.test( email ) ) {
    $("#userForm\\:emailMsg").text("Valid Email");
    $("#userForm\\:emailMsg").attr("class", "ui-messages-info
      ui-widget ui-corner-all ui-messages-info-summary");
  } else {
    $("#userForm\\:emailMsg").text("Invalid Email");
    $("#userForm\\:emailMsg").attr("class", "ui-message-error
      ui-widget ui-corner-all ui-message-error-detail");
  }
}
```

2. Add the `validateEmail()` function as an event handler for the `onchange` event on the e-mail input field:

```
<h:form id="userForm">
    <p:outputLabel value="Email:"/>
  <p:inputText id="email" value="#{userController.user.email}"
    onchange="validateEmail();" />
    <p:message id="emailMsg" for="email"/>

</h:form>
```

What just happened?

We have created a JavaScript function to validate e-mail using Regex. Using the jQuery API we have added an info/error message notifying us whether the e-mail is valid or invalid. We have hooked up this function to the `onchange` event of the e-mail `inputText` element. So `validateEmail()` gets invoked as soon as the e-mail value is changed and shows the message.

We got the e-mail field using $("#userForm\\:email"), where userForm is the ID of the form and email is the ID of the e-mail inputText field. JSF generates the IDs with colon (:) separator, but jQuery has a special meaning for colon .So we have replaced the colon (:) with \\:

Instead of replacing the colon by yourself, you can use the PrimeFaces.escapeClientId() utility function as follows:

```
function validateEmail()
{
  var emailReg = /^([\w-\.]+@([\w-]+\.)+[\w-]{2,4})?$/;
  var email = $.trim($(PrimeFaces.escapeClientId("userForm:email"))
    .val());
  if(email ==''){
    $(PrimeFaces.escapeClientId("userForm:emailMsg")).text("");
    $(PrimeFaces.escapeClientId("userForm:emailMsg")).attr("class",
"");
    return;
  }
  if( emailReg.test( email ) ) {
    $(PrimeFaces.escapeClientId("userForm:emailMsg")).
      text("Valid Email");
    $(PrimeFaces.escapeClientId("userForm:emailMsg")).
      attr("class", "ui-messages-info ui-widget ui-corner-all ui-
      messages-info-summary");
  } else {
    $(PrimeFaces.escapeClientId("userForm:emailMsg")).
      text("Invalid Email");
    $(PrimeFaces.escapeClientId("userForm:emailMsg")).
    attr("class", "ui-message-error ui-widget ui-corner-all ui-
    message-error-detail");
  }
}
```

Since JSF2.x, we can also change the JSF ID separator character using the following <context-param> configuration in web.xml:

```
<context-param>
    <param-name>javax.faces.SEPARATOR_CHAR</
param-name>
    <param-value>-</param-value>
</context-param>
```

The preceding client-side validation process involves performing manual validations using JavaScript/jQuery. PrimeFaces-4.0 introduced the **Client Side Validation (CSV)** framework with more powerful features, which we will discuss in *Chapter 4, Introducing the PrimeFaces Client Side Validation Framework*.

Understanding partial page rendering (PPR)

PrimeFaces provides a generic **partial page rendering (PPR)** mechanism to update specific JSF components with AJAX.

PrimeFaces provides process, `update` attributes to indicate which view components need to be processed or updated. Partial processing also provides some keywords which has some special meaning.

Keyword	Description
`@this`	Component that triggers the PPR is processed.
`@parent`	Parent of the PPR trigger is processed.
`@form`	Encapsulating form of the PPR trigger is processed.
`@namingcontainer`	Encapsulating naming container.
`@none`	No component is processed, useful to revert changes to form.
`@all`	Whole component tree is processed just like a regular request.

Sometimes, we may need to process the form partially based on the action triggered on the form. A very common scenario is, there can be multiple submit buttons in a form and you need to perform validations based on the action performed and ignore other field validations that are irrelevant to the action invoked.

For example, assume we are viewing a **User Detail Form** and we can update the user details or delete the user record using **Update** and **Delete** submit buttons. For updating, the user fields, `userId`, `userName`, and `firstName` are mandatory where as for deleting, only `userId` is required. So, when the **Update** button is clicked, validations should be performed on `userId`, `userName`, and `firstName` fields. But when the **Delete** button is clicked, validations on `userName` and `firstName` should be skipped.

Time for action – partial processing on the user details form

In this section, we will demonstrate how to process only a subset of components based on the action performed.

1. Create `userDetails.xhtml` with the **User Details Form** containing update and delete actions:

```
<h:form id="userDetailsForm">
<p:panel header="User Details Form" style="width: 800px;">
  <p:messages/>
  <h:panelGrid columns="3">

    <p:outputLabel value="UserId:*"/>
```

```
      <p:inputText id="userId" value="#{userController.loginUser.
id}" required="true" label="UserId" />
      <p:message id="userIdMsg" for="userId"/>

      <p:outputLabel value="UserName:*"/>
      <p:inputText id="userName" value="#{userController.loginUser.
userName}" required="true"
    label="UserName" />
      <p:message id="userNameMsg" for="userName"/>

      <p:outputLabel value="Password:*"/>
      <p:password id="password"
        value="#{userController.loginUser.password}"
        required="true" label="Password"/>
      <p:message id="passwordMsg" for="password"/>

      <p:outputLabel value="FirstName:*"/>
      <p:inputText id="firstName"
        value="#{userController.loginUser.firstName}"
        required="true"    label="FirstName"/>
      <p:message id="firstNameMsg" for="firstName"/>

      <p:commandButton value="Update"
        action="#{userController.updateUser()}"
        update="userDetailsForm"/>
      <p:commandButton value="Delete"
        action="#{userController.deleteUser()}"
        update="userDetailsForm"/>

  </h:panelGrid>
 </p:panel>
</h:form>
```

2. Create a managed bean UserController.java to perform update and delete actions:

```
@ManagedBean
@RequestScoped
public class UserController
{
  private User loginUser;

  public UserController()
  {
    this.loginUser = new User();
  }
```

```
public User getLoginUser()
{
  return loginUser;
}

public void setLoginUser(User loginUser)
{
  this.loginUser = loginUser;
}

public String  updateUser() {
  System.out.println("Updating User Id:
    "+this.loginUser.getId());
  String msg = "User updated Successfully";
  FacesContext.getCurrentInstance().addMessage(null, new
    FacesMessage(FacesMessage.SEVERITY_INFO, msg, msg));
  return "userDetails.jsf";
}

public String  deleteUser() {
  System.out.println("deleting User Id:
    "+this.loginUser.getId());
  String msg = "User deleted Successfully";
  FacesContext.getCurrentInstance().addMessage(null, new
    FacesMessage(FacesMessage.SEVERITY_INFO, msg, msg));
  return "userDetails.jsf";
}
}
```

3. Run the application and point your browser to `http://localhost:8080/ chapter01/userDetails.jsf`.

When you click on the **Delete** button, the whole form will be processed, and displays a form with error messages if any required fields are blank. To resolve this issue, we can use the `process` attribute to specify only the `UserId` field to be processed and invoke the `deleteUser()` method:

```
<p:commandButton value="Delete"
  action="#{userController.deleteUser()}"
process="@this,userId"  update="userDetailsForm"/>
```

What just happened?

We have used the `process` attribute to specify which components to be processed so that we can bypass the other fields' validations, which are irrelevant to the invoked action. Also note that `<p:commandButton>` issues an AJAX request by default. So if you want to redirect to a different page after action logic is executed make it a non-AJAX request by setting `ajax="false"`.

Submitting partial data to the server

Both JSF AJAX implementation and PrimeFaces serializes the whole form data, and post it to server even for AJAX requests that will process only partial components. In the case of forms with more number of input components, we will be sending huge payload even though only few specific components will be processed on server side. This process unnecessarily consumes server resources.

PrimeFaces provides `partialSubmit` feature, which enables to serialize and send only the components data that will be processed on server side. By default `partialSubmit` feature is disabled, and we can enable this feature globally by configuring the following context parameter in `web.xml`:

```xml
<context-param>
  <param-name>primefaces.SUBMIT</param-name>
  <param-value>partial</param-value>
</context-param>
```

The preceding configuration enables `partialSubmit` feature globally. We can override this `partialSubmit` behavior for specific command components or AJAX events as follows:

```xml
<p:commandButton value="Delete"
  action="#{userController.deleteUser()}" process="@this,userId"
  partialSubmit="true"  update="userDetailsForm"/>
<p:inputText id="userName"
  value="#{userController.registrationUser.userName}" required="true"
  label="UserName">
  <p:ajax event="keyup"
  listener="#{userController.checkUserNamesExists()}"
  update="userNameMsg" partialSubmit="true"/>
</p:inputText>
```

You can see the difference between payload data sending to server when `partialSubmit` is enabled and disabled using firebug or chrome developer tools.

Updating the view using AJAX

AJAX support became a must for any framework or library used for building rich and interactive web applications. AJAX features make the web application more responsive by updating parts of the page without requiring full page reload.

PrimeFaces has in-built AJAX support and is based on JSFs server-side APIs. On client side, PrimeFaces use the most popular JavaScript library jQuery.

Processing a form submission and updating the portions of view using AJAX is very commonly used feature in web applications. Let us see how we can submit a form and update the view using AJAX.

Time for action – updating the view using AJAX

Let us create a **Login Form** with user name and password. When form is submitted, show the login status using AJAX. Perform the following steps for the same:

1. Create a `login.xhtml` page with login form as follows:

```
<h:form id="loginForm">
  <p:panel header="Login Form" style="width: 500px;">
    <h:panelGrid columns="2">
      <p:outputLabel value="UserName"/>
      <p:inputText value="#{userController.loginUser.
        userName}"/>

      <p:outputLabel value="Password"/>
      <p:password value="#{userController.loginUser.
        password}"/>

      <p:commandButton action="#{userController.login}"
        value="Login" update="loginStatusMsg"/>
      <p:commandButton type="reset" value="Reset"/>

      <p:outputLabel value="#{userController.loginStatus}"
        id="loginStatusMsg"/>
    </h:panelGrid>
  </p:panel>
</h:form>
```

2. Create a `UserController.java` managed bean as follows:

```
@ManagedBean
@RequestScoped
public class UserController
{
```

```
private User loginUser;
private String loginStatus;

public UserController() {
  this.loginUser = new User();
}

public User getLoginUser() {
  return loginUser;
}

public void setLoginUser(User loginUser) {
  this.loginUser = loginUser;
}

public String getLoginStatus() {
  return loginStatus;
}

public void setLoginStatus(String loginStatus) {
  this.loginStatus = loginStatus;
}

public String login() {
  boolean validCredentials = "admin".equals(loginUser.
getUserName()) &&
  "admin".equals(loginUser.getPassword());
  this.loginStatus  = validCredentials? "Login Successful" :
    "Login failed";
  return null;
}
}
```

3. Point the browser to `http://localhost:8080/chapter01/login.jsf`.

When you enter **UserName** and **Password** and click on the **Login** button, the login status should be displayed using AJAX. Have a look at the following screenshot:

What just happened?

We have created a **Login Form** with **UserName** and **Password** fields. When we submit the form, the model gets updated and login status will be set based on the provided credentials. As we have specified to update the view component with the ID `loginStatusMsg` through `update="loginStatusMsg"`, when you click on the **Login** button, the login status will be displayed without complete page refresh.

Updating the view using AJAX listeners

Sometimes we may need instant feedback to be shown as and so user fills the form, instead of showing error messages after form submission. For example, in user **Registration Form**, we may want to check whether the **UserName** is already in use and show an error message immediately.

PrimeFaces provides AJAX listener support to invoke method on JSF managed bean. We can use this feature to check whether the entered **UserName** is already in use or not, and update the view to show error message using AJAX, even before submitting the entire form.

Time for action – validate the UserName using AJAX listeners

Let's add AJAX event listener `keyup` event to the **UserName** input field so that as you type, it will check if the username entered is already in use or not.

1. Create `viewAjaxListener.xhtml` with registration form to validate the **UserName** using AJAX Listener as follows:

```
<h:form id="registrationForm">
  <p:panel header="Registration Form" style="width: 800px;">
  <h:panelGrid columns="3">
    <p:outputLabel value="UserName:*"/>
    <p:inputText id="userName"
      value="#{userController.registrationUser.userName}"
      required="true" label="UserName">
      <p:ajax event="keyup"
        listener="#{userController.checkUserNamesExists()}"
        update="userNameMsg"/>
    </p:inputText>
    <p:message id="userNameMsg" for="userName"/>

    <p:outputLabel value="Password:*"/>
    <p:password id="password"
      value="#{userController.registrationUser.password}"
      required="true" label="Password"/>
    <p:message id="passwordMsg" for="password"/>
```

```
<p:outputLabel value="FirstName:*"/>
<p:inputText id="firstName"
   value="#{userController.registrationUser.firstName}"
   required="true" label="FirstName"/>
<p:message id="firstNameMsg" for="firstName"/>

<p:commandButton action="#{userController.register}"
   value="Register" update="registrationForm"/>

   </h:panelGrid>
   </p:panel>
</h:form>
```

2. Create a `UserController.java` managed bean with the `checkUserNamesExists()` method to check whether the entered **UserName** is already in use or not and add the error message accordingly:

```
public void checkUserNamesExists()
{
  String userName = this.registrationUser.getUserName();
  if("admin".equals(userName) || "test".equals(userName))
  {
    String msg = "UserName ["+userName+"] already in use.";
    FacesContext.getCurrentInstance().addMessage
      ("registrationForm:userName",
        new FacesMessage(FacesMessage.SEVERITY_ERROR, msg,
          msg));
  }
}
```

3. Point your browser to `http://localhost:8080/chapter01/viewAjaxListener.jsf`.

Enter `admin` or `test` in the **UserName** field then you should see the error message displayed immediately as in the following screenshot:

What just happened?

We have used AJAX listener in conjunction with `keyup` event on the **UserName** input field. So for each `keyup` event the callback method `checkUserNamesExists()` will be invoked to check whether the entered **UserName** value is `admin` or `test`, and adds error message if it is. As we are updating the view component with ID `userNameMsg` using `update="userNameMsg"`, the error message is displayed immediately using the AJAX update.

Performing tasks periodically using a poll component

PrimeFaces provides poll component, which can be used to perform actions via JSF managed bean methods, periodically on regular intervals.

Suppose we want to display current time on web pages. We can do it by using poll component. We can update the `currentTime` view component using `<p:poll>` component to display current time for every second without reloading the entire page.

Time for action – using the poll component to display the current time

Let's display live time by polling server time for every second and display it using the poll component.

1. Create `poll.xhtml` with a poll component to display `currentTime` as follows:

```
<h:form>
  <p:outputLabel value="Current Time:" /> <p:outputLabel
    id="currentTime" value="#{serverTimeBean.time}"/>
  <p:poll interval="1"
    listener="#{serverTimeBean.updateTime()}"
    update="currentTime"/>
</h:form>
```

2. Create `ServerTimeBean.java` managed bean with the `updateTime()` method to set the `currentTime` value as follows:

```
@ManagedBean
@RequestScoped
public class ServerTimeBean
{
  private String time;
  public void setTime(String time) {
    this.time = time;
  }
```

```
public String getTime() {
    return time;
}
public void updateTime() {
    SimpleDateFormat sdf = new SimpleDateFormat("yyyy-MM-dd
hh:mm:ss");
    this.time = sdf.format(new Date());
}

}
```

What just happened?

We have used the `<p:poll>` component to call listener method `updateTime()` on `ServerTimeBean` for every second by specifying `interval="1"`, and updated the view to display current time using AJAX.

The poll component provides the following attributes, which provides additional control on its behavior:

AttributeName	Description
onstart	JavaScript handler to execute before AJAX request begins.
oncomplete	JavaScript handler to execute when AJAX request is completed.
onsuccess	JavaScript handler to execute when AJAX request succeeds.
onerror	JavaScript handler to execute when AJAX request fails.
autoStart	In autoStart mode, polling starts automatically on page load, to start polling on demand set it to false.
stop	Stops polling when true.

Controlling the polling process using external triggers

Sometimes, we may want to have control on when to start/stop the polling process, stop polling based on some criteria, and so on. The PrimeFaces poll component provides these features with additional attributes giving you full control on polling process.

For example, we want to start polling when the **Start** button is clicked, and stop polling when the **Stop** button is clicked.

Time for action – manually start and stop polling

We will now demonstrate how to start and stop polling using external triggers such as start and stop buttons using following steps:

1. Create a form with a poll component and start/stop buttons to start and stop polling using following code:

```
<h:form>
    <p:outputLabel value="Current Time:" /> <p:outputLabel
      id="currentTime" value="#{serverTimeBean.time}"/>
    <p:poll interval="1"
      listener="#{serverTimeBean.updateTime()}"
      update="currentTime" widgetVar="currentTimePoller"
      autoStart="false"/> <br/>
    <p:button value="Start" onclick="currentTimePoller.start()"
      href="#" />
    <p:button value="Stop" onclick="currentTimePoller.stop()"
      href="#"/><br/>
</h:form>
```

What just happened?

We have set the `autoStart` attribute to false, so that polling does not start automatically on page load. We have given a name for the poll component using `widgetVar ="currentTimePoller"` so that we can invoke `start()` and `stop()` methods on the poll component. We have associated the `start()` and `stop()` methods to the button's `onclick` events. So when we click on the **Start** button, polling will start and when we click on the **Stop** button, polling will be stopped.

> PrimeFaces provides PrimeFaces push, which is better suitable for asynchronous processing. Prefer using PrimeFaces push over <p:poll> component. For more information see http://www.primefaces.org/showcase/push/index.jsf.

Invoking server-side methods from JavaScript using RemoteCommand

RemoteCommand component provides an option to invoke server-side methods, say JSF managed bean methods, from JavaScript client-side code directly. This feature comes in handy when some task needs some client-side action and server-side logic. When you declare a `RemoteCommand` component to invoke a JSF managed bean method, then you can call it like a JavaScript function, with the `remoteCommand` name from the JavaScript code.

Suppose in our user **Registration Form**, we want to validate e-mail format first on client side using Regex and if it is in valid e-mail format, then we want to check whether the e-mail is already in use or not using server-side logic. We can do this by using the RemoteCommand component.

Time for action – validate e-mail using RemoteCommand

We will now take a look at how to invoke server-side logic from JavaScript code using RemoteCommand. First we will check the e-mail format on client side using JavaScript, and then invoke server-side logic to check if the user provided e-mail already in use or not. Perform the following steps:

1. Create a method using following code in the UserController managed bean to check whether the given e-mail is already in use or not:

```
@ManagedBean
@RequestScoped
public class UserController
{

  public void checkEmailExists()
  {
    String email = this.registrationUser.getEmail();
    if("admin@gmail.com".equals(email) || "test@gmail.com".
equals(email))
    {
      String msg = "Email ["+email+"] already in use.";
      FacesContext.getCurrentInstance().addMessage
        ("registrationForm:email",
        new FacesMessage(FacesMessage.SEVERITY_ERROR,
        msg, msg));
    }
  }
}
```

2. On the user registration page, create validateEmail() JavaScript function for checking e-mail format, and use a remoteCommand component to invoke the checkEmailExists() actionListener method to check whether the given e-mail is already in use or not:

```
<!DOCTYPE html>
<html xmlns="http://www.w3.org/1999/xhtml"
      xmlns:h="http://java.sun.com/jsf/html"
      xmlns:f="http://java.sun.com/jsf/core"
      xmlns:ui="http://java.sun.com/jsf/facelets"
      xmlns:p="http://primefaces.org/ui">
```

```
<h:head>
  <title>Home</title>
  <script>
  function validateEmail()
  {
    var emailReg = /^([\w-\.]+@([\w-]+\.)+[\w-]{2,4})?$/;
    var email = $.trim($(PrimeFaces.escapeClientId
      ("registrationForm:email")).val());
    if(email ==''){
      $(PrimeFaces.escapeClientId("registrationForm:emailMsg"))
        .text("");
      $(PrimeFaces.escapeClientId("registrationForm:emailMsg"))
        .attr("class", "");
      return;
    }
    if( emailReg.test( email ) ) {
      checkDuplicateEmail();
    } else {
      $(PrimeFaces.escapeClientId("registrationForm:emailMsg")).
  text("Invalid Email");
      $(PrimeFaces.escapeClientId("registrationForm:emailMsg"))
        .attr("class", "ui-message-error ui-widget ui-corner-
        all ui-message-error-detail");
    }
  }
  </script>
</h:head>
<body>

  <h:form id="registrationForm">
    <p:panel header="Registration Form" style="width: 800px;">
      <h:panelGrid columns="3">

        <p:outputLabel value="Email:"/>
        <p:inputText id="email"
          value="#{userController.registrationUser.email}"
          onblur="validateEmail();" />
        <p:message id="emailMsg" for="email"/>

        <p:commandButton action="#{userController.register}"
          value="Register" update="registrationForm"/>

      </h:panelGrid>
    </p:panel>
    <p:remoteCommand name="checkDuplicateEmail"
      actionListener="#{userController.checkEmailExists()}"
      update="emailMsg"/>
  </h:form>
</body>
</html>
```

What just happened?

We have created a validateEmail() JavaScript function to check the e-mail format using Regex and will be called on onblur event on e-mail input element. In the validateEmail() function, if the e-mail format is invalid we are showing the error message as **"Invalid email!!"**, otherwise we are invoking the remoteCommand checkDuplicateEmail as JavaScript function, which invokes the UserController.checkemailExists() method and add error message if the e-mail is already in use.

Summary

You have now been introduced to the PrimeFaces component library and did hands-on with some cool PrimeFaces features, but this is just the beginning. There are plenty more powerful yet easy to use Rich UI components, which we will be looking in further chapters. In this chapter, we took a glance at the PrimeFaces features and learned how to install and configure PrimeFaces. We have started by creating a simple HelloWorld application and learned performing validations and various AJAX features. We also learned how to use PrimeFaces PPR feature. Lastly, we have learned about polling and RemoteCommand components, which come very handy at times.

In the next chapter, we will take a look into the sample application TechBuzz that we will be building incrementally throughout the book. We will also discuss the application's domain model, creating the project structure and some sample screenshots of the application.

2
Introducing Sample Application TechBuzz

If all concepts were explained with an example, then they would be much easier to understand. That's what we are going to do here!

As you progress through the book, if you could apply the knowledge in building a sample application, then you will get not only theoretical knowledge on PrimeFaces, but also hands-on experience on how to use PrimeFaces in your real projects. So, we will be building a sample application called TechBuzz incrementally throughout this book.

TechBuzz is a knowledge sharing system wherein users can post about what is going on in the field of technology read others' posts, rate others' posts, and so on. You should note that this application is purposely very simple, and indeed many of its features were conceived so that we could highlight a particular piece of PrimeFaces functionality. As our primary focus is on how to use PrimeFaces, we will be discussing more about building the user interface using PrimeFaces, and you can find the complete backend logic implementation in the source code of this book.

In this chapter, we will cover:

◆ Understanding the requirements of the TechBuzz application
◆ Understanding the high-level design of the TechBuzz application
◆ Understanding the TechBuzz data model
◆ Looking at TechBuzz screenshots
◆ Setting up of the development environment for TechBuzz

In this chapter, we will discuss the functional requirements of the TechBuzz application and describe how we will be using PrimeFaces features to implement them.

Understanding the requirements of the TechBuzz application

TechBuzz is a community website where people can share their thoughts, ideas, and experiences on various technology-related topics. The user can post information such as when a new framework is released, upcoming technology training, information on newly published books, and so on. Also users can view others' posts, rate others' posts, view other users' profiles, and search for posts based on keywords or tags.

The TechBuzz system will have role-based access control security, and users with three types of roles: Administrator, Moderator, and Normal. TechBuzz users will be able to perform various actions based on his/her role.

Normal users can perform the following actions:

- New users can register
- Existing users can log in
- View a list of posts from all the users
- View the details of a post
- Add comments to a post
- Rate other user's posts
- Create a new post
- Update his/her own post
- Search posts by text, tag(s)
- View other user's profiles

Moderators can perform the following actions:

- Edit other user's posts
- Add/Remove tags for posts

Administrators can perform the following actions:

- Disable a user account
- Assign/Revoke the Moderator privilege to/from a user
- Create, update, and delete tags
- Make any user post visible or invisible

Understanding the high-level design of the TechBuzz application

The TechBuzz application will be developed using the **MVC (Model View Controller)** design pattern. For the Model layer, we will use the Spring framework to provide various business layer services. The View layer will be developed using JSF Facelets and PrimeFaces components. The Controller layer will be implemented using JSF managed beans. The following diagram depicts how each layer will communicate with other layers:

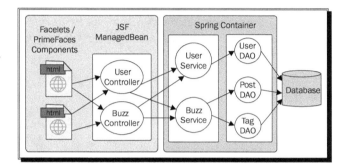

Understanding the TechBuzz data model

The following diagram depicts the database model for the TechBuzz application:

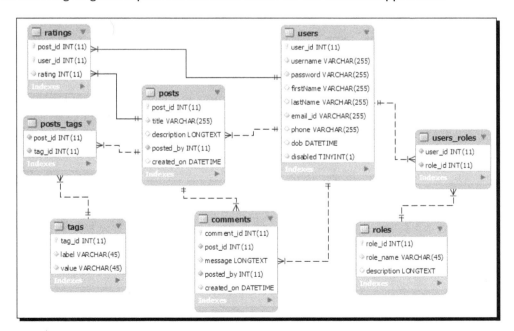

Looking at TechBuzz screenshots

In this section, we will see the sample screenshots of the TechBuzz application which we are going to build incrementally throughout the book.

User authentication

New users can register with the TechBuzz application and then log in to the system. To implement registration and login screens, we can use various PrimeFaces input components, Calendar, and Message components. Also we will learn how to perform form validations as well using the techniques described in the *Performing form validations* section of *Chapter 1, Introduction to PrimeFaces,* and *Chapter 4, Introducing the PrimeFaces Client Side Validation Framework.*

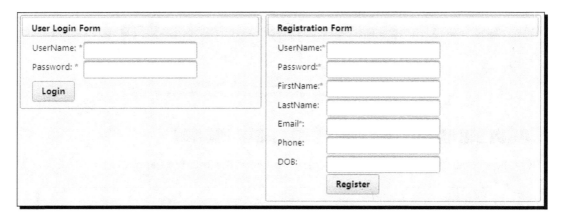

TechBuzz home page

When the user successfully logs in to TechBuzz, the **Home** page will be displayed with the list of posts posted by all the users, in reverse chronological order in a paginated manner. To implement this, we will use the DataList component along with pagination.

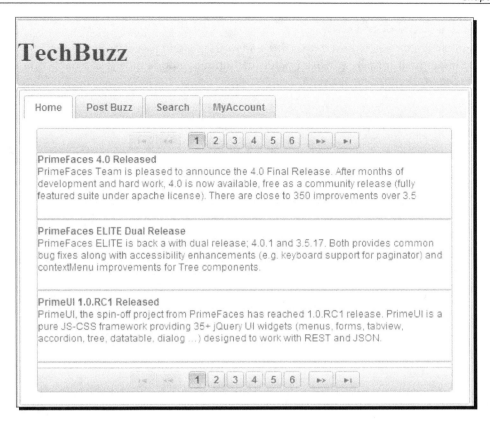

User account screen

Users can view his/her own and other user's account details such as their name, e-mail, and the posts he/she posted, and so on. For this, we will be using the TabView component.

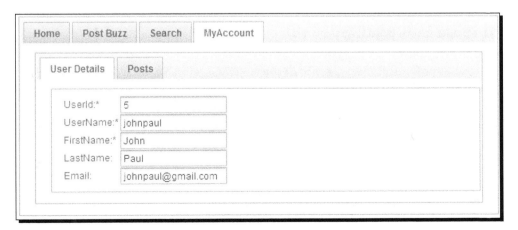

Creating a post screen

The user can create a new post with a title and message, and associate relevant tags to the post. To implement this, we will use PrimeFaces input components and the AutoComplete component while choosing **Tags**.

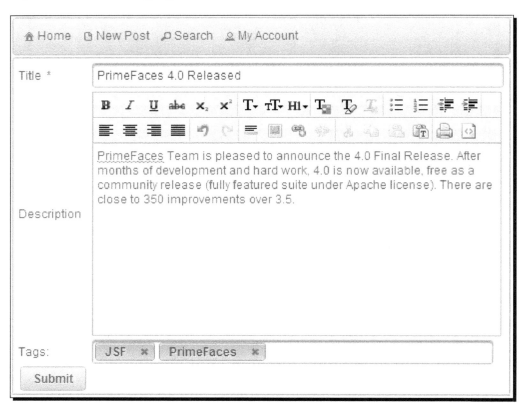

User roles management

The TechBuzz application will have role-based authentication and authorization security, which enables only authorized users to perform actions. For this, we will be creating privileges and roles, and associate privileges to roles. Administrators can add or remove roles to/from users. To implement this, we will use the PickList component.

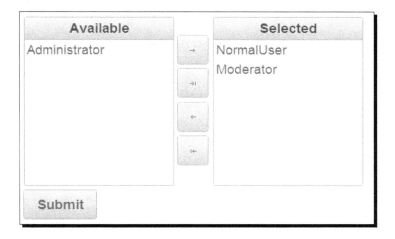

Posts in tree view

Sometimes, the user would like to see the posts based on year, month, and date. For this, we will use the Tree component to show posts in the tree format as follows:

Posts frequency charts

Administrators can view the frequency of posts per day/month/year in a graphical representation using Chart components.

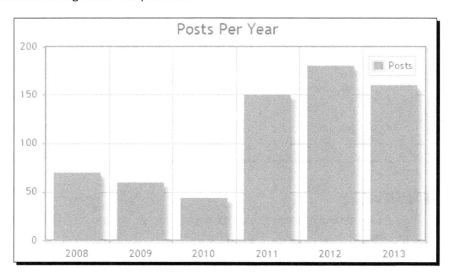

Setting up of the development environment for TechBuzz

In this section, we will go through the development environment setup process to get ready for developing the TechBuzz application. As PrimeFaces is a lightweight UI component framework for JSF-based applications, there are no specific requirements for particular IDEs, web servers, or databases. You can use your favorite IDE, servlet container, and database.

The TechBuzz application will be developed following three-tier architecture. We will be using JSF/PrimeFaces for the presentation tier, Spring for the business tier, and Spring JDBC for the persistence tier.

Time for action – installing the required software

For developing the TechBuzz application, we will be using the following software and tools:

1. **JDK**: PrimeFaces needs JDK 1.5 or later. We can download and install JDK from `http://www.oracle.com/technetwork/java/javase/downloads/index.html`.

2. **IDE**: We will be using Eclipse as the IDE, but if you want to use the NetBeans IDE, IntelliJ IDEA or any other IDEs, you can import and use them without any changes, as TechBuzz is a Maven-based web application. You can download and install the Eclipse IDE from `http://www.eclipse.org/downloads/`.

3. **Application server**: PrimeFaces can run on any servlet container such as Apache Tomcat, Jetty, JBoss, Glassfish, and so on. We will be using Apache Tomcat for TechBuzz but you can deploy and run on any of the servlet containers. You can download Apache Tomcat 7.0.39 from `http://tomcat.apache.org/download-70.cgi`.

4. **Database**: For the TechBuzz application, we will be using the MySQL database. You can use any other relational databases such as Oracle, Postgres, and so on, as per your choice. You can download and install the MySQL database from `http://dev.mysql.com/downloads/`.

5. **Build tool**: We will be using Maven as a build tool for the TechBuzz application. You can download and install Maven from `http://maven.apache.org/download.cgi`.

6. **Browser tools**: As we are going to learn a lot more about UI design using PrimeFaces components, it would be really helpful to have tools such as the Firebug plugin for Firefox or Chrome Developer Tools for the Google Chrome browser.

What just happened?

We have installed all the required software and tools for developing the TechBuzz sample application. As you progress through this book, you can add features to the TechBuzz application.

Once all the required software are installed, start your IDE and create a sample JSF project, and configure PrimeFaces as specified in the *Installing and configuring PrimeFaces* section of *Chapter 1, Introduction to PrimeFaces*. You can create a sample Facelets page, include a PrimeFaces namespace and use any PrimeFaces component such as `<p:editor/>` or `<p:calendar mode="inline"/>`. Now, you can run the application by choosing an application server that you have configured in your IDE. If you have configured PrimeFaces correctly, you should see the PrimeFaces component with a rich theme support.

Summary

In this chapter, we have discussed the functional requirements for the sample application TechBuzz, seen some sample UI screenshots, and prepared the development environment by installing the required software and tools.

In the next chapter, we will look into commonly used PrimeFaces components such as Dialog, Growl, Message, Tooltip, BlockUI, and so on, so that we will be familiar with these components and use them while developing the TechBuzz application.

3
Using PrimeFaces Common Utility Components

Most of the web applications need some common features such as displaying alerts, confirmation dialogs, error messages, tooltips and so on. JavaScript provides many of these features but those features are basic and limited. PrimeFaces provides some utility components such as Dialog, Tooltip, Growl, BlockUI and so on, that are commonly used with enhanced features and theming capabilities.

In this chapter we will cover the following topics:

- Displaying FacesMessages using Message, Messages, and Growl
- Displaying tooltips using the Tooltip component
- Partial Processing and Rendering using the Fragment component
- Introducing the Sticky component
- Using the RequestContext Utility
- Using the Dialog and ConfirmDialog components
- Displaying notification messages using NotificationBar
- Blocking UI components using BlockUI
- Working with the PrimeFaces Selectors API
- Introducing the search expression framework

Introducing the Message component

Message is an enhanced version of the standard JSF Message component with additional features and skinning capabilities. The `<p:message>` component is similar to the standard JSF's `<h:message>`, and is used to output a single message for a specific component as follows:

```
<p:message for="email"/>
```

The `<p:message/>` component provides the following attributes, which can be used to customize message display:

- `showSummary`: This specifies whether the summary of `FacesMessages` should be displayed. Default value is `false`
- `showDetail`: This specifies whether the detail of `FacesMessages` should be displayed. Default value is `true`
- `for`: ID of the component whose message is to be displayed
- `display`: Display mode can be `text`, `icon`, or `both`. Default is `both`.
  - `text`: Only message text is displayed
  - `icon`: Only message severity is displayed and message text is visible as a tooltip
  - `both`: Both icon and text are displayed
- `escape`: This defines whether HTML would be escaped or not. Default value is true.
- `severity`: This only displays a comma-separated list of severities.

Time for action – displaying FacesMessage using <p:message>

Let us see how to display FacesMessages with different display modes and severity levels.

1. Create a form with three required input fields and display validation errors using `<p:message>` as follows:

```
<h:form id="userRegForm" style="width: 500px; padding-left:
10px;">
  <p:panel header="Messages - Using 'display' modes" >
    <h:panelGrid columns="3">
      <p:outputLabel value="EmailId"/>
      <p:inputText id="emailId"
        value="#{messagesController.user.emailId}" required="true"
        requiredMessage="Enter EmailId"/>
      <p:message for="emailId"/>
```

```
            <h:outputText value="Password" />
            <p:password id="password"
              value="#{messagesController.user.password}"
    required="true"
                requiredMessage="Enter Password"/>
            <p:message  for="password" display="text"/>

            <h:outputText value="FirstName" />
            <p:inputText id="firstName"
              value="#{messagesController.user.firstName}"
    required="true"
                requiredMessage="Enter FirstName"/>
            <p:message for="firstName" display="icon" severity="warn,
              error" />

            <p:commandButton value="Submit"
              actionListener="#{messagesController.doRegister}"
              update="userRegForm"/>
          </h:panelGrid>
        </p:panel>
      </h:form>
```

What just happened?

We have displayed error messages using the `<p:message>` component for each of the input fields. We have also used different types of `display` modes. We have restricted **FirstName** input field messages to display only `warn` and `error` severity messages.

Displaying messages with HTML content

The Message component replaces the HTML content by default. You can use the `escape` attribute to turn on/off this behavior. By default, escape is set to `TRUE`.

Time for action – displaying FacesMessage with HTML content

Let us see how to use the `escape` attribute, while displaying `FacesMessages` with HTML content. Perform the following steps:

1. Create a form with two input fields as follows:

```
<h:form id="form1" style="width: 500px; padding-left: 10px;">
  <p:panel header="Messages with HTML content - Using 'escape'
    attribute">
  <h:panelGrid columns="3">
    <h:outputText value="FirstName" />
    <p:inputText id="fName"
      value="#{messagesController.user.firstName}"/>
    <p:message for="fName" escape="false" />

    <h:outputText value="LastName" />
    <p:inputText id="lName"
      value="#{messagesController.user.lastName}"/>
    <p:message for="lName" escape="true" />

    <p:commandButton value="Submit"
      actionListener="#{messagesController.addHtmlMessages}"
      update="form1"/>
  </h:panelGrid>
  </p:panel>
</h:form>
```

2. In action Handler method, `addHtmlMessages()`, add `FacesMessage` with HTML content:

```
public void addHtmlMessages()
{
  FacesContext.getCurrentInstance().addMessage("form1:fName",
    new FacesMessage(FacesMessage.SEVERITY_INFO, "<font
      size='4'>FirstName : "+user.getFirstName()+"</font>",
      null));
  FacesContext.getCurrentInstance().addMessage("form1:lName",
    new FacesMessage(FacesMessage.SEVERITY_INFO, "<font
      size='4'>LastName :"+user.getLastName()+"</font>",
      null));
}
```

What just happened?

We have added `FacesMessages` with HTML content for both `fName` and `lName` clientIds. For `fName`, we haven't escaped HTML content, so the message displayed is with font size 4. But for `lName`, we set `escape="true"` and hence, the HTML content is displayed as it is (with HTML tags).

Introducing the Messages component

The Messages component `<p:messages>` is an enhanced version of the standard JSF `<h:messages>` component with skinning capabilities. The `<p:messages>` component can be used to display multiple messages corresponding to UI elements.

The `<p:messages/>` component supports the following additional attributes in addition to the attributes supported by `<p:message>`:

- `globalOnly`: When `true`, only `FacesMessage` with no clientIds are displayed. Default value is `false`.

- `autoUpdate`: This enables the autoupdate mode if set to `TRUE`. Default value is `false`.

- `for`: This specifies the name of associated key, takes precedence when used with `globalOnly`.

- `closable`: This adds a close icon to hide the messages.

Time for action – displaying FacesMessage using `<p:messages>`

Let us see how to display multiple `FacesMessage` using `<p:messages>`:

1. Create a form with two `commandButton elements` and the `<p:messages/>` component using the following code:

```
<h:form style="width: 500px; padding-left: 10px;">
```

```
        <p:panel header="Messages with All Severity levels">
        <p:messages globalOnly="true" autoUpdate="true"/>
        <p:commandButton value="Show FacesMessages"
          actionListener="#{messagesController.addMultipleMsgs}"/>
        </p:panel>
    </h:form>
```

2. Add `FacesMessage` in the `actionListener` method as follows:

```
public void addMultipleMsgs()
{
  FacesContext.getCurrentInstance().addMessage(null, new
    FacesMessage(FacesMessage.SEVERITY_INFO,"Sample Info Msg",
    null));
  FacesContext.getCurrentInstance().addMessage(null, new
    FacesMessage(FacesMessage.SEVERITY_WARN,"Sample Warn Msg",
    null));
  FacesContext.getCurrentInstance().addMessage(null, new
    FacesMessage(FacesMessage.SEVERITY_ERROR,"Sample Error
    Msg", null));
  FacesContext.getCurrentInstance().addMessage(null, new
    FacesMessage(FacesMessage.SEVERITY_FATAL,"Sample Fatal
    Msg", null));
}
```

What just happened?

We added `FacesMessage` objects with various severity levels in the `actionListener` method `addMultipleMsgs()`, and updated the form using `autoUpdate="true"`. Then `<p:messages/>` displays all of those errors as follows:

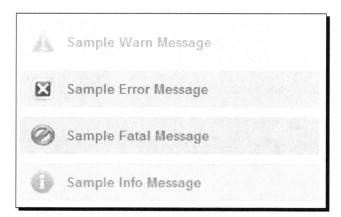

Displaying notifications using the growl component

The PrimeFaces Growl component is similar to MAC OS's growl notification widget, which can be used to display `FacesMessage`. The Growl component is similar to the Messages component, and thus have similar attributes to customize its behavior.

We can use the following attributes to customize the Growl components behavior:

- `autoUpdate`: When enabled, growl is updated for each AJAX request implicitly.
- `severity`: It is a comma-separated list of severity levels for display purposes only.
- `globalOnly`: When `true`, only the `FacesMessage` without client IDs are displayed. Default is `false`.
- `sticky`: It specifies whether the message should stay instead of being hidden automatically. Default is `false`.
- `life`: It is the duration in milliseconds to display non-sticky messages. Default is 6000 ms.
- `for`: Identifier of the component whose messages to display only, takes precedence when used with `globalOnly`.
- `escape`: It defines whether HTML would be escaped or not, defaults to `true`.

Let us see how to use the `<p:growl>` component to display the `FacesMessage objects` as follows:

Time for action – displaying FacesMessages with growl

We will see how to display `FacesMessages` with different severity levels as Growl notifications using `<p:growl>`. Perform the following steps:

1. Create a JSF page with a form and growl component:

```
<p:growl id="growl1" autoUpdate="true"
  severity="info,warn,error, fatal" sticky="true"
  globalOnly="true"/>
<h:form>
  <p:commandButton
  actionListener="#{messagesController.addMultipleMsgs}"
  value="Add Multiple Messages"/>
</h:form>
```

What just happened?

When the button is clicked, we have added `FacesMessages`. The growl component gets updated automatically and displayed notifications because we have set `autoUpdate` mode to `true`.

Displaying tooltips using the Tooltip component

Browsers provide native support for showing tooltips using the `title` attribute, but it is too primitive. PrimeFaces provides a Tooltip component with enhanced features and various customization options such as effects, events and custom content support.

By default, tooltips will be displayed on the `mouseover` event and hides on the `mouseout` event. We can customize this behavior using the `showEvent` and `hideEvent` attributes:

```
<p:tooltip for="emailId" showEvent="focus" hideEvent="blur"
  value="Please enter Email Id (Ex: admin@gmail.com)"/>
```

We can also specify tooltip text using the `title` attribute on the component itself:

```
<p:inputText id="emailId" value="" title="Please enter Email Id (Ex:
  admin@gmail.com)"/>
<p:tooltip for="emailId" showEvent="focus" hideEvent="blur" />
```

We can apply different styles of effects while showing or hiding tooltips using the `showEffect` and `hideEffect` attributes:

```
<p:tooltip for="emailId" showEffect="slide" hideEffect="explode"
  showEvent="focus" hideEvent="blur" value="Please enter Email Id
  (Ex: admin@gmail.com)"/>
```

In addition to plain text, we can also display HTML content, images, and so on as tooltips.

Time for action – displaying tooltip for UI components

Let us see how to display tooltips on various events, with different effects and containing HTML elements, such as images, by performing the following steps:

1. Create a form with input fields and add a `<p:tooltip>` component to display the tooltip using the following code:

```
<h:form title="Tooltip demo form">
  <p:panel header="Form with Tooltips">

    <h:panelGrid columns="3">
      <p:outputLabel value="EmailId:"/>
      <p:inputText id="emailId" value=""/>
      <p:tooltip for="emailId" value="Please enter Email Id (Ex:
        admin@gmail.com)"/>

      <p:outputLabel value="FirstName:"/>
      <p:inputText id="firstName" value=""/>
      <p:tooltip for="firstName" showEvent="focus"
hideEvent="blur"
        value="Please enter FirstName"/>

      <p:outputLabel value="LastName:"/>
      <p:inputText id="lastName" value=""/>
      <p:tooltip for="lastName" showEffect="slide"
        hideEffect="explode" value="Please enter LastName"/>

      <p:commandLink id="photo" value="OptimusPrime"/>
      <p:tooltip for="photo">
        <p:graphicImage value="/resources/images/optimusprime.
jpg"/>
      </p:tooltip>
    </h:panelGrid>

  </p:panel>
</h:form>
```

What just happened?

We have used the `<p:tooltip>` component to display tooltips with custom effects and events. Also, we have used the `<p:tooltip>` component to display HTML content such as images using `<p:graphicImage>`.

Using global tooltips

We can bind tooltips globally to all clickable elements with the `title` attribute instead of specifying for each element separately.

Time for action – using global tooltips

Let us see how we can use global tooltips to display tooltips for all the components, which are specifying the `title` attribute. Perform the following steps:

1. Include a global Tooltip component and specify tooltips for various components using the `title` attribute as follows:

```
<p:tooltip />
<h:form>
    <h:panelGrid id="grid" columns="2" cellpadding="5">
        <h:outputText value="Input: " />
        <p:inputText id="focus" title="Tooltip for an input"/>

        <h:outputText value="Link: " />
        <h:outputLink id="fade" value="#" title="Tooltip for a
          link">
            <h:outputText value="Fade Effect" />
        </h:outputLink>

        <h:outputText value="Button: " />
        <p:commandButton value="Update" title="Update
          Components" update="@parent"/>
    </h:panelGrid>
</h:form>
```

What just happened?

We have used a global `<p:tooltip/>` component to display tooltips for all the components, which have a `title` attribute set. This is a preferable approach to using a `<p:tooltip>` component for each component separately. You can customize tooltips for any specific component by adding `<p:tooltip>` to the respective component individually.

Partial Processing and Rendering using the Fragment component

The Fragment component can be used to define a segment of components that should be partially processed, and updated when an AJAX request is triggered by any descendant component. This comes in very handy when there are multiple sections of the form with different actions for each segment.

By using fragments, **Partial Processing and Rendering** becomes very easy because we don't need to specify the component IDs to be processed using the `process` attribute, and component IDs to be updated using the `update` attribute.

For example, in the **User Account** screen we can have **User Details** and **Contact Details** sections, each with a command button to update the respective sections' fields.

Time for action – using the Fragment component

Let us look at how we can use two fragments for the **User Details** and **Contact Details** sections and partially process each of them individually. Perform the following steps for using two fragment components:

1. Create a form with two fragments for **User Details** and **Contact Details** sections as follows:

```
<h:form>
  <p:panel header="User Account>
  <p:fragment autoUpdate="true">
  <p:fieldset legend="User Details">
  <h:panelGrid columns="3">
    <h:outputLabel for="emailId" value="EmailId:" />
    <p:inputText id="emailId" value="#{userController.emailId}"
      required="true" label="emailId"/>
    <p:message for="emailId" display="icon"/>

    <h:outputLabel for="firstName" value="FirstName:" />
    <p:inputText id="firstName" value="#{userController.
      firstName}" required="true" label="FirstName"/>
    <p:message for="firstName" display="icon"/>

    <h:outputLabel for="lastName" value="LastName:" />
    <p:inputText id="lastName" value="#{userController.
      lastName}" />
    <p:message for="lastName" display="icon"/>
    <p:commandButton value="Save"
      actionListener="#{userController.updateUserDetails()}"/>
    </h:panelGrid>
  </p:fieldset>
  </p:fragment>

  <p:fragment autoUpdate="true">
   <p:fieldset legend="Contact Details">
      <h:panelGrid columns="3">
    <h:outputLabel for="phone" value="Phone:" />
    <p:inputText id="phone" value="#{userController.phone}"
      required="true" label="Phone"/>
    <p:message for="phone" display="icon"/>
```

```
        <h:outputLabel for="fax" value="Fax:" />
        <p:inputText id="fax" value="#{userController.fax}" />
        <p:message for="fax" display="icon"/>

        <p:commandButton value="Save" actionListener="#
        {userController.updateContactDetails()}"/>
        </h:panelGrid>
    </p:fieldset>
    </p:fragment>
    </p:panel>
</h:form>
```

What just happened?

We have created two `<p:fragment>` components to wrap each of the **User Details** and **Contact Details** sections. Have a look at the following screenshot:

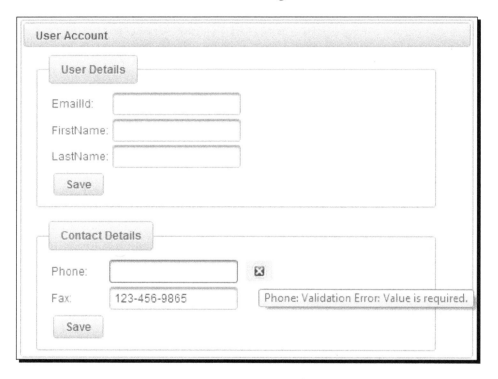

When you click on the **Save** button in the **User Details** section, only `EmailId`, `FirstName`, and `LastName` fields will be processed and updated. Similarly, when you click on the **Save** button in the **Contact Details** section, only **Phone** and **Fax** fields will be partially processed and updated. Even though some required fields in other fragments are blank, they won't be processed and hence no error messages will be displayed.

Introducing the Sticky component

Sticky component can be used to make other components stick within the viewport while scrolling. For example, we may want to stick the top header and navigation menu bar section of the web page while scrolling.

Let us see how we can make the header and menu bar sticky with a `<p:sticky>` component using the following code:

```
<h:body>
  <div class="wrapper">
  <p:panel id="headerSection">
  <p:panel id="header"  style="height: 80px; margin-bottom: 2px;">
    <h1>TechBuzz</h1>
  </p:panel>
  <h:form id="mainMenuForm">
    <p:menubar>
    <p:menuitem value="Home" url="home.jsf"/>
    <p:menuitem value="New Post" url="createPost.jsf"/>
    <p:menuitem value="Search" url="search.jsf"/>
    <p:menuitem value="My Account" url="userAccount.jsf"/>
      <p:menuitem value="Administration" url="admin.jsf"/>
      </p:menubar>
  </h:form>
  </p:panel>
  <p:panel style="margin-bottom: 3px; min-height: 500px;">
    <ui:insert name="bodyContent"/>
  </p:panel>
  </div>
  <p:sticky target="headerSection" margin="3"/>
</h:body>
```

Here we have specified the header section panel with the component ID `headerSection` as the target of the `<p:sticky>` component. So, when you scroll through the web page, the `headerSection` panel content will stick at the top of the page. Also, we have specified the margin in pixels for the Sticky component via the `margin` attribute.

 The DataTable component has out-of-the-box support for the Sticky header by setting the attribute `stickyHeader="true"`.

Introducing the RequestContext utility

`RequestContext` is a utility class provided by PrimeFaces with the following features, which come in handy at times:

- Update UI components from Managed Bean methods programmatically
- Execute JavaScript from Managed Bean methods
- Add AJAX callback parameters
- ScrollTo a specific component after the AJAX update

The `RequestContext` utility class can be used with both AJAX and Non-AJAX requests. We can also use the `requestContext.isAjaxRequest()` method to determine whether the current request is an AJAX or Non-AJAX request.

Updating UI components

Normally we use the `update` attribute to specify the component ID(s) that needs to be updated after an AJAX request is completed.

We can also update the components using the `org.primefaces.context.RequestContext` utility function.

Time for action – updating UI components using RequestContext.update()

In this section, we will demonstrate how to update client-side view components from the server side using the following steps:

1. Create a form with an input field and a submit button as follows:

```
<h:form id="form1">
  <h:panelGrid columns="2">
    <h:outputLabel value="EmailId" />
    <p:inputText id="emailId" value="#{requestContextController.
emailId}"/>

    <p:commandButton id="submitBtn" value="Submit" actionListener=
"#{requestContextController.handleSubmit}" />
  </h:panelGrid>
  <h:outputText value="You have Entered :
#{requestContextController.emailId}" />
</h:form>
```

2. In the action handler method, update the form component using the `RequestContext.update()` method as follows:

```
public void handleSubmit(ActionEvent ae)
{
   RequestContext.getCurrentInstance().update("form1");
}
```

What just happened?

We got a `RequestContext` instance using `RequestContext.getCurrentInstance()` and used the `update()` method to update the form component with `id="form1"`. So, if you enter `admin@gmail.com` in the e-mail input field and click on the **Submit** button, you will see the updated text as **You have Entered: admin@gmail.com**.

Executing JavaScript from server-side code

You can execute JavaScript code using the `RequestContext.execute()` method.

Suppose you want to display a dialog box once the form submission request is completed successfully.

Time for action – executing JavaScript using RequestContext.execute()

We will now take a look at how to execute client-side JavaScript code from server-side code by performing the following steps:

1. Create a form with a Dialog component using the following code:

```
<h:form id="form1">
  <h:panelGrid columns="2">
    <h:outputLabel value="EmailId" />
    <p:inputText id="emailId" value="#{requestContextController.emailId}"/>

    <p:commandButton id="submitBtn" value="Submit" actionListener="#{requestContextController.handleSubmit}" />
  </h:panelGrid>

  <p:dialog header="Information" widgetVar="dlg" closeOnEscape="true" modal="true">
    You have Entered : #{requestContextController.emailId}
  </p:dialog>
</h:form>
```

2. In the action handler method, execute the JavaScript call, dlg.show(), to display a dialog widget using the RequestContext.execute() method. Use the following code for the same:

```
public void handleSubmit(ActionEvent ae)
{
  RequestContext context = RequestContext.getCurrentInstance();
  context.update("form1");
  context.execute("dlg.show()");
}
```

What just happened?

When the **Submit** button is clicked, we have updated the form and executed the JavaScript code dlg.show() which displays a dialog widget.

Adding AJAX callback parameters

Sometimes, we may need to execute an AJAX request and perform some UI updates based on the callback parameters received from managed bean methods.

Let us see how we can add a basic parameter and a **Plain Old Java Object** (**POJO**), which will be serialized into JSON as a callback parameter.

Time for action – adding callback parameters using RequestContext.addCallbackParam()

In this section, we will see how to add callback parameters to an AJAX response payload by performing the following steps:

1. Create a form with an input field and submit button using the following code:

```
<h:form id="form1">
  <h:panelGrid columns="2">
    <h:outputLabel value="EmailId" />
    <p:inputText id="emailId"
  value="#{requestContextController.emailId}" required="true"/>

    <p:commandButton id="submitBtn" value="Submit"
  actionListener="#{requestContextController.handleSubmit}"
    oncomplete="handleComplete(xhr, status, args)"/>
  </h:panelGrid>
  <h:outputText value="You have Entered :
#{requestContextController.emailId}" />

</h:form>
```

2. Implement the `oncomplete` callback JavaScript function `handleComplete()` as follows:

```
<script type="text/javascript">
  function handleComplete(xhr, status, args)
  {
    if(args.validationFailed) {
      alert("Validation Failed");
    }
    else {
      var text = "Email Id :"+ args.emailId + "\n"+"FirstName
  :"+args.user.firstName+"\nLastName "+args.user.lastName;
      alert(text);
    }
  }
</script>
```

3. In the action handler method, add callback parameters using the `RequestContext.addCallbackParam()` method as follows:

```
public void handleSubmit(ActionEvent ae)
{
  RequestContext context = RequestContext.getCurrentInstance();
  context.update("form1");

  context.addCallbackParam("emailId", emailId);
  User user = new User();
  user.setFirstName("Optimus");
  user.setLastName("Prime");
  context.addCallbackParam("user", user);
}
```

What just happened?

In the action handler method, we have added callback parameters using `RequestContext.addCallbackParam("paramName", paramValue)`.

We have created a JavaScript callback function `handleComplete(xhr, status, args)` to be executed on completion of the AJAX request.

By default, the `validationFailed` callback parameter is added implicitly if JSF validation fails. So, initially we are checking whether there are any validation failures and then we will display, `emailId`, user's `firstName` and `lastName` extracted from the `args` parameter, which we have added using the `RequestContext.addCallbackParam()` method. The `user` object that we added as a callback parameter is converted into JSON format as `{"firstName":"Optimus", "lastName":"Prime"}`.

Scrolling to a component

We can use the `RequestContext.scrollTo()` method to scroll to a component after an AJAX request is completed:

```
RequestContext.getCurrentInstance().scrollTo("clientId");
```

Internally, this method will call the JavaScript function `PrimeFaces.scrollTo ("clientId")`. So you can directly use this in your JavaScript to scroll to any component.

Displaying pop-up dialogs using the Dialog component

Dialog is a container component that can contain other components, and overlay other elements on the page. By default, the Dialog component will not be visible. We can use a client-side API to show or hide the dialog.

Time for action – displaying a dialog

Let us see how to create a basic Dialog component and show/hide based on button click events by performing the following steps:

1. Create a form with a Dialog component and two buttons to show and hide the dialog using the following code:

```
<h:form>
  <p:commandButton value="ShowDialog" onclick="dlg1.show();"
    type="button" />
  <p:commandButton value="HideDialog" onclick="dlg1.hide();"
    type="button" />
  <p:dialog id="simpleDialog" header="Simple Dialog"
    widgetVar="dlg1" width="300" height="50">
    <h:outputText value="PrimeFaces Simple Dialog" />
  </p:dialog>
</h:form>
```

What just happened?

We have created a Dialog component using `<p:dialog>` and used two `<p:commandButton>` components to perform `show` and `hide` actions on the dialog box using client-side API calls `dlg1.show()` and `dlg1.hide()`.

The Dialog component has the following attributes, which can be used to customize its behavior:

◆ `widgetVar`: This specifies the n Name of the client-side widget.
◆ `visible`: When enabled, the dialog is visible by default. The default is `false`.

- ◆ `header`: This is the text of the header.
- ◆ `footer`: This is the text of the footer.
- ◆ `modal`: It enables modality, default is false.
- ◆ `draggable`: This specifies drag ability, default is true.
- ◆ `resizable`: It specifies resizability, default is true.
- ◆ `closable`: This defines if close icon should be displayed or not, default is true .
- ◆ `position`: This defines where the dialog should be displayed. By default, dialog is positioned at the center of the viewport. We can change the location by setting the position value using the following ways:
    - ❑ Single string value representing the position within viewport, such as position= "center". Other possible values are left, right, top, and bottom.
    - ❑ Comma - separated x and y co-ordinate values such as position="150, 450".
    - ❑ Comma - separated position values such as position="right,top".
- ◆ `showEffect`: This specifies the effect to use when showing the dialog.
- ◆ `hideEffect`: This specifies the effect to use when hiding the dialog.
- ◆ `onShow`: This determines the client-side callback to execute when dialog is displayed.
- ◆ `onHide`: This determines the client-side callback to execute when dialog is hidden.
- ◆ `minimizable`: This determines whether a dialog is minimizable or not, default is `false`.
- ◆ `maximizable`: This determines whether a dialog is maximizable or not, default is `false`.
- ◆ `appendToBody`: This appends Dialog component as a child of the document body. Default is `false`.
- ◆ `closeOnEscape`: This defines whether dialog should close on the escape key, default is `false`.
- ◆ `dynamic`: This enables lazy loading of the content with AJAX, default is `false`.
- ◆ `focus`: This defines which component to have focus by default.

We can apply different styles of effects while displaying or hiding the dialog using the `showEffect` and `hideEffect` attributes:

```
<p:dialog id="simpleDialog" header="Simple Dialog" widgetVar="dlg1"
  width="300" height="50"
      showEffect="bounce"  hideEffect="explode">
  <h:outputText value="PrimeFaces Simple Dialog" />
</p:dialog>
```

Available options for `showEffect` and `hideEffect` are: blind, bounce, clip, drop, explode, fade, fold ,highlight, puff, pulsate, scale, shake, size, slide, and transfer.

Using the Dialog component's client-side callbacks

Let us see how we can hook-up client-side JavaScript functions as callbacks using the `onShow` and `onHide` attributes.

Time for action – client-side callbacks for onShow and onHide

Here we will demonstrate how to trigger JavaScript functions when dialog show and hide events happen. Perform the following steps:

1. Create a Dialog component and two JavaScript functions to be called as callback functions for `onShow` and `onHide` events:

```
<h:head>
  <script>
    function simpleDlgOnShowCallback()
    {
      alert('Simple Dialog displayed successfully');
    }

    function simpleDlgOnHideCallback()
    {
      alert('Simple Dialog is closed successfully');
    }

  </script>
</h:head>


<h:form>

    <p:commandButton value="ShowDialog" onclick="dlg1.show();"
      type="button" />
    <p:commandButton value="HideDialog" onclick="dlg1.hide();"
      type="button" />

    <p:dialog id="simpleDialog" header="Simple Dialog"
      widgetVar="dlg1"
      width="300" height="50"
        onShow="simpleDlgOnShowCallback()"
          onHide="simpleDlgOnHideCallback()">
      <h:outputText value="PrimeFaces Simple Dialog" />
    </p:dialog>

</h:form>
```

What just happened?

We have created two JavaScript functions, `simpleDlgOnShowCallback()` and `simpleDlgOnHideCallback()` and hooked-up as callback functions using the `onShow` and `onHide` attributes. When you click on the **ShowDialog** button, the dialog will be shown and `simpleDlgOnShowCallback()` will be invoked. Similarly, when you click on the **HideDialog** button or close the dialog using the close icon, then the dialog will be closed and `simpleDlgOnHideCallback()` will be invoked.

Handling the dialog close event

For the Dialog component, you can also register event listeners for `close`, `minimize`, and `maximize` events.

Time for action – the Dialog component close event listener

Let us see how we can register a listener for the `close` event using the following steps:

1. Create a Dialog component and register a `close` event listener using the `<p:ajax>` tag:

```
<h:form id="form3" style="width: 400px;">
  <p:messages id="msgs" for="SampleDialog"/>
  <p:panel header="Dialog - Close Event Listener">
    <p:commandButton value="ShowDialog" onclick="dlg3.show();"
      type="button" />

    <p:dialog id="SampleDialog" header="Sample Dialog"
      widgetVar="dlg3" width="300" height="50"
        showEffect="bounce"  hideEffect="explode"
          closeOnEscape="true">
      <p:ajax event="close" update="msgs"
        listener="#{dialogController.handleDialogClose}"/>
      <p:outputLabel value="PrimeFaces Dialog"/>
    </p:dialog>
  </p:panel>
</h:form>
```

2. Implement the `handleDialogClose()` method to handle the close event:

```
public void handleDialogClose(CloseEvent event)
{
  String msg = event.getComponent().getId() + " dialog is
    closed";
  FacesContext facesContext =
    FacesContext.getCurrentInstance();
  FacesMessage message = new FacesMessage
    (FacesMessage.SEVERITY_INFO, msg, msg);
  facesContext.addMessage("SampleDialog", message);
}
```

What just happened?

We have created a dialog and hooked-up a close event listener using `<p:ajax event="close" update="msgs" listener="#{dialogController.handleDialogClose}"/>`. So when dialog is closed, the event listener method `handleDialogClose()` will be invoked. In `handleDialogClose()` we have added a INFO `FacesMessage` to `FacesContext`. As we have specified to update the `<p:messages id="msgs"/>` component with `update="msgs"`, the message is displayed as **SampleDialog dialog is closed**. Similarly, we can register event listeners for minimize and maximize events.

Working with a Dialog component containing forms

We can create Dialog components containing other complex components including forms, data tables, and so on. In our TechBuzz application, we will have a register link in the menu bar and when the user clicks on the register link, we will show a dialog containing a registration form. If there are any validation errors, the registration form should be redisplayed with error messages, otherwise the user should be registered, close the dialog, and display a registration success message.

Time for action – creating dialog with a registration form

In this section, we will demonstrate how to use forms in Dialog components and close the dialog conditionally such as in a successful form submission.

1. Create a dialog containing a user **Registration Form** using the following code:

```
<p:messages id="globalMsgs" globalOnly="true"
  autoUpdate="true"/>
<h:outputLink id="registerLink" value="javascript:void(0)"
  onclick="registrationDlg.show()" title="Registration">
  <p:outputLabel value="Register"/>
</h:outputLink>

<p:dialog id="registrationDlgId" widgetVar="registrationDlg"
  header="Registration Form"
  focus="registrationFormDlg:firstName">

  <h:form id="registrationFormDlg">
    <p:messages id="regmsgs" severity="error"/>
    <h:panelGrid columns="2" width="400px">
      <p:outputLabel value="EmailId:"/>
      <p:inputText
        value="#{dialogController.registerUser.emailId}"
        required="true" label="EmailId"/>
```

```
<p:outputLabel value="Password"/>
<p:password
   value="#{dialogController.registerUser.password}"
   required="true" label="Password"/>

<p:outputLabel value="FirstName:*" />
   <p:inputText id="firstName"
      value="#{dialogController.registerUser.firstName}"
          required="true" label="FirstName"/>

<p:outputLabel value="LastName:" />
<p:inputText id="lastName"
   value="#{dialogController.registerUser.lastName}" />

<p:outputLabel value="Phone:" />
<p:inputText id="phone"
   value="#{dialogController.registerUser.phone}" />

<p:outputLabel value="DOB:" />
<p:calendar
   value="#{dialogController.registerUser.dob}"
      id="dob"/>

   <p:commandButton value="Register"
      actionListener="#{dialogController.doRegister}"
          update="@form" oncomplete=
             "handleRegistrationRequest(xhr, status, args)"/>
   </h:panelGrid>
 </h:form>
</p:dialog>
```

2. Create an `oncomplete` event handler callback JavaScript function
    `handleRegistrationRequest()`:

```
function handleRegistrationRequest(xhr, status, args)
{
  if(args.validationFailed || !args.registered) {
    $("#registrationDlgId").effect("shake", { times:3 }, 100);
  } else {
    registrationDlg.hide();
    $("#registerLink").fadeOut();
  }
}
```

3. Create the `doRegister()` method in the `DialogController` managed bean:

```
public void doRegister()
{
  boolean registered = false;
  try {
    System.out.println("Register User "+registerUser);//write
      code for persisting user data into database
    String msg = "User Registered successfully";
    FacesContext.getCurrentInstance().addMessage(null, new
      FacesMessage(FacesMessage.SEVERITY_INFO, msg, msg));
    registerUser = new User();
    registered = true;
  } catch (Exception e) {
    String msg = e.getMessage();
    String componentId = "registrationFormDlg";
    FacesContext.getCurrentInstance().addMessage(componentId,
      new FacesMessage(FacesMessage.SEVERITY_ERROR, msg, msg));
  }
  RequestContext.getCurrentInstance().addCallbackParam
    ("registered", registered);
}
```

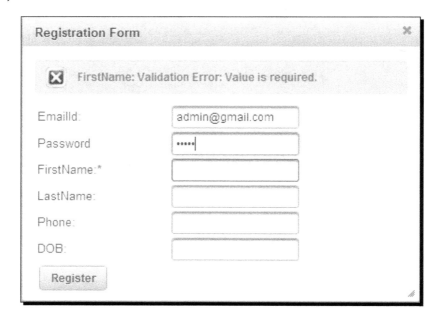

What just happened?

We have created a complex dialog box, which contains the user's **Registration Form**. By default, focus will be on the `FirstName` field as we have specified `focus="registrationFormDlg:firstName"`. We hooked-up a JavaScript callback function `handleRegistrationRequest(xhr, status, args)` for the `oncomplete` event. When the registration form is submitted, we are checking whether there are any validation errors using `args.validationFailed`. Also, we are checking whether registration is successful or not with `args.registered`, which we have added in the `DialogController.doRegister()` handler method. In case of validation errors or registration failed, we have applied a `shake` effect for dialog and displayed errors using `<p:messages>`. On successful registration, we are closing the dialog using `registrationDlg.hide()` and hiding the register link using `$("#registerLink").fadeOut()`.

Here, we have used a JavaScript - centric approach to conditionally close the dialog. There is another approach to close the dialog conditionally.

If registration is successful then we can close the dialog in the `DialogController.doRegister()` method using `RequestContext.execute("script")` as follows:

```
<p:commandButton value="Register" actionListener="#{dialogController.
doRegister}" update="msgs"/>

public void doRegister()
{
  try {
    userService.register(registerUser);
    FacesContext.getCurrentInstance().addMessage(null, new
      FacesMessage(FacesMessage.SEVERITY_INFO, "User Registered
      successfully", null));
    RequestContext.getCurrentInstance().execute
      ("registrationDlg.hide();");
    RequestContext.getCurrentInstance().execute
      ("$('#registerLink').fadeOut();");
    registerUser = new User();
  } catch (Exception e) {
    FacesContext.getCurrentInstance().addMessage
      ("registrationFormDlg", new
      FacesMessage(FacesMessage.SEVERITY_ERROR,
      e.getMessage(), null));
  }
}
```

We will learn more features of the `RequestContext` utility in the next dialog framework section.

> We should keep in mind the following important tips from the official PrimeFaces User Guide while using the Dialog component:

◆ Use `appendToBody` with care as the page definition and HTML DOM would be different, for example if the dialog is inside a `<h:form>` component and `appendToBody` is enabled, on the browser, dialog would be outside the form and may cause unexpected results. In this case, nest a form inside a dialog.

◆ Do not place dialog inside tables, containers as in `divs` with relative positioning or with non - visible overflow defined. In cases such as these, functionality might be broken. This is not a limitation but a result of the DOM model. For example, dialog inside a layout unit, tab view, and accordion are a few of examples. The same applies to `confirmDialog` as well.

Introducing dialog framework

PrimeFaces 4.0 introduces a new dialog framework, which can be used to generate dynamic dialog components at runtime with the content from any external facelets page.

In order to use a dialog framework, first we need to configure `DialogActionListener`, `DialogNavigationHandler`, and `DialogViewHandler` in `faces-config.xml` as follows:

```
<faces-config ...>
  <application>
    <action-listener>
    org.primefaces.application.DialogActionListener
  </action-listener>
    <navigation-handler>
    org.primefaces.application.DialogNavigationHandler
  </navigation-handler>
    <view-handler>
    org.primefaces.application.DialogViewHandler
  </view-handler>
  </application>
</faces-config>
```

We can use the `RequestContext.openDialog()` and `RequestContext.closeDialog()` methods to open and close the dialog components.

Time for action – showing the search users screen in dialog

Let us see how we can display the search users page (searchUsers.xhtml) in the
Dialog component.

1. Create a CommandButton button whose actionListener triggers open the dialog
using the RequestContext.openDialog() method:

```
<p:commandButton value="Search Users" actionListener="#{userContro
ller.searchUsersForm}" />

public void searchUsersForm()
{
  RequestContext.getCurrentInstance().
    openDialog("searchUsers");
}
```

2. Create the search users page searchUsers.xhtml as follows:

```
<!DOCTYPE html>
<html xmlns="http://www.w3.org/1999/xhtml"
      xmlns:h="http://java.sun.com/jsf/html"
      xmlns:f="http://java.sun.com/jsf/core"
      xmlns:ui="http://java.sun.com/jsf/facelets"
      xmlns:p="http://primefaces.org/ui">
    <h:head>
        <title>Search Users</title>
    </h:head>
    <h:body>
        <h:form>
          <p:inputText value="#{userController.searchName}"/>
          <p:commandButton value="Search" actionListener="#{use
rController.searchUsersByName}" update="usersTbl"/>
          <p:dataTable id="usersTbl" value="#{userController.
searchUsers}" var="user">
              <p:column headerText="EmailId">
                  #{user.emailId}
              </p:column>
              <p:column headerText="Name">
                  #{user.firstName} #{user.lastName}
              </p:column>
          </p:dataTable>
        </h:form>
    </h:body>
</html>
```

What just happened?

When you click on the **Search Users** button, a new dialog will be opened with the response of `searchUsers.xhtml` page content.

We can also use the other overloaded `openDialog()` method to pass optional configuration parameters:

```
RequestContext.openDialog(String outcome, Map<String,Object>
  options, Map<String,List<String>> params);
```

The following is the list of supporting options:

- `modal`: This controls modality of the dialog. Default value is `false`.

- `resizable`: When enabled, this makes dialog resizable. Default value is `true`.

- `draggable`: When enabled, this makes dialog `draggable`. Default value is `true`.

- `width`: This specifies the width of the dialog. Default value is `auto`.

- `height`: This specifies the height of the dialog. Default value is `auto`.

- `contentWidth`: This specifies the width of the dialog content. Default value is `640`.

- `contentHeight`: This specifies the height of the dialog content. Default value is `auto`.

We can open the dialog with customization options as follows:

```
public void searchUsersForm()
{
  Map<String,Object> options = new HashMap<String, Object>();
  options.put("modal", true);
  options.put("resizable", false);
  options.put("contentHeight", 800);
  RequestContext.getCurrentInstance().openDialog("searchUsers",
    options,null);
}
```

Passing data from the dialog back to the source page

The dialog framework also supports passing data from the dialog back to the parent page. The trigger component, which opens the dialog, needs to have a `dialogReturn` AJAX event listener registered to receive data returned from the dialog.

Time for action – passing data from the search users dialog to the source page

Let us add a new column Select to the DataTable in the searchUsers.xhtml page to select a user, and pass the selected user's details back to source page. Perform the following steps:

1. Create a DataTable component with a Select column to choose a user row using the following code:

    ```
    <p:dataTable id="usersTbl"
      value="#{userController.searchUsers}" var="user">
      <p:column headerText="EmailId">
        #{user.emailId}
      </p:column>
      <p:column headerText="Name">
        #{user.firstName} #{user.lastName}
      </p:column>
      <p:column headerText="Select">
        <p:commandButton icon="ui-icon-search"
          actionListener="#{userController.selectSearchUser
          (user)}" />
      </p:column>
    </p:dataTable>
    ```

2. When the user selects a row (user), close the dialog by passing the selected user object as data:

    ```
    public void selectSearchUser(User user){
      RequestContext.getCurrentInstance().closeDialog(user);
    }
    ```

3. Register the dialogReturn AJAX listener to the **Search Users** button, which will receive the SelectEvent object as a parameter. We can obtain the selected user object from SelectEvent with event.getObject(), and update the **UserDetails** PanelGrid to display the selected user details:

    ```
    <p:commandButton value="Search Users"
      actionListener="#{userController.searchUsersForm}">
      <p:ajax event="dialogReturn"
      listener="#{userController.handleSelectSearchUser}"
      update="UserDetails"/>
    </p:commandButton>

    <h:panelGrid id="UserDetails" columns="2">
      <h:outputLabel value="EmailId" />
      <h:outputText value="#{userController.searchUser.emailId}" />
      <h:outputLabel value="FirstName" />
    ```

```
        <h:outputText value="#{userController.searchUser.firstName}" />
      </h:panelGrid>

      public void handleSelectSearchUser(SelectEvent event){
        this.searchUser = (User) event.getObject();
      }
```

What just happened?

We have created a `CommandButton` button to open a dialog with the **Search Users** form. When the user searches for users, the results will be populated in a data table. When you select any user by clicking on the **Select** button, the selected user object will be passed back to the source page and display the results in the **User Details** panel grid.

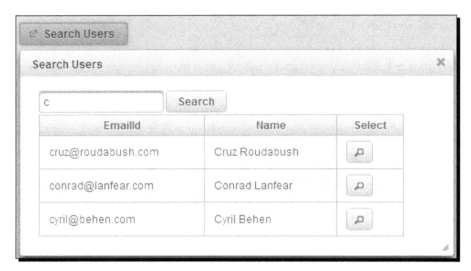

Displaying FacesMessage in dialog

The dialog framework also provides a simple utility method, `RequestContext.showMessageInDialog(FacesMessage)` to display `FacesMessage` in a dialog. This comes in very handy when displaying the user action status once the application logic is executed:

```
<p:commandButton value="Delete" actionListener="#{userController.
deleteUser}" />

public void deleteUser() {
  //logic to delete user
  RequestContext.getCurrentInstance().showMessageInDialog(new
FacesMessage("User deleted successfully"));
}
```

- At the moment, `<p:commandButton>` and `<p:commandLink>` supports `dialogReturn`
- Nested dialogs are not supported
- Calls to the `DialogFramework` API within a non-AJAX are ignored

Introducing the ConfirmDialog component

The `ConfirmationDialog` component is a replacement for the traditional JavaScript confirm dialog with skinning and customization features.

Very common scenarios to display the confirm dialog box is when the user tries to delete some data.

Time for action – creating a confirmation dialog

Let us see how to create a confirmation dialog with **Yes** and **No** options.

1. Create a confirmation dialog using `<p:confirmDialog>` with two buttons for **Yes** and **No** options:

```
<h:form id="form1" style="width: 300px; margin-left: 5px;">
  <p:growl/>
  <p:panel header="User Form">
    <h:panelGrid columns="2">
      <h:outputText value="EmailId:" />
      <p:inputText value="admin@gmail.com"/>
      <p:commandButton value="Delete" onclick="cnfDlg.show()"
        />
    </h:panelGrid>
  </p:panel>
  <p:confirmDialog widgetVar="cnfDlg" header="Confirmation"
    message="Are you sure to delete?" >
```

```
      <p:commandButton value="Yes"
        actionListener="#{confirmDialogController.handleDelete}"
        oncomplete="cnfDlg.hide();" update="form1"/>
      <p:commandButton value="No" onclick="cnfDlg.hide();"/>
    </p:confirmDialog>

  </h:form>
```

2. Implement the action handler method using the following code:

```
public void handleDelete(ActionEvent event)
{
  FacesMessage msg = new
    FacesMessage(FacesMessage.SEVERITY_INFO, "Deleted
    Successfully",null);
  FacesContext.getCurrentInstance().addMessage(null, msg);
}
```

What just happened?

We have created a ConfirmDialog box using the `<p:confirmDialog>` component with **Yes** and **No** buttons. As ConfirmDialog is hidden by default, we have created a **Delete** button to display the confirmation dialog. When a **Delete** button is clicked, we will display the ConfirmationDialog using a client-side JavaScript API call cnfDlg.show(). When the **Yes** button is clicked, the action handler method handleDelete() will be executed. Once the AJAX request is completed, the oncomplete event callback gets invoked where we are closing the ConfirmationDialog box using the cnfDlg.hide() method. If the **No** button is clicked, then we are simply closing the **Confirmation** dialog box using the cnfDlg.hide() method.

Using the global ConfirmDialog component

In our applications we might want to display confirmation dialogs with **Yes** or **No** options in many scenarios. Instead of creating a separate `<p:confirmDialog>` component for each of the scenarios, we can use a single global confirm dialog box.

We can create a global ConfirmationDialog as follows:

```
<p:confirmDialog global="true">
  <p:commandButton value="Yes" type="button" styleClass="ui-
confirmdialog-yes" icon="ui-icon-check"/>
  <p:commandButton value="No" type="button" styleClass="ui-
confirmdialog-no" icon="ui-icon-close"/>
</p:confirmDialog>
```

Note that in the global `ConfirmDialog` component, the command component with `styleClass="ui-confirmdialog-yes"` triggers a **Yes** action, and the command component with `styleClass="ui-confirmdialog-no"` triggers a **No** action.

Once the global `ConfirmDialog` component is defined, any trigger component, such as the **Delete** button in the preceding example, can use `<p:confirm>` behavior by passing specific header text, dialog messages and icon values:

```
<p:commandButton value="Delete"
  actionListener="#{userController.deleteUser()}">
  <p:confirm header="Confirmation" message="Are you sure to delete?"
    icon="ui-icon-alert"/>
</p:commandButton>
```

Suppose you want to display a confirm dialog while deleting a Tag. We no longer need to create a `<p:confirmDialog>`, instead we can just use `<p:confirm>` to trigger the global `ConfirmDialog` as follows:

```
<p:commandButton value="Delete" actionListener="#{adminController.
deleteTag()}">
  <p:confirm header="Confirmation" message="Are you sure to delete
Tag?" icon="ui-icon-alert"/>
</p:commandButton>
```

The global `ConfirmDialog` component is very useful as we can define the global `ConfirmDialog` component in the main layout page and can use `<p:conrfirm>` to show `ConfirmDialog` whenever required.

Displaying notifications using the NotificationBar component

The `NotificationBar` is a component to display notifications as a fixed positioned panel either on top or bottom of the page. As the notification bar is a Panel component, you can place other JSF components inside it. You can use client-side API methods `show()` and `hide()` respectively to show and hide the notification bar through the `widgetVar` value.

Time for action – displaying notification messages

Let us see how to create a simple notification bar to display a message using JavaScript `show()` and `hide()` methods.

1. Create a NotificationBar component to display notification messages and two buttons to `show` and `hide` the notification bar widget:

```
<p:notificationBar id="bar" widgetVar="notifBar" style="height:
    20px; background-color: #8B0000;">
    <h:outputText value="There are New Unread Emails in your
        MailBox." style="color:#FFF;font-size:20px;"/>
</p:notificationBar>
<h:form>
    <p:commandButton value="Show" onclick="notifBar.show()"/>
    <p:commandButton value="Hide" onclick="notifBar.hide()"/>
</h:form>
```

What just happened?

We have created a notification bar widget using a `<p:notificationBar>` component. When the **Show** and **Hide** buttons are clicked, we have displayed and closed `NotificationBar` using the client-side JavaScript API calls `notifBar.show()` and `notifBar.hide()`.

By default, `NotificationBar` is hidden. If you want to display `NotificationBar` on page load set autoDisplay="true".

You can apply effects while displaying and hiding the NotificationBar using the `effect` attribute. Default is fade. If you don't want to apply any effects, you can set effect="none" which will turn off the animation effects. Also you can set the speed of effect using the `effectSpeed` attribute that can take normal, slow or fast as its value:

```
<p:notificationBar id="bar" widgetVar="notifBar" effect="slide"
effectSpeed="slow" style="height: 20px; background-color: #8B0000;">
    <h:outputText value="There are New Unread Emails in your MailBox."
        style="color:#FFF;font-size:20px;"/>
</p:notificationBar>
```

By default, `NotificationBar` will be placed at the top of the page. You can set position="bottom" to display `NotificationBar` at the bottom of the page. As the `NotificationBar` positioning is fixed, even if you scroll the page, the notification bar will not scroll.

Hiding NotificationBar automatically

Once the notification bar is displayed, you may want to hide it automatically with a delay. You can do this using the JavaScript `setTimeout()` method as follows:

Time for action – automatically hiding NotificationBar

In this section we will demonstrate how to display the PrimeFaces NotificationBar component and automatically hide it using the JavaScript `setTimeout()` function.

Create a NotificationBar widget and buttons to show and hide it using the following code:

```
<p:notificationBar id="bar" widgetVar="notifBar" position="top"
  effect="slide" effectSpeed="slow" style="height: 20px;
  background-color: #8B0000;">
  <h:outputText value="There are New Unread Emails in your
    MailBox." style="color:#FFF;font-size:20px;"/>
</p:notificationBar>

<h:form>
  <p:commandButton value="Show" onclick="notifBar.show()"/>
  <p:commandButton value="Hide" onclick="notifBar.hide()"/>
  <p:commandButton value="Show &amp; Auto Hide"
    onclick="showNotifBar()"/>
</h:form>
```

2. Create an `onclick` event handler JavaScript function `showNotifBar()` using the following code:

```
<script>
  var timeoutID = null;
  function showNotifBar()
  {
    notifBar.show();
    timeoutID = window.setTimeout(hideNotifBar, 5000);
  }

  function hideNotifBar()
  {
    notifBar.hide();
    if(timeoutID != null)
    {
      window.clearTimeout(timeoutID);
    }
  }
</script>
```

What just happened?

When the **Show & Auto Hide** button is clicked, the showNotifBar() function gets invoked and the notification bar is displayed by calling notifBar.show(). Also, we are using the window.setTimeout() function to call hideNotifBar() with a delay of 5000 milliseconds, which will close the notification bar using the notifBar.hide() method.

Blocking a region using the BlockUI component

The BlockUI component can be used to block other JSF UI components during AJAX processing. With the special AJAX integration, AJAX requests from any of the trigger components will block the UI component for the onstart event and unblock for the oncomplete event.

We may want to block a particular UI component or even entire page while some background processing is running. For example, when we submit a form, we may want to block the form to prevent users from doing any action on the form until the response is received from the server.

Time for action – blocking the form

In this section, we will demonstrate how to block a specific region, such as a form, while the form submission background process is still running.

1. Create a user **Registration Form** and BlockUI component to block the form while registration is inprocess using the following code:

```
<p:growl autoUpdate="true"/>
<h:form id="form1">
  <p:panel header="BlockUI">
  <h:panelGrid columns="2">
    <h:outputLabel value="EmailId" />
    <p:inputText value="#{blockUIController.
      registerUser.emailId}"/>

    <h:outputLabel value="Password" />
    <p:password value="#{blockUIController.registerUser.
      password}"/>

    <p:commandButton id="submitBtn" value="Register"
      actionListener="#{blockUIController.doRegister}"/>
  </h:panelGrid>
  </p:panel>
  <p:blockUI block="form1" trigger="submitBtn"/>
</h:form>
```

2. Create an action handler method `doRegister()`:

```
public void doRegister()
{
  //To simulate 5 seconds delay from server
  try {
    Thread.sleep(5000);
  } catch (InterruptedException e) {
    e.printStackTrace();
  }
  System.out.println("Register User :"+registerUser);
  FacesContext.getCurrentInstance().addMessage(null,
      new FacesMessage(FacesMessage.SEVERITY_INFO, "User
        Registered successfully", null));
}
```

What just happened?

We have used the `<p:blockUI>` component to block the **Registration Form** when the form is submitted by the user, and automatically unblock when the response is received from the server.

The `block` attribute needs to be set to the `id` of the component to be blocked, and the `trigger` attribute needs to be set to the ID(s) of the component(s), which triggers the blocking action.

- ◆ BlockUI supports multiple triggers by setting comma - separated component ids to trigger blocking
- ◆ BlockUI doesn't support blocking absolute or fixed positioned components such as `Dialog` or `ConfirmDialog` components

You can also display custom content such as loading or processing animation images when the UI component is blocked as follows:

```
<p:blockUI block="regForm" trigger="submitBtn">
  Processing<br />
  <p:graphicImage value="/resources/images/ajax-loader.gif"/>
</p:blockUI>
```

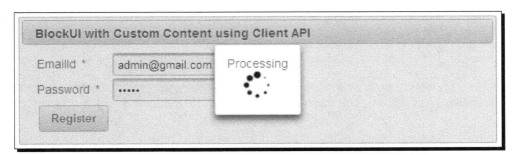

You can also use a client-side JavaScript API to block UI components as follows:

```
<p:commandButton id="submitBtn" value="Register"
  actionListener="#{userController.doRegister}" onclick="bui.show()"
  oncomplete="bui.hide()"/>

<p:blockUI block="regForm" widgetVar="bui">
  Processing<br />
  <p:graphicImage value="/resources/images/ajax-loader.gif"/>
</p:blockUI>
```

Here, instead of using the `trigger` attribute on the `<p:blockUI>` component, we triggered blocking and unblocking actions with `show()` and `hide()` JavaScript methods using `onclick` and `oncomplete` events on `commandButton`.

Understanding PrimeFaces selectors

The jQuery library has great support for selecting DOM elements based on various criteria such as ID, name, or CSS class and so on.

Following are a few examples on how to use jQuery Selectors to select DOM elements:

- `$("p")`: All `<p>` elements
- `$("#userId")`: The element with `id="userId"`
- `$(".navbar")`: All elements with `class="navbar"`

PrimeFaces has integration with the jQuery Selector API for referencing JSF component models. So you can use the jQuery Selector API to choose components to be processed or updated.

In most of the scenarios, using the jQuery Selector API for finding UI components yields better performance as the components are picked by navigating through the DOM tree on the client side instead of navigating through the JSF component tree on the server side and hence reduce the load on the server.

You can give a selector expression to update and process UI components using the following syntax:

```
process="@(expression)" update="@(expression)"
```

For example, `process="@(.ui-panel :input)" update="@(.ui-panel)"`

Here, the `process` selector selects all input components in panel components and proceses them. Similarly, the `update` selector selects all panel components and updates them.

Time for action – updating UI components using jQuery Selectors

Let us see how to use the jQuery Selector API to update JSF UI components.

1. Create a form with some mandatory input fields and `commandButtons`. When buttons are clicked, update the form or fields using jQuery Selector expressions as follows:

```
<h:form id="loginForm" styleClass="myform" style="width: 500px;">
  <p:panel header="Login Form">
  <p:messages/>
  <h:panelGrid columns="2">
    <h:outputText value="EmailId:" />
    <p:inputText value="#{jQuerySelectorController.user.emailId}"
    required="true" label="EmailId"/>

    <h:outputText value="Password:" />
    <p:password value="#{jQuerySelectorController.user.password}"
    required="true" label="Password"/>

      <p:commandButton value="Update Form" actionListener="#{jQueryS
electorController.doLogin}"
    update="@(#loginForm)"/>
      <p:commandButton value="Update Fields" actionListener="#{jQuer
ySelectorController.doLogin}"
    process="@(:input)" update="@(:input)"/>

  </h:panelGrid>
  </p:panel>
</h:form>
```

2. Implement the action handler method `doLogin()`:

```
public void doLogin()
{
  if("admin@gmail.com".equals(user.getEmailId()) && "admin".
equals(user.getPassword()))
  {
    FacesContext.getCurrentInstance().addMessage(null,
        new FacesMessage(FacesMessage.SEVERITY_INFO, "Login
          successful", null));
  } else {
    FacesContext.getCurrentInstance().addMessage(null,
        new FacesMessage(FacesMessage.SEVERITY_ERROR, "Login
          failed", null));
  }
}
```

What just happened?

When the **Update Form** button is clicked, we are updating the form component using the jQuery Selector `@(#loginForm)`. When we click on the **Update Fields** button, we are processing and updating only input fields using jQuery Selector expressions `process="@(:input)" update="@(:input)"`.

We can also update the `loginForm` using the style `class` instead of `id` as follows:

```
<p:commandButton value="Login"
  actionListener="#{jQuerySelectorController.doLogin}"
  update="@(.myform)"/>
```

The jQuery Selector API is feature rich and easy to use. You can find more information on jQuery Selectors at `http://api.jquery.com/category/selectors/`.

Following are some commonly used jQuery Selectors to find UI components in the DOM tree:

Expression	Description
`@(*)`	All elements in the document.
`@(#lastname)`	The element with `id="lastname"`.
`@(.header)`	All elements with `class="header"`.
`@(.header,.preview)`	All elements with the class "`header`" or "`preview`".
`@(p)`	All `<p>` elements.
`@(p:first)`	The first `<p>` element.
`@(p:last)`	The last `<p>` element.
`@(tr:even)`	All even `<tr>` elements.
`@(tr:odd)`	All odd `<tr>` elements.
`@(:focus)`	The element that currently has focus.
`@([href])`	All elements with a `href` attribute.
`@(:input)`	All input elements.
`@(:text)`	All input elements with `type="text"`.
`@(:selected)`	All selected input elements.
`@(:checked)`	All checked input elements.

We can use these selector expressions for the `update` and `process` attributes to specify which UI components have to be updated or processed.

Introducing the search expression framework

PrimeFaces 4.0 introduces a new search expression framework for referencing UI components on both the client and server side with more keywords. In addition to more keywords, the search expression framework also supports nested composite expressions as well, which gives finer control on selecting components.

JSF supports referencing UI components by using component identifiers and also provides some keywords to refer commonly used UI elements such as, @this, @all, @none, and @form.

- ◆ @this: Represents current component
- ◆ @all: Represents whole view
- ◆ @form: Represents closest ancestor form of current component
- ◆ @none: Represents no component

Look at the following form which uses identifiers for partial processing and updating the form:

```
<h:form id="loginForm">
...
<p:commandButton id="loginBtn" process="loginBtn"
  update="loginForm"/>
</h:form>
```

Instead of using component identifiers we can use the keywords so that if the identifiers are changed we don't need to update in all the places:

```
<h:form id="loginForm">
  ...
  <p:commandButton id="loginBtn" process="@this" update="@form"/>
</h:form>
```

But JSF supporting keywords are very limited. PrimeFaces provides the following additional keywords for many of the commonly used components:

- ◆ @parent: Represents parent of the current component
- ◆ @child(n): Represents nth child
- ◆ @previous: Represents previous sibling
- ◆ @next: Represents next sibling
- ◆ @widgetVar(name): Represents component with given widgetVar
- ◆ @namingcontainer: Represents closest ancestor naming container of current component
- ◆ @composite: Represents closest composite component ancestor

In addition to these new keywords, the PrimeFaces search expression framework also supports nested composite expressions such as `@this:@parent`, `@parent:@child(1)`, or `@widgetVar(registrationForm):@child(2):compId`.

Let us see how we can use these search expressions to partial process and update components:

```
<h:form widgetVar="registrationForm">
  <p:panel id="panel" header="User Registration Form" style="margin-
bottom:10px;">
    <p:messages id="messages" />
    <h:panelGrid columns="3">
      <h:outputLabel for="@next" value="EmailId: *" />
      <p:inputText id="emailId" value="#{userController.emailId}"
required="true" label="EmailId"/>
      <p:message for="@previous" />

      <h:outputLabel for="firstName" value="FirstName: *" />
      <p:inputText id="firstName" value="#{userController.firstName}"
required="true" label="FirstName"/>
      <p:message for="firstName" />

      <h:outputLabel for="lastName" value="LastName: *" />
      <p:inputText id="lastName" value="#{userController.lastName}"
required="true" label="LastName"/>
      <p:message for="lastName" />
    </h:panelGrid>
  </p:panel>
  <h:panelGrid columns="1">
    <p:commandButton value="Process Form" process="@parent:@parent"
update="@form"/>
    <p:commandButton value="Process LastName" process="@form:@
child(1):lastName" update="@all"/>
    <p:commandButton value="Process RegistrationForm Widget"
process="@widgetVar(registrationForm)" update="@form"/>
  </h:panelGrid>
</h:form>
```

In the preceding form, the **Process Form** button processes the form because `@parent` refers to the parent `<h:panelGrid>`; and `@parent:@parent` refers to the parent of `<h:panelGrid>`, which is `<h:form widgetVar="registrationForm">`.

The **Process LastName** processes the `LastName` component because `@form:child(1):lastName` represents the component whose ID is the `lastName` within the first child component of the enclosing form, which is `<p:panel id="panel" ..>`.

The **Process RegistrationForm Widget** button processes the `RegistrationForm` component because `@widgetVar(registrationForm)` refers to the component whose `widgetVar="registrationForm"`.

Also we have used `<h:outputLabel for="@next"..>` and `<p:message for="@previous" />` both referring to `<p:inputText id="emailId" ..>`.

Summary

In this chapter, we have learned about frequently used PrimeFaces UI components such as Messages, Growl, Fragment, Sticky, Dialog, ConfirmDialog, BlockUI, and NotificationBar. We learned how to use RequestContext utility methods and looked into the PrimeFaces jQuery Selectors API integration. Also, we have explored how to use a dialog framework and search expression framework.

In the next chapter, we will learn a very important and interesting topic, PrimeFaces Client Side Validation (CSV) framework, which is introduced in the latest PrimeFaces4.0.

4

Introducing the PrimeFaces
Client Side Validation Framework

In most of the web applications, getting input data from the user, validating, and converting the user-entered text into domain objects is an obvious process. So, JSF hooks up these common steps into a Request Processing Lifecycle of a web request. JSF provides input data conversions and validations on the server side. But many applications demand performing validations on the client side, to reduce the load on the server, as well as to provide immediate feedback on validation errors.

*PrimeFaces 4.0 introduces a brand new **Client Side Validation (CSV)** framework, which performs input data conversions and validations on the client side which is compatible with the server-side implementation. The PrimeFaces CSV framework not only supports built-in JSF validators and converters, but also provides extension points to work with custom validators and converters.*

In this chapter, we will cover:

- ◆ Configuring and using the Client Side Validation framework
- ◆ Triggering client-side validations based on events
- ◆ Supporting I18N for validation messages
- ◆ Extending the CSV framework with custom JSF validators and converters
- ◆ Using the CSV framework with the Bean Validation API
- ◆ Extending the CSV framework with custom Bean Validation annotations

Configuring and using the Client Side Validation framework

The PrimeFaces CSV feature is disabled by default. To enable the Client-side Validation framework, we need to configure `<context-param>` in the `web.xml` file as follows:

```
<context-param>
    <param-name>primefaces.CLIENT_SIDE_VALIDATION</param-name>
    <param-value>true</param-value>
</context-param>
```

We can trigger client-side validations by setting the `validateClient` attribute to `true` on command components such as `<p:commandButton>` or `<p:commandLink>`.

Time for action – performing client-side validations

Let us see how we can create a **User Registration** form with regular JSF validators and converters, and perform validations using the PrimeFaces Client-side Validation framework, by performing the following step:

> *1.* Create a **User Registration** form and enable client-side validations by setting the `validateClient` attribute to `true`:

```
<h:form id="registrationForm">
<p:panel header="User Registration">
    <h:panelGrid columns="3">
        <p:outputLabel value="EmailId:*"/>
        <p:inputText id="emailId"
            value="#{userController.registerUser.emailId}"
        label="EmailId" required="true">
        <f:validateRegex pattern="^[_A-Za-z0-9-\+]+(\.[_A-Za-
            z0-9-]+)*@[A-Za-z0-9-]+(\.[A-Za-z0-9]+)*(\.[A-Za-
            z]{2,})$" />
        </p:inputText>
        <p:message for="emailId"/>

        <p:outputLabel value="Password:*"/>
        <p:password id="password"
            value="#{userController.registerUser.password}"
            required="true" label="Password">
            <f:validateLength minimum="4" maximum="12"/>
        </p:password>
        <p:message for="password"/>
```

```
<p:outputLabel value="FirstName:*"/>
<p:inputText id="firstName"
    value="#{userController.registerUser.firstName}"
    required="true" label="FirstName"/>
<p:message for="firstName"/>

<p:outputLabel value="LastName:"/>
<p:inputText id="lastName"
    value="#{userController.registerUser.lastName}"/>
<p:message for="lastName"/>

<p:outputLabel value="Phone:"/>
<p:inputText id="phone"
    value="#{userController.registerUser.phone}"
    validatorMessage="Invalid Phone. Phone number
        should be in 999-999-9999 format">
    <f:validateRegex pattern="^\d{3}-\d{3}-\d{4}$"/>
</p:inputText>
<p:message for="phone"/>

<p:outputLabel value="DOB:"/>
<p:inputText id="dob"
    value="#{userController.registerUser.dob}"
    label="DOB"
    validatorMessage="Invalid DOB. Date should be in
        MM/dd/yyyy format">
<f:convertDateTime pattern="MM/dd/yyyy" />
</p:inputText>
<p:message for="dob"/>

<p:commandButton action="#{userController.doRegister}"
value="Register" update="@form" validateClient="true"/>
</h:panelGrid>
</p:panel>
</h:form>
```

What just happened?

The **User Registration** form performs conversions and validations on the client side instead
of regular JSF server-side conversions and validations, as we have enabled the PrimeFaces
Client-side Validation framework by setting the `validateClient="true"` attribute on
`<p:commandButton>`.

The PrimeFaces CSV framework works with PrimeFaces components only and doesn't support standard JSF components such as <h:inputText>, <h:inputSecret>, and so on.

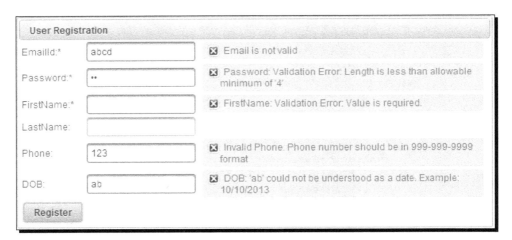

With the client-side validations enabled, all required field validations, length validation, the **DOB** (Date of Birth) value conversion/validation, and the **EmailId** or **Phone** values regex validations will be performed on the client side. Similarly, you can use other JSF validations such as <f:validateDoubleRange/>, <f:validateLongRange/>, and the <f:convertNumber/> converter as well.

Triggering client-side validations based on events

The client-side validations get triggered when the form is submitted, that is when you click on the command component with the validateClient attribute set to true. But sometimes, we may want to show validation errors immediately instead of waiting for the user to submit the form.

We can enable instant validations using <p:clientValidator/> for various events such as change(default), blur, keyup, and so on, as follows:

```
<p:inputText id="emailId"
    value="#{userController.registerUser.emailId}" label="EmailId"
    required="true" validatorMessage="#{msg['invalid.email']}">
    <f:validateRegex pattern="^[_A-Za-z0-9-\+]+(\.[_A-Za-z0-9-
        ]+)*@[A-Za-z0-9-]+(\.[A-Za-z0-9]+)*(\.[A-Za-z]{2,})$" />
    <p:clientValidator />
</p:inputText>
<p:password id="password"
    value="#{userController.registerUser.password}"
```

```
        required="true" label="Password">
        <f:validateLength minimum="4" maximum="12"/>
        <p:clientValidator event="blur"/>
    </p:password>
```

In the preceding form, the **EmailId** input field will be validated if the values are changed as change, which is the default event. The **Password** field will be validated when it loses focus.

The PrimeFaces CSV framework supports AJAX and non-AJAX requests as well as **Partial Processing and Rendering**.

For non-AJAX requests, all the visible and editable input components in the form will be validated and message components must be placed inside the form.

The following CommandButton component triggers the non-AJAX request, and all the input fields will be processed and redisplay the **User Registration** page along with error messages, if any validations or conversions failed:

```
<p:commandButton action="#{userController.doRegister}" ajax="false"
    validateClient="true" value="Register"/>
```

The following CommandButton component triggers an AJAX request and only the **EmailId** and **Password** fields will be processed and the enclosing form will be updated:

```
<p:commandButton action="#{userController.doRegister}"
    value="Register" validateClient="true" process="emailId,
    password" update="@form"/>
```

Supporting I18N for validation messages

The PrimeFaces CSV framework displays conversion or validation errors in the same way as the JSF server-side conversion or validation error messages, and also supports Internationalization (I18N). You can find more information on Internationalization in the *Understanding Internationalization (I18N) and Localization (L10N)* section of *Chapter 7, Introducing Advanced Input Components*.

You can have error messages in ResourceBundles that are registered in the `faces-config. xml` file and use them for validation or conversion messages as follows:

```
<p:inputText id="email"
    value="#{userController.registerUser.emailId}" label="EmailId"
    required="true" validatorMessage="#{msg['invalid.email']}">
    <f:validateRegex pattern="^[_A-Za-z0-9-\+]+(\.[_A-Za-z0-9-
        ]+)*@[A-Za-z0-9-]+(\.[A-Za-z0-9]+)*(\.[A-Za-z]{2,})$" />
    <p:clientValidator />
</p:inputText>
<p:message for="email"/>
```

Create the `messages.properties` file which contain messages for the English locale as follows:

```
invalid.email=EmailId is invalid
```

Also, create the `messages_fr.properties` file which contain messages for the French locale as follows:

```
invalid.email=Email est invalide
```

A validation error message will be displayed based on the current locale if **EmailId** is invalid.

 PrimeFaces only provides English translations for the built-in JSF conversion and validation error messages. You can find the PrimeFaces client-side validation message templates in the `primefaces-4.0.jar/META-INF/resources/primefaces/validation/validation.js` file.

Extending the CSV framework with custom JSF validators

In addition to built-in converters and validators, JSF supports creating custom converters and validators. We can also extend the PrimeFaces CSV framework to support custom converters and validators, and perform conversions and validations on the client side, similar to the built-in converters and validators.

To create a custom JSF validator, we need to implement `javax.faces.validator.Validator`. To make this custom validator work with the PrimeFaces CSV framework, we also need to implement the `org.primefaces.validate.ClientValidator` interface to provide a client validator ID and validation metadata.

Time for action – using the custom JSF validator on the client side

Let us see how we can create a custom JSF validator and use it with the PrimeFaces CSV framework, by performing the following steps:

1. Create the `CreditCardValidator` class to validate whether the credit card number is in the 9999 9999 9999 9999 format or not:

    ```
    import java.util.*;
    import java.util.regex.Pattern;
    import javax.faces.application.FacesMessage;
    import javax.faces.component.UIComponent;
    import javax.faces.context.FacesContext;
    ```

```
import javax.faces.validator.FacesValidator;
import javax.faces.validator.Validator;
import javax.faces.validator.ValidatorException;
import org.primefaces.validate.ClientValidator;

@FacesValidator("creditCardValidator")
public class CreditCardValidator implements Validator,
    ClientValidator
{
    private Pattern pattern;
    private static final String CC_PATTERN = "^\\d{4} \\d{4}
        \\d{4} \\d{4}$";

    public CreditCardValidator() {
        pattern = Pattern.compile(CC_PATTERN);
    }

    public void validate(FacesContext context, UIComponent
        component, Object value) throws ValidatorException {
        if(value == null) {
            return;
        }
        if(!pattern.matcher(value.toString().trim()).matches()) {
            throw new ValidatorException(new
                FacesMessage(FacesMessage.SEVERITY_ERROR,
                "Validation Error", value + " is not a valid
                creditcard number"));
        }
    }

    public Map<String, Object> getMetadata() {
        Map<String, Object> metadata = new HashMap<String,
            Object>();
        metadata.put("data-error-msg", "Invalid CreditCard
            Number");
        return metadata;
    }

    public String getValidatorId() {
        return "creditCardValidator";
    }
}
```

2. Implement the client-side `validator` function and configure it:

```
<script type="text/javascript">
    PrimeFaces.validator['creditCardValidator'] =
    {
        pattern: /\d{4} \d{4} \d{4} \d{4}/,
        validate: function(element, value) {
```

```
                        if(!this.pattern.test(value)) {
                            throw {
                                summary: 'Validation Error',
                                detail: element.data('error-msg')
                            }
                        }
                    }
                }
            };
        </script>
```

3. Register the `CreditcardValidator` class for the `CreditCard` input field:

```
<h:form>
    . . .
    <p:inputText id="cc" value="#{paymentController.cc}">
        <f:validator validatorId="creditCardValidator" />
    </p:inputText>
    <p:message for="cc"  />
    . . .
    <p:commandButton value="Submit" ajax="false"
        validateClient="true"/>
</h:form>
```

What just happened?

We have implemented the `validate()` method to check the credit card format using the Regular Expression API. Also, we have implemented the `getValidatorId()` method to return the name of the client-side validator ID and `getMetadata()` to return the metadata that will be used by the client-side `validate` function. In the preceding code snippets, we have configured the client-side `validator` function using `<script>` tags inside the facelets pages directly. But it is a better approach to put it in the separate JavaScript file and include them using the `<h:outputStylesheet>` tag.

 We need to add metadata with the key pattern `data-{keyname}` in order to obtain the value on the client side using `element.data('{keyname}')`.

Extending the CSV framework with custom JSF converters

Similarly, we can also create a custom JSF converter and extend the PrimeFaces CSV framework to perform conversions on the client side. To make this custom converter work with the PrimeFaces CSV framework, we also need to implement the `org.primefaces.convert.ClientConverter` interface to provide the client converter ID and validation metadata.

Time for action – using the custom JSF converter on the client side

Let us see how we can create a custom JSF converter and use it with the PrimeFaces CSV framework, by performing the following steps:

1. Create a bean named `CreditCardBean`:

    ```java
    public class CreditCardBean
    {
        private String number;
        public CreditCardBean(String number)
        {
            this.number = number;
        }
        public String toString()
        {
            return number;
        }
    }
    ```

2. Create the `CreditCardConverter` class to convert a string value into the `CreditCardBean` object and vice versa by implementing `javax.faces.convert.Converter` and `org.primefaces.convert.ClientConverter`:

    ```java
    @FacesConverter("creditCardConverter")
    public class CreditCardConverter implements Converter,
        ClientConverter
    {
        private static final String CC_PATTERN = "^\\d{4} \\d{4}
            \\d{4} \\d{4}$";

        @Override
        public Object getAsObject(FacesContext context, UIComponent
            component, String value)
        {
            if (value==null || value.trim().equals("")) {
                return null;
            }
            else {

                if(!Pattern.compile(CC_PATTERN).matcher(value).
                    matches()){
                    FacesMessage msg = new
                        FacesMessage(FacesMessage.SEVERITY_ERROR,
                        "Conversion Error", "Can't convert
                        "+value+" into CreditCard Number");
    ```

```java
                throw new ConverterException(msg);
            }
        return new CreditCardBean(value);
        }
    }

    @Override
    public String getAsString(FacesContext context, UIComponent
        component, Object value)
    {
        if (value == null || value.equals("")) {
            return "";
        } else if(value instanceof CreditCardBean){
            return String.valueOf(((CreditCardBean)
                value).toString());
        }
        return "";
    }

    @Override
    public Map<String, Object> getMetadata()
    {
        return null;
    }

    @Override
    public String getConverterId()
    {
        return "creditCardConverter";
    }
}
```

3. Implement and configure the client-side `CreditCard` converter:

```javascript
<script type="text/javascript">
    PrimeFaces.converter['creditCardConverter'] = {
        pattern: /\d{4} \d{4} \d{4} \d{4}/,
        convert: function(element, value) {
            if(!this.pattern.test(value)) {
            throw {
                summary: 'Conversion Error',
                detail: value + ' cannot be converted into
                    CreditCard Number'
            }
            }
        }
        return value;
    }
};
</script>
```

4. Register `CreditCardConverter` for the `CreditCard` input field:

```
<h:form>
    ...
    <h:outputLabel for="creditCardBean" value="CreditCard:" />
    <p:inputText id="creditCardBean"
        value="#{paymentController.creditCardBean}">
        <f:converter converterId="creditCardConverter"/>
        <f:validator validatorId="creditCardValidator" />
    </p:inputText>
    <p:message for="creditCardBean"/>
    ...
    <p:commandButton value="Submit" ajax="false"
        validateClient="true"/>
</h:form>
```

What just happened?

We have implemented the `getAsObject()` and `getAsString()` methods to convert the `CreditCard` bean into a string and vice versa. Also, we have implemented the `getConverterId()` method to return the name of the client-side converter ID and `getMetadata()` to return the metadata that will be used by the client-side `convert()` function. We have implemented the client-side `converter` function by checking the credit card number format using JavaScript regex. Here, we are not really converting the input into any other data type. But in real scenarios, you may have to convert the input string value into number, date, or currency types.

Using the CSV framework with the Bean Validation API

The Bean Validation API simplifies the data validation process using metadata constraint annotations on Java beans. The Bean Validation API also supports XML-based constraint definitions, but many prefer annotations due to its ease of use. The Bean Validation API provides most of the commonly used constraints and we can create our own custom validators also, if required.

JSF provides out-of-the-box integration with the Bean Validation API, which means instead of specifying the validations inside facelets pages, we can define the validation constraints on Java beans. When you submit the form, if there are any violations to the metadata constraints, those errors will be displayed as `FacesMessages` with `ERROR` severity.

The PrimeFaces Client-side Validation framework also supports Bean Validation API-based validations and performs the validations on the client side.

Time for action – using the CSV framework with the Bean Validation API

Let us see how we can use the Bean Validation API to specify validation constraints and perform validations using PrimeFaces client-side validations, by performing the following steps:

1. Create the `UserBean` class and specify the validation constraints using the Bean Validation API annotations:

```
public class UserBean
{
    private Integer id;
    @Pattern(regexp="^[_A-Za-z0-9-\\+]+(\\.[_A-Za-z0-9-]+)*@[A-
        Za-z0-9-]+(\\.[A-Za-z0-9]+)*(\\.[A-Za-z]{2,})$",
        message="Invalid Email Id")
    private String emailId;
    @Size(min=2,max=5)
    private String password;
    @Size(min=1, message="FirstName should not be empty")
    private String firstName;
    private String lastName;
    @Pattern(regexp="^\\d{3}-\\d{3}-\\d{4}$")
    private String phone;
    @Past
    private Date dob;
    @AssertTrue(message="You must agree to Terms and
        Conditions")
    private boolean agreeToTnc;

    //setters and getters
}
```

2. Create the **User Registration** form:

```
<h:form id="registrationForm">
    <p:panel header="User Registration">
        <h:panelGrid columns="3">
            <p:outputLabel value="EmailId:*"/>
            <p:inputText id="emailId"
                value="#{userController.userBean.emailId}"
                label="EmailId">
                <p:clientValidator event="blur"/>
            </p:inputText>
            <p:message for="emailId"/>

            <p:outputLabel value="Password:*"/>
```

```
<p:password id="password"
    value="#{userController.userBean.password}"
    label="Password">
    <p:clientValidator/>
</p:password>
<p:message for="password"/>

<p:outputLabel value="FirstName:*"/>
<p:inputText id="firstName"
    value="#{userController.userBean.firstName}"
    label="FirstName"/>
<p:message for="firstName"/>

<p:outputLabel value="LastName:"/>
<p:inputText id="lastName"
    value="#{userController.userBean.lastName}"/>
<p:message for="lastName"/>

<p:outputLabel value="Phone:"/>
<p:inputText id="phone"
    value="#{userController.userBean.phone}"/>
<p:message for="phone"/>

<p:outputLabel value="DOB:"/>
<p:inputText id="dob"
    value="#{userController.userBean.dob}"
    label="DOB">
    <f:convertDateTime pattern="MM/dd/yyyy" />
</p:inputText>
<p:message for="dob"/>

<h:outputLabel for="agreeToTnc" value="Agree to
    Terms and Conditions " />
<p:selectBooleanCheckbox id="agreeToTnc"
    value="#{userController.userBean.agreeToTnc}"
    />
<p:message for="agreeToTnc" />

<p:commandButton
    action="#{userController.doRegister}"
    value="Register" validateClient="true"
    update="@form"/>

    </h:panelGrid>

</p:panel>
</h:form>
```

What just happened?

We have specified the validation metadata on `UserBean` properties using various annotations such as `@Size`, `@Pattern`, `@AssertTrue`, and so on. We have not specified any validations in the registration form, and enabled client-side validations using the `validateClient="true"` attribute on `<p:commandButton>`.

When you click on the **Register** button, the form data will be validated on the client side and displays error messages accordingly. Also, note that we have used `<p:clientValidator/>` for the **EmailId** and **Password** fields to trigger validations immediately instead of waiting till the form is submitted.

User Registration		
EmailId:	abc	☒ Invalid Email Id
Password:*	.	☒ size must be between 2 and 5
FirstName:*		☒ FirstName should not be empty
LastName:		
Phone:		☒ must match "\d{3}-\d{3}-\d{4}"
DOB:	09/10/2014	☒ must be in the past
Agree to Terms and Conditions ☐		☒ You must agree to Terms and Conditions
Register		

Extending the CSV framework with custom Bean Validation annotations

The Bean Validation API also supports creating custom validation annotations and we can extend the PrimeFaces CSV framework to support custom Bean Validation annotations as well.

We can create a custom Bean Validation annotation and specify constraint validator using the `@Constraint` annotation. In order to make it work with the PrimeFaces CSV framework, we also need to specify the client-side constraint resolver using the `@ClientConstraint` annotation.

Time for action – using the custom Bean Validation annotation with the CSV framework

In this section, we will demonstrate how to create a custom `CreditCard` validator @ `CreditCard` using the Bean Validation API, and show how to extend the PrimeFaces CSV framework to work with the custom Bean Validation annotation @CreditCard, by performing the following steps:

1. Create a custom Bean Validation annotation @CreditCard:

```
@Target({METHOD,FIELD,ANNOTATION_TYPE})
@Retention(RUNTIME)
@Constraint(validatedBy=CreditCardConstraintValidator.class)
@ClientConstraint(resolvedBy=CreditCardClientValidation
    Constraint.class)
@Documented
public @interface CreditCard
{
    String message() default "{com.packtpub.techbuzz.validation.
creditcard.invalid}";
    Class<?>[] groups() default {};
    Class<? extends Payload>[] payload() default {};
}
```

2. Implement the `CreditCardConstraintValidator` class by implementing `ConstraintValidator<CreditCard, String>`:

```
public class CreditCardConstraintValidator implements
    ConstraintValidator<CreditCard, String>
{

    private Pattern pattern;
    private static final String CC_PATTERN = "^\\d{4} \\d{4}
        \\d{4} \\d{4}$";
    public void initialize(CreditCard a) {
        pattern = Pattern.compile(CC_PATTERN);
    }

    public boolean isValid(String value,
ConstraintValidatorContext cvc) {
        if(value == null)
            return true;
        else{
            return pattern.matcher(value.toString()).matches();
        }
    }
}
```

3. Implement `CreditCardClientValidationConstraint` by implementing `ClientValidationConstraint`:

```
public class CreditCardClientValidationConstraint implements
    ClientValidationConstraint
{
    public Map<String, Object> getMetadata(ConstraintDescriptor
        constraintDescriptor) {
        Map<String,Object> metadata = new HashMap<String,
            Object>();
        Map attrs = constraintDescriptor.getAttributes();
        String message = (String)attrs.get("message");
        if(message != null){
            metadata.put("data-cc-msg", message);
        }
        return metadata;
    }

    public String getValidatorId() {
        return "CreditCard";
    }
}
```

4. Implement the client-side `validator` and configure it:

```
<script type="text/javascript">
    PrimeFaces.validator['CreditCard'] = {
        pattern: /\d{4} \d{4} \d{4} \d{4}/,
        MESSAGE_ID:
            'com.packtpub.techbuzz.validation.
            creditcard.invalid',
        validate: function(element, value) {
            var vc = PrimeFaces.util.ValidationContext;
            if(!this.pattern.test(value)) {
                var msgStr = element.data('cc-msg');
                var msg = msgStr ? {summary:msgStr, detail:
                    msgStr} : vc.getMessage(this.MESSAGE_ID);
                throw msg;
            }
        }
    };
</script>
```

5. Use a custom `@CreditCard` annotation for validating the `creditCard` property:

```
public class PaymentController
{
    @CreditCard(message="Invalid CreditCard Number")
    private String creditCard;
    ...
}
<h:form>
    ...
    <h:outputLabel value="CreditCard:" />
    <p:inputText id="creditCard"
        value="#{paymentController.creditCard}" />
    <p:message for="creditCard"/>
    ...
    <p:commandButton value="Submit" ajax="false"
        validateClient="true"/>
</h:form>
```

What just happened?

We have created a custom Bean Validation constraint annotation `@CreditCard` and implemented `ConstraintValidator`. We have also implemented the `ClientValidationConstraint` resolver `CreditCardClientValidationConstraint` to return a client validator ID and metadata that will be used by the client-side validator. We have implemented the client-side `validator` JavaScript function and configured it. Finally, we have used the `@CreditCard` annotation with the `creditCard` property and provided a custom validator error message using the `message` attribute. We have enabled the client-side validations using `validateClient="true"` for the form submission command component.

◆ We need to add the custom Bean Validation message keys in the `ValidationMessages.properties` file which should be available in the root classpath.

◆ PrimeFaces only provides English translations for built-in Bean Validation error messages. You can find the corresponding PrimeFaces client-side validation message templates in the `primefaces-4.0.jar/META-INF/resources/primefaces/validation/beanvalidation.js` file.

Summary

In this chapter, we have learned how to use the PrimeFaces **Client-side Validation (CSV)** framework to perform conversions and validations on the client side. We looked at how to use the Bean Validation API along with the CSV framework. Also, we learned how to extend the CSV framework to work with custom JSF converters/validators and custom Bean Validation annotations.

In the next chapter, we will learn about the most important topic, PrimeFaces input UI components. Also, we will learn about some advanced input components such as InputMask, Editor, and AutoComplete widgets.

5
Introducing Text Input Components

PrimeFaces provides several text input components, among them some that are enhanced versions of standard JSF UI components with additional features and theming support. In addition to that, PrimeFaces also provides its own advanced input components such as InputText, InputTextarea, Password, InputMask, Editor, Inplace, AutoComplete, and so on, which will help to build the applications with a rich look and feel.

In this chapter we will cover:

- Getting text input with the InputText component
- Advanced uses of InputTextarea
- Getting input in specific format using InputMask
- Using the Password component along with strength indicator and match mode
- Rich text editing using Editor
- Advanced editing using the Inplace editor
- Providing suggestions using AutoComplete

Getting text input with the InputText component

InputText is an extension of the standard JSF `<h:inputText>` component with skinning capabilities:

```
<p:inputText id="emailId" value="#{userController.loginUser.emailId}"
  required="true"/>
```

PrimeFaces provides an additional `type` attribute for the `<p:inputText>` component, which can be used to generate other types of input fields such as the `hidden` input text field, which is similar to the standard JSF `<h:inputHidden>` component:

```
<p:inputText id="id" value="#{userController.registerUser.id}"
type="hidden" />
```

Similar to the JSF `<h:inputText>` component, PrimeFaces `<p:inputText>` supports various JavaScript events such as `onclick`, `onmouseover`, `onfocus`, and so on.

Time for action – using the InputText component

Let us see how we can use various features of the `<p:inputText>` component such as creating `text`, `hidden` type input fields, JavaScript event handlers, and so on:

1. Create a form with input fields of type `text` and `hidden`:

```
<h:form id="form1">
    <p:panel header="InputText Components">
        <h:panelGrid columns="2">
        <h:outputLabel value="EmailId" />
            <p:inputText id="emailId"
                value="#{userController.registerUser.emailId}"
                required="true" onclick="$(this).select();"/>

        <h:outputLabel for="firstName" value="FirstName"/>
            <p:inputText id="firstName"
                value="#{userController.registerUser.firstName}"
                required="true" label="FirstName"
                onchange="firstNameChanged()" />

            <p:inputText id="id"
                value="#{userController.registerUser.id}"
                type="hidden" />
            <p:commandButton value="Submit" update="@form"/>
        </h:panelGrid>
    </p:panel>
</h:form>
```

2. Create the JavaScript event handler method, `firstNameChanged()`, as follows:

```
function firstNameChanged ()
{
    alert("FirstName value changed");
}
```

What just happened?

We have used `<p:inputText>` components to create `text` type input fields: `emailId` and `firstName`, and `hidden` type input field `id`. Also, we have used JavaScript callback event handlers for the `onclick` and `onchange` events. We can also register AJAX event listeners to execute server-side logic using `<p:ajax>`, as follows:

```
<p:inputText id="lastName"
  value="#{userController.registerUser.lastName}">
  <p:ajax event="change"
    listener="#{userController.handleLastNameChanged}"/>
</p:inputText>
```

We can also make InputText components as read-only input fields by setting the `readonly` attribute to `true`:

```
<p:inputText id="userId" value="#{userController.registerUser.id}"
  readonly="true" />
```

Introducing the InputTextarea component

InputTextarea is an extension to the standard JSF `<h:inputTextarea>` component with support for AutoComplete, autoResize, remaining characters counter, and theming features:

```
<p:inputTextarea cols="50" rows="5"
  value="#{userController.loginUser.bio}"/>
```

The `<p:inputTextarea>` component provides the following additional attributes in addition to the JSF `<h:inputTextarea>` attributes:

- ◆ `autoResize`: Specifies auto growing when being typed. Default is true.
- ◆ `maxlength`: Maximum number of characters that can be entered in this field.
- ◆ `counter`: ID of the output component to display remaining characters.
- ◆ `counterTemplate`: Template text to display in counter.
- ◆ `completeMethod`: Method to provide AutoComplete suggestions.
- ◆ `minQueryLength`: Minimum number of characters to be typed to run a query. Default is 3.
- ◆ `queryDelay`: Delay in milliseconds before sending each query. Default is 700.
- ◆ `scrollHeight`: Height of the viewport for AutoComplete suggestions.

In our TechBuzz application, we will use the `<p:inputTextarea>` component for various screens such as **My Account**, **Add Comment**, and so on.

In the **My Account** screen, we will have an InputTextarea field to enter the user's biography with maximum limit of 500 characters and AutoComplete suggestions for some commonly used words. We will also display the number of characters remaining, as shown in the following screenshot:

Time for action – using InputTextarea

In this section, we will demonstrate how to use the AutoComplete feature with InputTextarea and show how many more characters can be entered into that field, which is shown as follows:

1. Create the user account form with `<p:inputTextarea>` to enter the user's biography:

```
<h:form id="myAccountForm">
    <p:panel header="My Account">
        <h:panelGrid columns="2">
            <p:outputLabel for="bio" value="About Me"/>
            <p:inputTextarea id="bio"
                value="#{userController.loginUser.bio}"
                cols="50" rows="5"
                completeMethod="#{userController.completeBio}"
                    minQueryLength="4" scrollHeight="100"
                counter="counter" counterTemplate="{0}
                    characters remaining" maxlength="500"
                    autoResize="true" />
            <h:outputText id="counter" value="" />
            <p:commandButton value="save"
                actionListener="#{userController.updateUser}"
                update="@form"/>
        </h:panelGrid>
    </p:panel>
</h:form>
```

2. Implement the `completeBio()` method to provide suggestions as follows:

```java
public List<String> completeBio(String query)
{
    List<String> values = new ArrayList<String>();
    if("soft".equalsIgnoreCase(query))
    {
        values.add("Software");
        values.add("Software Engineer");
        values.add("Software Developer");
        values.add("Software Architect");
        values.add("Software Development");
        values.add("Software Solutions");

        values.add("Software Development Methodologies");
        values.add("Software Development Process");
        values.add("Software Development Life Cycle");
        values.add("Software Design");
        values.add("Software Design Guidelines");
        values.add("Software Design Strategies");
        values.add("Software Testing");
        values.add("Software Testing Tools");

        values.add("Soft skills");
    }
    else if("java".equalsIgnoreCase(query))
    {
        values.add("Java");
        values.add("Java Programming");
        values.add("Java Platform");
        values.add("JavaScript");
    }
    return values;
}
```

What just happened?

We have created an InputTextarea field with a maximum size of 500 characters, using the `maxlength="500"` attribute to enter the biography details, along with a `counter` component to display the number of characters remaining, using the `counter` attribute. The counter template is customized to display text as **{0} characters remaining**. The default `counterTemplate` value is `{0}`, which means it will display only the number of characters remaining. The InputTextarea component height will be automatically increased if required as the `autoResize` attribute is set to `true`.

We have used the `completeMethod` attribute to provide AutoComplete suggestions. The search query will be triggered only after typing a minimum of four characters in a word because we have specified `minQueryLength="4"`. If the number of suggestions is more, then it will display all the suggestions and the list size will be overflowed. We have set the height of viewport for the AutoComplete suggestions box using `scrollHeight="100"`, so if there are more suggestions then the suggestion box will be displayed with a scrollbar.

Getting formatted input using the InputMask component

The InputMask component can be used to read input in a specific format. For example, we may want the user to enter a phone number in the XXX-XXX-XXXX format. We can use the `<p:inputMask>` component to read the input in the given format, restricting the user from entering invalid data:

```
<p:inputMask value="#{userController.registerUser.phone}" mask="999-
    999-9999"/>
```

The `mask` template can have the following characters, which have special meaning:

◆ 9: Represents a single digit, that is from 0 to 9.

◆ a: Represents an alphabetic character, that is from A to Z and a to z.

◆ *: Represents any alphanumeric character, that is 0 to 9, A to Z, or a to z.

Let us see a few examples of `mask` templates:

```
<p:inputMask mask="(999) 999-99-9999"/>
```

This `mask` template `(999) 999-99-9999` restricts the input to contain any digit in place of 9 in the template. It won't allow the user to enter any non-digit character in place of 9.

Some valid inputs are: (111) 123-45-6789, (435) 222-99-0987.

```
<p:inputMask mask="aaa999"/>
```

This `mask` template `mask="aaa999"` only allows three alphabetic characters followed by three digits.

Some valid inputs are: ABC123, pqr321, eFh234.

```
<p:inputMask mask="a*-a999"/>
```

This `mask` template `a*-a999` restricts the input to contain any digit in place of 9, any alphabetic character in place of a, and any alphanumeric in place of * in the template.

Some valid inputs are: A8-d123, da-a321, x2-t234, XY-Z123.

We can set some portions of the input as optional using the ? symbol. Anything mentioned after ? in the `mask` template is optional.

Suppose we want the user to enter a phone number, and optionally he/she can enter an extension:

```
<p:inputMask mask="(999) 999-9999? x9999" />
```

In this `mask` template, `(999) 999-9999? x9999`, we have `x9999` after the ? symbol, which means this part is optional.

Some valid values are: (122) 222-2222 x222, (122) 222-2222, (122) 222-2222 x2.

By default, the placeholder will be displayed as underscore (_), as shown in the following screenshot:

We can customize the placeholder character using the `placeHolder` attribute:

```
<p:inputMask id="phone" value="#{userController.loginUser.phone}"
    mask="999-999-9999? (Ext:9999)" placeHolder="X"/>
```

Phone: xxx-xxx-xxxx (Ext:xxxx)

In our TechBuzz application, the user can update his/her phone number in the **My Account** screen. We will use the `<p:inputMask>` component to enter the phone number in a predefined format.

Time for action – reading formatted input using InputMask

Let's look at how to get phone number input in the `999-999-9999? (Ext:9999)` format using the InputMask component:

1. Create a form with a **Phone** input field to read a phone number in the `999-999-9999? (Ext:9999)` format, by using the following code:

```
<h:form id="form1">
    <p:panel header="My Account">
        <h:panelGrid columns="2">
            <p:outputLabel for="phone" value="Phone"/>
            <p:inputMask id="phone"
                value="#{userController.loginUser.phone}"
                mask="999-999-9999? (Ext:9999)"
                placeHolder="X"/>
        </h:panelGrid>
    </p:panel>
</h:form>
```

What just happened?

We have used the `<p:inputMask>` component to read a phone number in the `999-999-9999` format. To set the extension number as optional, we have mentioned the extension part after the `?` symbol. As we have set the placeholder to `X`, when you put the cursor in the **Phone** input field, the mask is displayed as `XXX-XX-XXXX? (Ext:XXXX)`.

Introducing the Password component

The Password component is an extended version of the standard JSF `<h:inputSecret>` component with theme integration, strength indicator, and match mode support.

A basic Password component can be created as follows:

```
<p:password value="#{userController.registerUser.password}" />
```

We can also provide feedback on the strength of the password using the `feedback` attribute. As you type in the password field, it will provide feedback on whether the entered password is **Weak**, **Good**, or **Strong** based on the combination of characters used.

Password strength is determined by the characters used in the ranges [0-9], [a-z, A-Z], and [!@#$%^&*?_~.,;=]:

```
<p:password value="#{userController.loginUser.password}"
    feedback="true"/>
```

By default, when feedback is on and the **Password** field is blank it will show a tooltip with the text **Please enter a password**. Based on the strength of the password entered, it will display tooltips as **Weak**, **Good**, or **Strong**. You can customize these tooltip values as follows:

```
<p:password value="#{userController.loginUser.password}"
    feedback="true"
                promptLabel="Please enter Password"
                    weakLabel="Weak password"
                goodLabel="Good Password" strongLabel="Strong
                    Password" />
```

Instead of displaying the feedback in tooltips, you can also display the feedback inline, just under the Password field, using the `inline` attribute as follows:

```
<p:password value="#{userController.loginUser.password}"
    feedback="true" inline="true"/>
```

Password matching is a very common requirement for many web applications. Generally for the user registration or change password features, we would like to enter a password and confirm the password and both of them should match with each other. The `<p:password>` component provides a password matching feature with the `match` attribute. We have to set the `match` attribute to `id` of the other Password component against which we want to match.

In our TechBuzz application, we will use the <p:password> component in user registration and change password screens. In the **Change Password** screen, we want the user to enter **Current Password**, **New Password**, and **Confirm Password**. We will display the strength of the new password and verify whether the new password and the confirm password values are matching or not.

Time for action – using password strength indicator and match mode

Let us see how to implement the **Change Password** screen using <p:password> components:

1. Create the **Change Password** form:

```
<h:form id="changePwdForm">
    <p:messages id="messages" showDetail="true"
autoUpdate="true"/>
    <p:panel header="Change Password">
    <h:panelGrid columns="2">

        <p:outputLabel for="oldPwd" value="Current Password"/>
        <p:password id="oldPwd"
            value="#{userController.changePwd.currentPwd}"
            required="true"/>

        <p:outputLabel for="newPwd" value="New Password"/>
        <p:password id="newPwd"
            value="#{userController.changePwd.newPwd}"
                        feedback="true"
                        promptLabel="Enter New Password"
                        weakLabel="Weak Password"
                        goodLabel="Good Password"
                        strongLabel="Strong Password"
                        match="confPwd" required="true"/>

        <p:outputLabel for="confPwd" value="Confirm Password"/>
        <p:password id="confPwd"
            value="#{userController.changePwd.newPwd}"
            required="true"/>

        <p:commandButton value="Submit"
            actionListener="#{userController.changePassword}"
            update="@form"/>

    </h:panelGrid>
    </p:panel>
</h:form>
```

What just happened?

We have created three password fields using the <p:password> component. For the **New Password** input field, we have enabled feedback support using the feedback="true" attribute. Also, we have used the match attribute for the **New Password** field to match with the **Confirm Password** field.

If the **New Password** value is weak, then the feedback will be displayed as shown in the following screenshot:

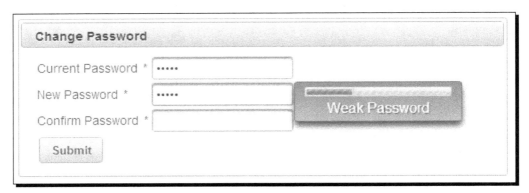

If the **New Password** and **Confirm Password** values are not matching, then you will see the error message as shown in the following screenshot:

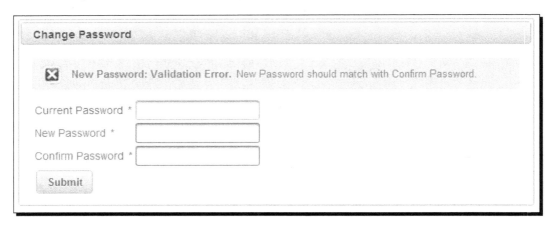

Make sure the `showDetail` attribute value is set to `true` to display the detailed error message.

The Password component's `match` attribute should be specified on the **New Password** field to match against the **Confirm Password** field. Password matching doesn't work if you specify the `match` attribute on the **Confirm Password** field to match against the **New Password** field. That means the following code doesn't work:

```
<p:password id="newPwd"
        value="#{userController.changePwd.newPwd}"
        required="true"/>
<p:password id="confPwd"
        value="#{userController.changePwd.newPwd}"
        required="true" match="newPwd"/>
```

Introducing the Editor component

Editor is an input component with rich text editing capabilities. The Editor component comes with a toolbar containing various options to apply HTML styles. The Editor component can be created as follows:

```
<p:editor id="buzzText"
    value="#{postController.newPost.description}"/>
```

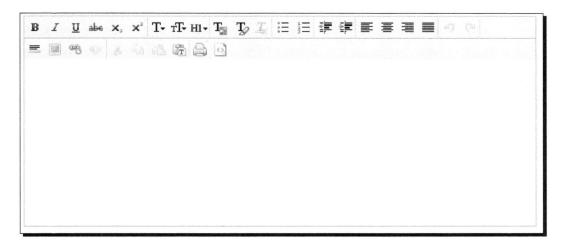

We can customize the toolbar options using the `controls` attribute as follows:

```
<p:editor id="buzzText" value="#{postController.newPost.description}"
    controls="bold italic underline strikethrough font numbering size
    color source" />
```

With this customization, the Editor looks like the following screenshot:

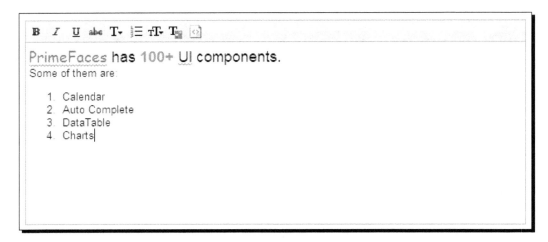

The following is the full list of all available controls:

◆ bold	◆ justify
◆ italic	◆ undo
◆ underline	◆ redo
◆ strikethrough	◆ rule
◆ subscript	◆ image
◆ superscript	◆ link
◆ font	◆ unlink
◆ size	◆ cut
◆ style	◆ copy
◆ color	◆ paste
◆ highlight	◆ pastetext
◆ bullets	◆ print
◆ numbering	◆ source
◆ alignleft	◆ outdent
◆ center	◆ indent
◆ alignright	◆ removeFormat

The <p:editor> component provides the following client-side API methods:

Method	Description
init()	Initializes a lazy editor, subsequent calls do not reinitialise the editor.
saveHTML()	Saves HTML text in iframe back to the textarea.
clear()	Clears the text in the editor.
enable()	Enables editing.
disable()	Disables editing.
focus()	Adds cursor focus to the edit area.
selectAll()	Selects all text in the editor.
getSelectedHTML()	Returns selected text as HTML.
getSelectedText()	Returns selected text in plain format.

Time for action – using editor client-side API methods

Let us create an Editor component and see how to use it as a rich text editor and perform various operations using client-side API methods:

1. Create a form with the <p:editor> component and buttons to invoke various client-side API methods.

```
<h:form id="form1">
    <p:editor id="buzzText" widgetVar="editor"
        value="#{postController.newPost.description}"
        controls="bold italic underline strikethrough font
        numbering size color source"/>

    <p:commandButton type="button" value="Submit"
        update="display" oncomplete="dlg.show()" />
    <p:commandButton type="button" value="Clear"
        onclick="editor.clear()"/>
    <p:commandButton type="button" value="Enable"
        onclick="editor.enable()" />
    <p:commandButton type="button" value="Disable"
        onclick="editor.disable()" />
    <p:commandButton type="button" value="SelectAll"
        onclick="editor.selectAll()" />
    <p:commandButton type="button" value="Get Selected HTML"
        onclick="alert(editor.getSelectedHTML());" />
    <p:commandButton type="button" value="GetSelectedText"
        onclick="alert(editor.getSelectedText());" />
```

```
<p:dialog header="Content" widgetVar="dlg"
    showEffect="fade" hideEffect="fade" modal="true">
    <h:outputText id="display"
        value="#{postController.newPost.description}"
        escape="false" />
</p:dialog>

</h:form>
```

What just happened?

We have created a rich text editor component using `<p:editor>` and invoked various client-side API methods through the `widgetVar` attribute value.

 Editor is not integrated with `ThemeRoller` since there is only one icon set for the controls. At the time of writing this book, `<p:editor>` doesn't support internationalization and all the tooltips for the controls will be displayed in English.

Inplace editing using the Inplace component

The Inplace editor provides easy Inplace editing and inline content display. The Inplace editor consists of two elements: display element is the initial clickable label, and inline element is the hidden content that is displayed when display element is toggled.

Let us see how we can use the `inplace` editor for an input text field:

```
<p:inplace emptyLabel="Enter Email Here">
    <p:inputText value="admin@gmail.com"/>
</p:inplace>
```

Here, an **admin@gmail.com** e-mail ID will be displayed as a label. When you click on that label, then an input text field will be displayed with the **admin@gmail.com** value.

The Inplace editor component `<p:inplace>` provides the following attributes to customize its behavior:

- `label`: Label to be shown in the display mode.
- `emptyLabel`: Label to be shown in the display mode when value is empty.
- `effect`: Effect to be used when toggling. Default is fade.
- `effectSpeed`: Speed of the effect. Default is normal.
- `editor`: Specifies the editor mode. Default is false.
- `saveLabel`: Tooltip text of the Save button in editor mode. Default is Save.
- `cancelLabel`: Tooltip text of the Cancel button in the editor mode. Default is Cancel.
- `event`: Name of the client-side event to display inline content. Default is click.
- `toggleable`: Defines whether Inplace is toggleable or not. Default is true.

In addition to text fields, we can also use other types of input components such as drop-down lists, checkboxes, radio buttons, and so on with the `inplace` editor.

We can use the `editor` attribute to display the **Save** and **Cancel** buttons next to the editor, to accept or reject the edited value. We can use the `saveLabel` and `cancelLable` attributes to override the default tooltip values of the **Save** and **Cancel** buttons. We can also register event listeners for the save and cancel events.

Time for action – using the Inplace editor

Let us see how to use the Inplace editor with the drop-down component along with editor support, and register event listeners for the `save` and `cancel` events:

1. Create a form using Inplace editor components, as follows:

```
<h:form id="inplaceForm">
    <p:panel header="Inplace Editing" >
        <h:panelGrid columns="2">
            <p:outputLabel for="email" value="Email"/>
            <p:inplace id="email" emptyLabel="Enter Email Here"
                editor="true" effect="slide"
                effectSpeed="fast">
                <p:ajax event="save"
                    listener="#{userController.handleSave}"/>
                <p:ajax event="cancel"
                    listener="#{userController.handleCancel}"/>
                <p:inputText
                    value="#{userController.user.emailId}"/>
            </p:inplace>

            <p:outputLabel for="gender" value="Gender"/>
```

```
                    <p:inplace id="gender" emptyLabel="Select Gender"
                        event="dblclick">
                        <p:selectOneMenu
                            value="#{userController.user.gender}">
                                <f:selectItem itemLabel="Male"
                                    itemValue="Male" />
                                <f:selectItem itemLabel="Female"
                                    itemValue="Female" />
                        </p:selectOneMenu>
                    </p:inplace>
                </h:panelGrid>
            </p:panel>
        </h:form>
```

2. Implement the `save` and `cancel` event listener methods:

```
public void handleSave()
{
    System.out.println("handleSave");
    //add custom logic here
}

public void handleCancel()
{
    System.out.println("handleCancel");
    //add custom logic here
}
```

What just happened?

We have used the Inplace editor with an input text field and a drop-down box. We have used the `dblclick` event to display **Gender** in the drop-down box instead of the default click event. For the `emailId` Inplace editor, we have set `editor="true"`, which displays the **Save** and **Cancel** buttons that can be used to apply or cancel editing. We have also registered event listeners for the `save` and `cancel` events on the editor using the `<p:ajax>` component, as shown in the following screenshot:

Providing completion suggestions using the AutoComplete component

The AutoComplete component provides a list of matching suggestions based on what you have already typed in the input field. This enables the user to quickly select available options without the need of completely typing the value.

In our TechBuzz application, we will use the `<p:autoComplete>` component in the **Search Users** screen. In the **Search Users** screen, we can search other users by their e-mail IDs. By using the AutoComplete component, we will display a list of e-mail IDs that start with what the user typed in the input field, by using the following code:

```
<p:autoComplete value="#{userController.searchEmail}"
    completeMethod="#{userController.completeEmail}"/>
```

The AutoComplete component provides the following attributes to customize its behavior:

- `maxResults`: Maximum number of results to be displayed.
- `minQueryLength`: Number of characters to be typed before starting to query. Default value is 1.
- `queryDelay`: Delay to wait in milliseconds before sending each query to the server. Default value is 300.
- `forceSelection`: When enabled, AutoComplete only accepts input from the selection list. Default value is false.
- `scrollHeight`: Defines the height of the item's viewport.
- `effect`: Effect to use when showing/hiding suggestions.
- `effectDuration`: Duration of effect in milliseconds. Default value is 400.
- `dropdown`: Enables the drop-down mode when set to true. Default value is false.
- `itemTipMyPosition`: Position of the itemtip corner relative to the item. Default value is `left top`.
- `itemTipAtPosition`: Position of the Item's corner relative to Itemtip. Default value is `right bottom`.
- `cache`: When enabled, AutoComplete caches the searched result list. Default value is false.
- `cacheTimeout`: Timeout value for cached results. Default value is 300000.
- `emptyMessage`: Text to display when there is no data to display.

Time for action – using basic AutoComplete

Let us see how to use the AutoComplete component in the **Search Users** screen to display a list of matching e-mail IDs:

1. Create a **Search Users** form with the AutoComplete component to search by e-mail ID:

```
<h:form id="searchUserForm">
    <h:panelGrid columns="2">

        <p:outputLabel for="searchUser" value="Search Users By
            Email"/>
        <p:autoComplete id="searchUser"
            value="#{userController.searchEmail}"

            completeMethod="#{userController.completeEmail}"/>

        <p:commandButton
            action="${userController.searchUsers()}"
            value="Submit" update="@form"/>
    </h:panelGrid>
</h:form>
```

2. Implement the `completeEmail()` method to provide suggestions:

```
public List<String> completeEmail(String query)
{
    List<String> emails = new ArrayList<String>();
    List<User> users = userService.findAllUsers();
    for (User user : users)
    {
        if(user.getEmailId().startsWith(query))
        {
            emails.add(user.getEmailId());
        }
    }
    return emails;
}
```

When you start typing in the search input field, a list of matching e-mail IDs will be displayed as shown in the following screenshot:

What just happened?

When you start typing in the input field, the `completeMethod` handler's `completeEmail`(query) gets invoked by passing the value you typed in the input field. We are fetching all the user e-mail IDs from the database and returning only those e-mail IDs that start with a query value. The AutoComplete component displays a list of suggestions that we have returned from the `completeEmail`(query) method.

We can also enable caching of AutoComplete search results using the `cache` and `cacheTimeout` attributes, as follows:

```
<p:autoComplete id="searchUser" value="#{userController.searchEmail}"
    completeMethod="#{userController.completeEmail}"
    cache="true" cacheTimeout="30000">
</p:autoComplete>
```

Here, AutoComplete results will be cached for 30,000 milliseconds. If you enter the same query, then results will be returned from cache instead of invoking the server-side `userController.completeEmail()` method.

Using AutoComplete with POJO support

In the preceding AutoComplete example, we have used `List<String>` objects returned from the `completeMethod` handler to populate suggestions. Instead of Strings, we can use **Plain Old Java Objects** (**POJO**) to populate AutoComplete suggestions with the use of a FacesConverter.

In our TechBuzz application, we will have a **Search Posts** screen where you can search posts by `Tag`. We can use the `<p:autoComplete>` component to provide suggestions for matching `Tag` names as user types in the input field. Instead of using `List<String>` values to populate suggestions, we will use `List<Tag>` POJOs, as shown in the following screenshot:

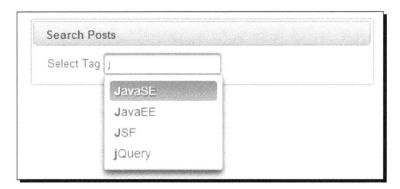

Time for action – using AutoComplete with POJO support

Let us see how we can use `List<Tag>` objects to populate the AutoComplete component:

1. Create the **Search Posts** form with the AutoComplete component:

```
<p:autoComplete value="#{postController.searchTag}"
                completeMethod="#{postController.completeTag}"
                var="t" itemLabel="#{t.label}" itemValue="#{t}"
                converter="tagConverter"/>
```

2. Implement the `completeMethod` handler method and the `completeTag()` method returning the `List<Tag>` object:

```
public List<Tag> completeTag(String query)
{
    if(query == null){
        return new ArrayList<Tag>();
    }
    List<Tag> tags = new ArrayList<Tag>();
    List<Tag> allTags = loadTagsFromDataSource();
    for (Tag tag : allTags)
    {
    if(tag.getLabel().toLowerCase().
        startsWith(query.toLowerCase()))
        {
            tags.add(tag);
        }
    }
    return tags;
}
```

3. Implement the `TagConverter` class:

```java
@FacesConverter(value="tagConverter", forClass=Tag.class)
public class TagConverter implements Converter
{
    @Override
    public Object getAsObject(FacesContext context, UIComponent
        component, String value)
    {
        if (value==null || value.trim().equals(""))
        {
            return null;
        }
        try
        {
            int id = Integer.parseInt(value);
            List<Tag> tags = loadTagsFromDataSource();
            for (Tag t : tags )
            {
                if (t.getId() == id)
                {
                        return t;
                 }
            }
        } catch(NumberFormatException exception)
        {
            throw new ConverterException(new
                FacesMessage(FacesMessage.SEVERITY_ERROR,
                "Conversion Error", "Not a valid Tag"));
        }
        return null;
    }

    @Override
    public String getAsString(FacesContext context, UIComponent
        component, Object value)
    {
        if (value == null || value.equals("")) {
            return "";
        } else {
            return String.valueOf(((Tag) value).getId());
        }
    }
}
```

What just happened?

In the `completeMethod` handler's `completeTag`(query), we are returning `List<Tag>` objects by loading the tag details from the database that start with the entered query. We have used the `<p:autoComplete>` component's `var` attribute to store `Tag` object while iterating through the collection, the `itemLabel` attribute to specify which property to display in the suggestion box, and the `itemValue` attribute to specify the value of the entry. We have used the `TagConverter` class to convert `String` to `Tag` and `Tag` to `String` by looking up against tag details loaded from the database.

You can also display custom content as labels using nested `<p:column>` elements:

```
<p:autoComplete value="#{postController.searchTag}"
          completeMethod="#{postController.completeTag}"
          var="t" itemLabel="#{t.label}" itemValue="#{t}"
          converter="tagConverter">
    <p:column>
        #{t.label} - #{t.value}
    </p:column>
    <p:column>
        <p:graphicImage value="/resources/images/tags/#{t.value}.png"
            width="40" height="50"/>
    </p:column>
</p:autoComplete>
```

Selecting multiple items

The AutoComplete component supports multiple item selection as well. We can use multiple item selection features by setting the `multiple` attribute to `true`.

In our TechBuzz application, while creating a new post, we can select multiple tags that are associated with the post content.

For example, if we are posting about PrimeFaces, then we can select the **JavaEE**, **JSF**, and **PrimeFaces** tags as shown in the following screenshot:

Time for action – selecting multiple items using AutoComplete

Let us see how to use the `<p:autoComplete>` component with multiple selection:

1. Create the new post form with the AutoComplete component to select multiple tags:

```
<p:autoComplete id="newPostTags"
    value="#{postController.newPost.tags}"
        completeMethod="#{postController.completeTag}"
        maxResults="10" minQueryLength="2" queryDelay="400"
        effect="slide"
        var="t" itemLabel="#{t.label}" itemValue="#{t}"
        converter="tagConverter" multiple="true">

</p:autoComplete>
```

What just happened?

We have used the `<p:autoComplete>` component with multiple selection support by setting the `multiple` attribute to `true`. We have also used various other attributes such as `maxResults`, `minQueryLength`, `queryDelay`, `forceSelection`, and `effect` to customize the `<p:autoComplete>` component behavior. As we have set `minQueryLength` to 2, the query gets triggered only after typing a minimum of two characters. Keep the sensible value for `queryDelay` to reduce the load on the server when you are typing the query quickly.

Handling the ItemSelect and ItemUnselect Events

The AutoComplete component supports the `itemSelect` and `itemUnselect` events in addition to the events inherited from the normal input text component. The `itemSelect` event get triggered when an item is selected from the list of suggestions. If the AutoComplete component is a multiple selection field then the `itemUnselect` event gets triggered when an item is removed by clicking on the close icon on one of the selected items. We can use the `itemSelect` event to check whether the user is trying to add a duplicate tag or not.

Time for action – using the ItemSelect and ItemUnselect events

Let us see how to use the AutoComplete component's `itemSelect` and `itemUnselect` events:

1. Create a form with the AutoComplete component and register the `itemSelect` and `itemUnselect` event listeners:

```
<p:autoComplete id="newPostTags"
    value="#{postController.newPost.tags}"
                completeMethod="#{postController.completeTags}"
```

```
                    maxResults="10" minQueryLength="1"
                        queryDelay="400"


                    var="t" itemLabel="#{t.label}" itemValue="#{t}"
                    converter="tagConverter" multiple="true">
              <p:ajax event="itemSelect"
                  listener="#{postController.handleTagSelected}"/>
              <p:ajax event="itemUnselect"
                  listener="#{postController.handleTagUnselected}"/>

      </p:autoComplete>
```

2. **Implement event listener methods:** `handleTagSelected()` **and**
   `handleTagUnselected()`:

```java
public void handleTagSelected(SelectEvent selectEvent)
{
    Tag selectedObj = (Tag) selectEvent.getObject();
    Integer tagid = selectedObj.getId();
    Tag duplicateTag = null;
    int count = 0;
    for(Tag t : selectedTags) {
        if(tagid == t.getId()){
            duplicateTag = t;
            count++;
        }
    }
    if(count > 1) {
        boolean removed = selectedTags.remove(duplicateTag);
        RequestContext.getCurrentInstance()
            .update("newPostForm:newPostTags");
        JSFUtils.addErrorMessage("You have selected duplicate
            Tag :"+selectedObj.getLabel());
    } else {
        JSFUtils.addInfoMessage("You have selected
            :"+selectedObj.getLabel());
    }
}


public void handleTagUnselected(UnselectEvent unselectEvent)
{
    Tag unselectedObj = (Tag) unselectEvent.getObject();
    FacesContext.getCurrentInstance().addMessage(null, new
        FacesMessage("You have unselected
        :"+unselectedObj.getLabel()));
}
```

What just happened?

We have registered event listeners for the `itemSelect` and `itemUnselect` events by using the `<p:ajax>` component. When the `itemSelect` event gets triggered, the `handleTagSelected(org.primefaces.event.SelectEvent selectEvent)` event listener method gets triggered. We obtained the selected the `Tag` object by calling `selectEvent.getObject()` and checked whether there was a duplicate tag and removing it. After removing the duplicate tag, we have updated the AutoComplete component using the `RequestContext.update()` utility method. Similarly, the `itemUnselect` event listener also gets triggered by the `org.primefaces.event.UnselectEvent` parameter, from which we obtained the removed `Tag` object.

Displaying tooltips using the Itemtip facet

When you mouse over the suggestion items, we can display tooltips using the Itemtip facet.

In the preceding example, when you mouse over the **Tags** label, we can display the tag description using Itemtip, as follows.

Time for action – displaying tooltips on suggested items using the Itemtip facet

In this section, we will take a look at how to display tooltips with custom content for AutoComplete suggestion items using the Itemtip facet:

1. Create the AutoComplete component for **Tags** and display the tag description using `itemTip`:

```
<p:autoComplete id="newPostTags"
    value="#{postController.newPost.tags}"
                completeMethod="#{postController.completeTags}"
                maxResults="10" minQueryLength="2"
                    queryDelay="400"
    var="t" itemLabel="#{t.label}" itemValue="#{t}"
    converter="tagConverter" multiple="true"
    itemTipMyPosition="left top" itemTipAtPosition="right
        bottom">

        <f:facet name="itemtip">
            <h:panelGrid columns="2" style="text-align: left">
                <f:facet name="header">
                    Tag Details
                    </f:facet>
                    <h:outputText value="Label: " />
                    <h:outputText value="#{t.label}" />
```

```
                              <h:outputText value="Description: " />
                              <h:outputText value="#{t.description}" />
                       </h:panelGrid>
                 </f:facet>

       </p:autoComplete>
```

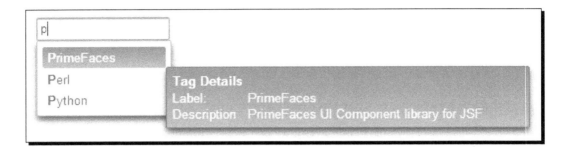

What just happened?

When you mouse over suggestion items, the tag description will be displayed as a tooltip using the Itemtip facet.

Summary

In this chapter, we have learned how to use PrimeFaces text input components that are very commonly used in web applications. We have looked into using the advanced features of InputTextarea, Password, InputMask, and Inplace components. Also, we learned how to use the AutoComplete component with POJO support, multiple selection, and Itemtip display features. In the next chapter, we will learn how to use selection input components such as SelectManyCheckbox, SelectOneRadio, SelectOneMenu, SelectOneListbox, SelectManyMenu, and so on.

6
Working with Selection Input Components

Selection components such as drop-down lists, checkboxes, and radio buttons are vey commonly used elements in web applications. But native HTML selection input components are very limited and don't provide enough features to build modern complex and rich user interfaces. To address this, PrimeFaces provides several selection input components with enhanced features and theming support.

In this chapter, we will cover the following components:

- ◆ Creating the toggle button using SelectBooleanButton
- ◆ Creating the On or Off options using SelectBooleanCheckbox
- ◆ Introducing SelectManyCheckbox
- ◆ Introducing SelectOneRadio
- ◆ Introducing SelectOneButton
- ◆ Introducing SelectManyButton
- ◆ Creating drop-down lists using SelectOneMenu
- ◆ Introducing SelectOneListbox
- ◆ Introducing SelectManyMenu
- ◆ Creating the overlay menu using SelectCheckboxMenu
- ◆ Creating the overlay menu with a default command using SplitButton
- ◆ Introducing the PickList component
- ◆ Introducing the MultiSelectListbox component

Creating the toggle button using SelectBooleanButton

The SelectBooleanButton component is used to select a yes or no decision with a toggle button:

```
<h:outputText value="Subscribe to Email Notifications: " />
<p:selectBooleanButton value="#{selectionController.subscribed}"
onLabel="Yes" offLabel="No" onIcon="ui-icon-check" offIcon="ui-icon-
close" />
```

Here, the onLabel and offLabel attributes are mandatory. We can change the labels and icons using the onLabel, offLabel, onIcon, and offIcon attributes.

We can also add an event listener to the `<p:selectBooleanButton>` component using a nested `<p:ajax>` element.

Time for action – using the SelectBooleanButton component

Let us see how to save user preferences on subscribing to weekly e-mail notifications using the `<p:selectBooleanButton>` component, by performing the following steps:

1. Create a **User Preferences** form:

```
<h:form>
    <p:panel header="User Preferences" style="width: 400px;
        margin: 0 auto;">
    <p:messages autoUpdate="true"/>
        <h:panelGrid columns="2" style="margin-bottom:10px"
            cellpadding="5">
        <h:outputText value="Subscribe to Email
            Notifications: " />
        <p:selectBooleanButton
            value="#{selectionController.
            subscribeToEmailNotif}" onLabel="Yes" offLabel="No"
            onIcon="ui-icon-check" offIcon="ui-icon-close">
            <p:ajax update="display"
                listener="#{selectionController.
                handleEmailSubscription}"/>
        </p:selectBooleanButton>
    </h:panelGrid>

    <h:panelGrid columns="1" id="display">
        <h:outputText value="Subscribed to Email Notification :
            #{selectionController.subscribeToEmailNotif}" />
    </h:panelGrid>
    </p:panel>
</h:form>
```

2. Implement the `handleEmailSubscription()` event listener method:

```
@ManagedBean
@RequestScoped
public class SelectionController
{
    private boolean subscribeToEmailNotif;
    //setters & getters

    public void handleEmailSubscription()
    {
        if(subscribeToEmailNotif){
            //logic to subscribe
        } else {
            //logic to unsubscribe
        }
    }
}
```

What just happened?

We have used the `<p:selectBooleanButton>` component to create a **Yes** or **No** type boolean button and registered an event listener using the `<p:ajax>` element. When you click on the button, the `handleEmailSubscription()` method gets invoked and updates the user preferences, as shown in the following screenshot:

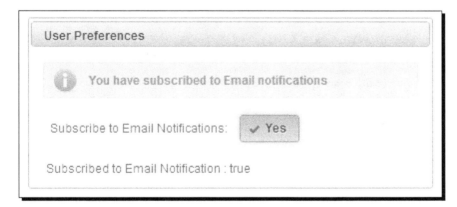

Creating the On or Off options using SelectBooleanCheckbox

The SelectBooleanCheckbox component is an extended version of the standard checkbox with theme integration. We can also add an event listener to the `<p:selectBooleanCheckbox>` component using a nested `<p:ajax>` element.

Time for action – using the SelectBooleanCheckbox component

Let us see how to use `<p:selectBooleanCheckbox>` along with the AJAX listener support, by performing the following step:

1. Create the **User Preferences** form using `<p:selectBooleanCheckbox>` components:

```
<h:form>
    <p:panel header="User Preferences" style="width: 500px;">
    <p:messages/>
    <h:panelGrid columns="2" style="margin-bottom:10px"
        cellpadding="5">

        <h:outputText value="Show Online Status: " />
        <p:selectBooleanCheckbox
            value="#{selectionController.showOnlineStatus}" />

        <h:outputText value="Accept Private Messages: " />
        <p:selectBooleanCheckbox
            value="#{selectionController.recievePrivateMsgs}">
            <p:ajax update="display"
                listener="#{selectionController.
                updateUserpreferences}"/>
        </p:selectBooleanCheckbox>

    </h:panelGrid>
    <p:commandButton value="Submit" update="@form"
        actionListener="#{selectionController.
        updateUserpreferences}"/>

    <h:panelGrid columns="1" id="display">
        <h:outputText value="Show Online Status :
            #{selectionController.showOnlineStatus}" />
        <h:outputText value="Accept Private Messages :
            #{selectionController.recievePrivateMsgs}" />
    </h:panelGrid>
    </p:panel>

</h:form>
```

What just happened?

We have used `<p:selectBooleanCheckbox>` components to create checkboxes representing the user preferences on **Show Online Status** and **Accept Private Msgs**. We have registered a click event listener on the **Accept Private Messages** checkbox using `<p:ajax>`. When you check or uncheck the **Accept Private Messages** checkbox, then `updateUserpreferences()` gets invoked, as shown in the following screenshot:

Introducing SelectManyCheckbox

The SelectManyCheckbox component is an extended version of the JSF standard SelectManyCheckbox component with theme integration.

Time for action – using the SelectManyCheckbox component

Let us see how we can use the `<p:selectManyCheckbox>` component, by performing the following steps:

1. Create a form using the `<p:selectManyCheckbox>` components:

```
<h:form id="form1" style="width:500px; margin: 0 auto;">
    <p:messages autoUpdate="true"  escape="false" />
    <p:panel header="SelectManyCheckBox">
    <h:panelGrid columns="2" style="margin-bottom:10px"
        cellpadding="5">
```

```
<h:outputText value="Favourite Tags: " />
<p:selectManyCheckbox
    value="#{selectionController.favoriteTags}">
    <f:selectItem itemLabel="JSF" itemValue="jsf" />
    <f:selectItem itemLabel="PrimeFaces"
        itemValue="primefaces" />
    <f:selectItem itemLabel="Spring" itemValue="spring"
        />
</p:selectManyCheckbox>

<h:outputText value="Popular Tags: " />
<p:selectManyCheckbox value="#{selectionController.
    selectedPopularTags}">
<f:selectItem itemLabel="Web2.0" itemValue="web2.0" />
<f:selectItems
    value="#{selectionController.popularTags}" />
</p:selectManyCheckbox>

<h:outputText value="Tags: " />
<p:selectManyCheckbox
    value="#{selectionController.selectedTags}"
    layout="pageDirection" >
    <f:selectItems value="#{selectionController.tags}"
        />
</p:selectManyCheckbox>

<h:outputText value="Tags(Pojo): " />
<p:selectManyCheckbox value=
    "#{selectionController.selectedTagsFromPojos}"
    layout="pageDirection" converter="#{tagConverter}">
    <f:selectItems value=
        "#{selectionController.tagPojos}" var="tag"
        itemLabel="#{tag.label}" itemValue="#{tag}"/>
</p:selectManyCheckbox>


</h:panelGrid>
<p:commandButton value="Submit" update="@form"
    actionListener="#{selectionController.
    handleSelectMany}"/>
</p:panel>
</h:form>
```

2. Implement data initialization and the `actionListener` method in the
`SelectionController` managed bean:

```java
@ManagedBean
@RequestScoped
public class SelectionController
{
    private List<String>  tags;
    private Map<String, String> popularTags = null;
    private List<String>  selectedTags;
    private List<String>  favoriteTags;
    private List<String>  selectedPopularTags;

    private List<Tag> tagPojos;
    private List<Tag> selectedTagsFromPojos;

    public SelectionController()
    {
        tags = new ArrayList<String>();
        tags.add("JSF");
        tags.add("PrimeFaces");
        tags.add("JPA");
        tags.add("jQuery");

        popularTags = new HashMap<String, String>();
        popularTags.put("Java","java");
        popularTags.put("JavaScript","javascript");
        popularTags.put("PrimeFaces","primefaces");

        tagPojos = new ArrayList<Tag>();
        tagPojos.add(new Tag(1, "JavaSE", "java-se", "Java
            Programming Language"));
        tagPojos.add(new Tag(2, "JavaEE", "java-ee", "Java
            Enterprise Edition"));
        tagPojos.add(new Tag(3, "Spring", "spring", "Spring
            Framework"));

    }
    //setters & getters

    public void handleSelectMany()
    {
        String msg = "Selected Values :";
        msg += "";//logic to append selected Options
        FacesContext.getCurrentInstance().addMessage(null, new
            FacesMessage(msg));
    }

}
```

What just happened?

We have created **Favorite Tags** checkboxes using the `<p:selectManyCheckbox>` component with options using inline `<f:selectItem>` tags. For **Popular Tags** checkboxes, we have used the `Map<String, String>` object to populate options where key becomes `itemLabel` and value becomes `itemValue`. Similarly we have seen how to use `List<String>` objects to populate options for **Tags** checkboxes along with `layout="pageDirection"` to display checkboxes vertically. Default value for the `layout` attribute is `lineDirection`. Also, we have used `List<Tag>` POJOs to populate **Tags(Pojo)** checkboxes by using `TagConverter`:

Introducing SelectOneRadio

The SelectOneRadio component is an extended version of the JSF standard SelectOneRadio component with theme integration.

Time for action – using the SelectOneRadio component

Let us see how to use the `<p:selectOneRadio>` component, by performing the following steps:

1. Create a form with `<p:selectOneRadio>` components:

    ```
    <h:form id="form" style="width: 500px; margin: 0 auto;">
        <p:panel header="SelectOneRadio">
        <h:panelGrid columns="2" style="margin-bottom:5px"
            cellpadding="2">
    ```

```
<h:outputText value="Gender: " />
<p:selectOneRadio id="gender"
    value="#{selectionController.gender}">
    <f:selectItem itemLabel="Male" itemValue="M" />
    <f:selectItem itemLabel="Female" itemValue="F" />
</p:selectOneRadio>

<h:outputText value="Favourite Server: " />
<p:selectOneRadio id="server"
    value="#{selectionController.selectedServer}"
    layout="pageDirection">
    <f:selectItems
        value="#{selectionController.servers}"/>
</p:selectOneRadio>

<h:outputText value="Favourite Tag: " />
<p:selectOneRadio id="tag"
    value="#{selectionController.selectedTag}"
    converter="#{tagConverter}">
    <f:selectItems
        value="#{selectionController.tagPojos}"
        var="tag" itemLabel="#{tag.label}"
        itemValue="#{tag}"/>
</p:selectOneRadio>

</h:panelGrid>
<p:commandButton value="Submit" update="@form"/>
<p:separator/>
<h:outputText value="Gender :
    #{selectionController.gender}, Server :
    #{selectionController.selectedServer}, Tag :
    #{selectionController.selectedTag.label} " />
</p:panel>
</h:form>
```

2. Initialize data in the managed bean:

```
@ManagedBean
@RequestScoped
public class SelectionController
{
    private String gender;
    private List<String> servers;
    private String selectedServer;
    private List<Tag> tagPojos;
    private Tag selectedTag;
    //setters & getters
```

```
        public SelectionController()
        {
            tagPojos = loadTagsFromDatabase();
            servers = new ArrayList<String>();
            servers.add("Tomcat");
            servers.add("Glassfish");
            servers.add("JBoss");
        }
    }
```

What just happened?

We have created the radio button selection components using `<p:selectOneRadio>`.
For the **Gender** radio button, we have used static options using inline `<f:selectItem>`
tags. For the **Favourite Server** radio button, we have used dynamic data along with
`layout="pageDirection"` to display options vertically. The default `layout`
attribute's value is `lineDirection`, which displays options horizontally. We have also
used POJOs to populate `<p:selectOneRadio>` options using converter. By default,
`<p:selectOneRadio>` displays radio buttons with theme support. If you want to turn
off theming and display as native HTML radio buttons, set the attribute `plain` to `true`:

Introducing SelectOneButton

SelectOneButton is an input component to select options using regular buttons instead of radio buttons. The SelectOneButton component's behavior is similar to the SelectOneRadio component, except options are displayed as buttons instead of radios, as shown in the following screenshot:

Time for action – using the SelectOneButton component

Let us see how to use the `<p:selectOneButton>` component, by performing the following step:

1. Create a form with the `<p:selectOneButton>` component with multiple options:

```
<h:form>
    <p:panel header="SelectOneButton">
        <h:panelGrid style="margin-bottom:5px" cellpadding="3">
            <p:selectOneButton
                value="#{selectionController.number}">
                <f:selectItem itemLabel="One" itemValue="1"/>
                <f:selectItem itemLabel="Two" itemValue="2"/>
                <f:selectItem itemLabel="Three" itemValue="3"/>
            </p:selectOneButton>
        </h:panelGrid>
        <p:commandButton value="Submit" update="display"/>
        <h:outputText id="display" value=" Value :
            #{selectionController.number}" />
    </p:panel>
</h:form>
```

What just happened?

We have used the `<p:selectOneButton>` component to display options as toggle buttons. When you click on any option button and submit the form, then the selected option value is displayed.

Introducing SelectManyButton

SelectManyButton is a multiselect component similar to the SelectManyCheckbox component, except options will be displayed as buttons instead of checkboxes, as shown in the following screenshot:

Time for action – using the SelectManyButton component

Let us see how to use the `<p:selectManyButton>` component, by performing the following step:

1. Create a form with the `<p:selectManyButton>` component with multiple options:

```
<h:form>
    <p:panel header="SelectManyButton">
    <h:panelGrid style="margin-bottom:5px" cellpadding="3">
        <p:selectManyButton
            value="#{selectionController.numbers}">
            <f:selectItem itemLabel="One" itemValue="1"/>
            <f:selectItem itemLabel="Two" itemValue="2"/>
            <f:selectItem itemLabel="Three" itemValue="3"/>
    </p:selectManyButton>
    </h:panelGrid>

    <p:commandButton value="Submit" update="display"/>
    <h:outputText id="display"value="  Value :
        #{selectionController.numbers}" />
    </p:panel>
</h:form>
```

What just happened?

We have used the `<p:selectManyButton>` component to display options as toggle buttons. When you select multiple option buttons and submit the form, then the selected options values are displayed.

Creating drop-down lists using SelectOneMenu

The SelectOneMenu component is an extended version of the standard SelectOneMenu component with theme integration. We can create a basic drop-down list using `<p:selectOneMenu>` as follows:

```
<p:selectOneMenu value="#{selectionController.number}">
    <f:selectItem itemLabel="Select One" itemValue="" />
    <f:selectItem itemLabel="One" itemValue="1" />
    <f:selectItem itemLabel="Two" itemValue="2" />
    <f:selectItem itemLabel="Three" itemValue="3" />
</p:selectOneMenu>
```

The `<p:selectOneMenu>` component provides the following attributes to customize it's behavior:

- ◆ `effect`: Name of the toggle animation. Default value is `fade`. Available effect options are `blind`, `bounce`, `clip`, `drop`, `explode`, `fold`, `highlight`, `puff`, `pulsate`, `scale`, `shake`, `size`, `slide`, and `none`.

- ◆ `effectSpeed`: Duration of toggle animation in milliseconds. Default value is `400`.

- ◆ `editable`: If true, selected items become editable. Default value is `false`.

- ◆ `maxlength`: Maximum number of characters allowed in editable SelectOneMenu.

- ◆ `filter`: Renders filter input field. Default value is `false`.

- ◆ `filterMatchMode`: Match mode for filtering, valid values are `startsWith`, `contains`, `endsWith`, and `custom`. Default value is `startsWith`.

- ◆ `filterFunction`: Client-side function to use in custom filtering. Filter function will take `itemLabel` and `filterValue` as arguments.

- ◆ `caseSensitive`: Defines whether filtering would be case sensitive. Default value is `false`.

Let us see how to use the `<p:selectOneMenu>` component with editable and filter features.

Time for action – using SelectOneMenu with editable and filter features

Let's look at how to create a drop-down menu with editable options, by performing the following step:

1. Create a SelectOneMenu drop-down list using the `editable` and `filter` attributes:

```
<p:selectOneMenu value="#{selectionController.selectedOption}"
    effect="fade" editable="true" filter="true"
    filterMatchMode="startsWith">
    <f:selectItem itemLabel="Select One" itemValue="" />
    <f:selectItem itemLabel="One" itemValue="One" />
    <f:selectItem itemLabel="Two" itemValue="Two" />
    <f:selectItem itemLabel="Three" itemValue="Three" />
</p:selectOneMenu>
```

What just happened?

As we have set the `editable` attribute to `true`, we can select an existing option, select and edit an existing option, or write an entirely new option. When you click on the drop-down list icon, it will display the list of options along with a filter input textbox. When you type in the filter text, options will be filtered based on the filter mode that we are using, as shown in the following screenshot:

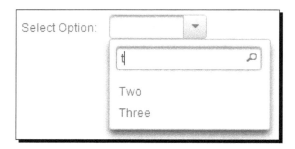

Using SelectOneMenu with POJOs

The `<p:selectOneMenu>` component can also be used with POJO instead of plain Strings. You can populate SelectOneMenu options with the list of POJOs and get the selected value as a POJO using converter.

Time for action – using SelectOneMenu with POJOs

In this section, we will demonstrate how to use SelectOneMenu backed by a collection of POJOs by using a converter, by performing the following steps:

1. Create a SelectOneMenu component using `List<Tag>` POJOs:

```
<p:selectOneMenu value="#{selectionController.selectedTag}"
    converter="tagConverter">
    <f:selectItem itemLabel="Select One" itemValue="" />
    <f:selectItems value="#{selectionController.tagPojos}"
        var="tag" itemLabel="#{tag.label}" itemValue="#{tag}"/>
</p:selectOneMenu>
```

2. Initialize `List<Tag>` POJOs in the managed bean:

```
@ManagedBean
@RequestScoped
public class SelectionController
{
    private List<Tag> tagPojos;
    private Tag selectedTag;

    public SelectionController()
    {
    tagPojos = new ArrayList<Tag>();
        tagPojos.add(new Tag(1, "JavaSE", "java-se", "Java
            Programming Language"));
        tagPojos.add(new Tag(2, "JavaEE", "java-ee", "Java
            Enterprise Edition"));
        tagPojos.add(new Tag(3, "Spring", "spring", "Spring
            Framework"));
    }
    //setters & getters
}
```

What just happened?

We have initialized the `List<Tag>` POJOs in the managed bean and populated options using `<f:selectItems value="#{selectionController.tagPojos}" var="tag" itemLabel="#{tag.label}" itemValue="#{tag}"/>`. It will iterate through the collection and uses `label` as `itemLabel` and `tag` object as `itemValue`. We have used `tagConverter` to convert `String` to `Tag` and `Tag` to `String`.

> We should override the `equals()` and `hasCode()` methods in the POJO class so that the SelectOneMenu component will be able to compare POJO objects and determine the selected POJO.

We can also display custom content using nested `<p:column>` facets. The advantage of using nested `<p:column>` facets for displaying options is that we can display custom content with rich content, also including images:

```
<p:selectOneMenu value="#{selectionController.selectedTag}" var="t"
    converter="tagConverter">
    <f:selectItem itemLabel="Select One" itemValue="" />
    <f:selectItems value="#{selectionController.tagPojos}" var="tag"
        itemLabel="#{tag.label}" itemValue="#{tag}"/>
    <p:column>
        #{t.label} - #{t.value}
    </p:column>
    <p:column>
        <p:graphicImage value="/resources/images/tags/#{t.value}.png"
            width="32px" height="32px"/>
    </p:column>
</p:selectOneMenu>
```

The preceding SelectOneMenu component displays options with custom content as shown in the following screenshot:

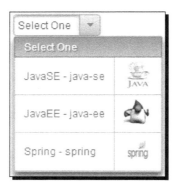

Grouping options in SelectOneMenu

We can group the options in the SelectOneMenu drop-down list using the `javax.faces.model.SelectItemGroup` and `javax.faces.model.SelectItem` objects.

Time for action – grouping options in SelectOneMenu

Let us see how to display SelectOneMenu options in groups, by performing the following step:

1. Create the SelectOneMenu component with option groups using the `SelectItemGroup` and `SelectItem` objects:

   ```
   @ManagedBean
   @RequestScoped
   ```

```
public class SelectionController
{
    private List<SelectItem> tagItems = new
        ArrayList<SelectItem>();
    private String selectedTagItem;

    public SelectionController()
    {
        SelectItemGroup g1 = new SelectItemGroup("JavaSE");
        g1.setSelectItems(new SelectItem[] {new
            SelectItem("Threads", "Threads"), new
            SelectItem("JDBC", "JDBC")});

        SelectItemGroup g2 = new SelectItemGroup("JavaEE");
        g2.setSelectItems(new SelectItem[] {new
            SelectItem("JPA", "JPA"), new SelectItem("JMS",
            "JMS"), new SelectItem("EJB", "EJB")});

        tagItems.add(g1);
        tagItems.add(g2);
    }
}
<p:selectOneMenu
    value="#{selectionController.selectedTagItem}">
    <f:selectItem itemLabel="Select One" itemValue="" />
    <f:selectItems value="#{selectionController.tagItems}" />
</p:selectOneMenu>
```

What just happened?

We have grouped the options using `javax.faces.model.SelectItemGroup`, and `javax.faces.model.SelectItem`, and used `List<SelectItem>` for populating drop-down list options to display the options in groups:

SelectOneMenu also provides the following client-side API functions that can be invoked on the `widgetVar` value to perform various operations:

- `show()`: Shows the overlay menu.
- `hide()`: Hides the overlay menu.
- `blur()`: Invokes the blur event.
- `focus()`: Invokes the focus event.
- `enable()`: Enables component.
- `disable()`: Disables component.
- `getSelectedValue()`: Returns value of the selected item.
- `getSelectedLabel()`: Returns label of the selected item.
- `selectValue(itemValue)`: Selects the option based on given value.

Introducing SelectOneListbox

The SelectOneListbox component is an extended version of the standard SelectOneListbox component with theme integration. Basic usage of `<p:selectOneListbox>` is as follows:

```
<p:selectOneListbox value="#{selectionController.number}">
    <f:selectItem itemLabel="One" itemValue="1" />
    <f:selectItem itemLabel="Two" itemValue="2" />
    <f:selectItem itemLabel="Three" itemValue="3" />
</p:selectOneListbox>
```

The preceding `<p:selectOneListbox>` component will be rendered as shown in the following screenshot:

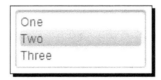

We can also use POJOs to populate `<p:selectOneListbox>` options. Let us see how to populate SelectOneListbox using POJOs.

Time for action – using SelectOneListbox with POJOs

Let's look at creating a SelectOneListbox backed by a collection of POJOs using a converter, by performing the following step:

1. Create a form with the SelectOneListbox component using POJOs:

```
<h:form>
    <p:panel header="SelectOneListbox">
    <h:panelGrid columns="2" style="margin-bottom:5px"
        cellpadding="3">
        <h:outputText value="Listbox Using POJO: " />
        <p:selectOneListbox
            value="#{selectionController.selectedTag}" var="t"
            converter="#{tagConverter}">
            <f:selectItems
                value="#{selectionController.tagPojos}"
                var="tag"
                itemLabel="#{tag.label}" itemValue="#{tag}"/>
            <p:column>
                #{t.label} - #{t.value}
            </p:column>
        </p:selectOneListbox>
    </h:panelGrid>

    <p:commandButton value="Submit" update="display" />
    <h:outputText id="display" value="Listbox Using POJO:
        #{selectionController.selectedTag.label}"/>
    </p:panel>
</h:form>
```

What just happened?

We have used List<Tag> POJOs to populate the <p:selectOneListbox> component options using tagConverter and displayed custom content using nested <p:column> facets:

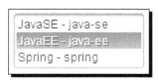

Introducing SelectManyMenu

The SelectManyMenu component is an extended version of the standard SelectManyMenu component with theme integration. SelectManyMenu is similar to SelectOneListbox but provides the ability to select multiple options. To select multiple options, you can press *Ctrl* and select **Options** or use the `showCheckbox="true"` attribute, which displays a checkbox for each option.

Time for action – using SelectManyMenu

Let us see how to use `<p:selectManyMenu>` with POJOs and the `showCheckbox` attribute, by performing the following step:

1. Create a form with `<p:selectManyMenu>` components:

```
<h:form>
    <p:panel header="SelectManyMenu">
    <h:panelGrid columns="2" style="margin-bottom:10px"
        cellpadding="5">
    <h:outputText value="Basic SelectManyMenu: " />
    <p:selectManyMenu  value="#{selectionController.numbers}">
        <f:selectItem itemLabel="One" itemValue="1" />
        <f:selectItem itemLabel="Two" itemValue="2" />
        <f:selectItem itemLabel="Three" itemValue="3" />
    </p:selectManyMenu>

    <h:outputText value="SelectManyMenu using POJO: " />
    <p:selectManyMenu
        value="#{selectionController.selectedTagsFromPojos}"
        var="t" showCheckbox="true"
        converter="#{tagConverter}">
    <f:selectItems value="#{selectionController.tagPojos}"
        var="tag" itemLabel="#{tag.label}" itemValue="#{tag}"/>
        <p:column>
            #{t.label} - #{t.value}
        </p:column>
    </p:selectManyMenu>
    </h:panelGrid>

    <p:commandButton value="Submit" update="display" />
    <h:panelGrid id="display">
    <h:outputText value="Basic: #{selectionController.numbers}" />
    <h:outputText value="POJO:
        #{selectionController.selectedTagsFromPojos}"/>
    </h:panelGrid>

    </p:panel>
    </h :form>
```

What just happened?

We have used `List<Tag>` POJOs to populate the `<p:selectManyMenu>` component options. As we have set the `showCheckbox` attribute to `true`, each option is displayed with a checkbox to select that option, as shown in the following screenshot:

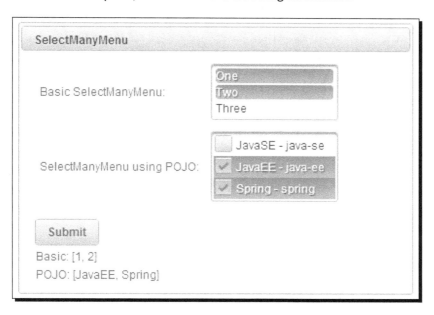

Creating the overlay menu using SelectCheckboxMenu

SelectCheckboxMenu is a multiselect component that displays options in an overlay. When you click on the SelectCheckboxMenu component, it will display a list of options each with a checkbox to select, and contains a filter text field to filter out the options.

Time for action – using SelectCheckboxMenu

Let us see how to use `<p:selectCheckboxMenu>` to select multiple options, by performing the following step:

1. Create a form with the `<p:selectCheckboxMenu>` component as follows:

```
<h:form>
    <p:panel header="SelectCheckboxMenu" style="width: 400px;
        height: 500px; margin: 0 auto;">
    <p:messages autoUpdate="true"/>
    <h:panelGrid style="margin-bottom:5px" cellpadding="3">
```

```
                        <p:selectCheckboxMenu
                            value="#{selectionController.
                            selectedSearchInOptions}"
                                label="Search In" filter="true"
                                    filterText="Filter"
                                    filterMatchMode="startsWith"
                                panelStyle="width:220px">
                            <f:selectItems
                                value="#{selectionController.searchInOptions}"
                                />
                        </p:selectCheckboxMenu>
                </h:panelGrid>
                <p:commandButton value="Submit" update="display"/>
                <h:outputText id="display" value="Value :
                    #{selectionController.selectedSearchInOptions}" />
            </p:panel>
        </h:form>
```

What just happened?

The preceding code displays SelectCheckboxMenu as shown in the following screenshot:

We have used List<String> type object searchInOptions to populate options. When the user selects options and clicks on submit, the selected options will be saved into the List<String> type object selectedSearchInOptions and is displayed on the form.

The SelectCheckboxMenu component supports two AJAX behavior events, change and toggleSelect. The toggleSelect event gets triggered when the Select all checkbox is checked or unchecked. The change event gets triggered if any of the options are checked or unchecked.

Creating the overlay menu with a default command using SplitButton

The SplitButton component displays a command button with an adjacent drop-down list icon. When you click on the button, the action associated with that button will be performed. When you click on the drop-down list icon it will display a list of other available options.

Time for action – using SplitButton

Let us see how we can use the `<p:splitButton>` component, by performing the following step:

1. Create a form with the `<p:splitButton>` component with **My Account** as the default action, and **Change Password** and **Logout** as other options:

```
<h:form>
    <p:splitButton value="My Account"
        actionListener="#{selectionController.showAccount}" >
        <p:menuitem value="Change Password" url="changePwd.jsf"
            />
        <p:menuitem value="Logout" ajax="false"
            actionListener="#{selectionController.logout}"/>
    </p:splitButton>
</h:form>
```

What the just happened?

The preceding code displays SplitButton as shown in the following screenshot:

We have used `<p:splitButton>` with default action **My Account,** which triggers the action listener method `selectionController.showAccount()`. We have provided the other action items using `<p:menuitem>` elements.

Introducing the PickList component

PickList is a dual list input component that is used for transferring data between two different collections with the following features:

- Drag-and-drop-based reordering
- Transition effects
- POJO support
- Filtering
- Captions
- Checkbox selection
- Client-server callbacks

PickList uses custom domain model `org.primefaces.model.DualListModel`, which contains source and target lists.

Time for action – using the basic PickList component

Let us see how we can create a PickList component to grant and revoke privileges to and from users, by performing the following steps:

1. Initialize `DualListModel` in the managed bean:

```
public class PickListController
{
    private DualListModel<String> privileges;
    public PickListController()
    {

        List<String> privilegesSource = new
            ArrayList<String>();
        List<String> privilegesTarget = new
            ArrayList<String>();

        privilegesSource.add("Create User");
        privilegesSource.add("Delete User");
        privilegesSource.add("Disable User");
        privilegesSource.add("Remove Buzz Post");

        privileges = new
            DualListModel<String>(privilegesSource,
            privilegesTarget);
    }
    //setter and getter for privileges
}
```

2. Use the `<p:pickList>` component to create a PickList component:

```
<p:pickList id="pickList"
            value="#{pickListController.privileges}"
            var="privilege"
            itemLabel="#{privilege}"
            itemValue="#{privilege}">
    <f:facet name="sourceCaption">Available
        Privileges</f:facet>
    <f:facet name="targetCaption">Granted Privileges</f:facet>
</p:pickList>
```

What just happened?

We have created a basic PickList component by creating a `DualListModel` instance as a backing bean and initialized with options. Now, we can transfer the options between the two lists using various transfer controls as shown in the following screenshot:

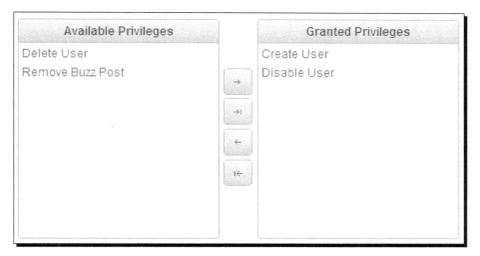

The PickList component provides the following attributes for customization:

◆ `addLabel`: Title of the the add button. Default is `Add`.

◆ `addAllLabel`: Title of the add all button. Default is `Add All`.

◆ `removeLabel`: Title of the remove button. Default is `Remove`.

◆ `removeAllLabel`: Title of the remove all button. Default is `Remove All`.

◆ `moveUpLabel`: Title of the move up button. Default is `Move Up`.

◆ `moveTopLabel`: Title of the move top button. Default is `Move Top`.

◆ `moveDownLabel`: Title of the move down button. Default is `Move Down`.

- ◆ moveBottomLabel: Title of the move bottom button. Default is Move Bottom.

- ◆ itemDisabled: Specifies whether an item can be picked or not.

- ◆ showSourceControls: Specifies visibility of reorder buttons of source list. Default is false.

- ◆ showTargetControls: Specifies visibility of reorder buttons of target list. Default is false.

- ◆ onTransfer: Client-side callback to execute when an item is transferred from one list to another.

- ◆ showSourceFilter: Displays and inputs filter for source list. Default is false.

- ◆ showTargetFilter: Displays and inputs filter for target list. Default is false.

- ◆ filterMatchMode: Match mode for filtering, valid values are startsWith, contains, endsWith, and custom. Default is startsWith.

- ◆ filterFunction: Name of the JavaScript function for custom filtering.

- ◆ showCheckbox: When true, a checkbox is displayed next to each item. Default is false.

Using the PickList component with POJO support

In addition to simple types such as String, PickList can be used with POJOs by using converter. Let us see how we can use a PickList component to assign and revoke roles to/from users.

Time for action – using the advanced PickList component

Let's look at creating a PickList component backed by a collection of POJOs using converter, by performing the following steps:

1. Create a user-role management form with the PickList component:

```
<p:growl id="msg" escape="false" />

<p:pickList id="pojoPickList"
    value="#{pickListController.roles}"
    converter="#{roleConverter}"
            var="role" itemValue="#{role}"
                itemLabel="#{role.roleName}"
            showSourceControls="true" showTargetControls="true"
            showSourceFilter="true" showTargetFilter="true"
            showCheckbox="true" filterMatchMode="contains"
                effect="bounce">
```

```
<f:facet name="sourceCaption">Available Roles</f:facet>
<f:facet name="targetCaption">Assigned Roles</f:facet>

<p:ajax event="transfer"
    listener="#{pickListController.onTransfer}"
    update="msg" />

<p:column style="width:100%">
    #{role.roleName}
</p:column>

</p:pickList>
```

2. Initialize DualListModel<Role> in the PickListController class and implement the onTransfer() listener method.

```
public class PickListController
{
    private DualListModel<Role> roles;
    public PickListController()
    {
        List<Role> source = loadRolesFromDatabase();
        List<Role> target = new ArrayList<Role>();
        roles = new DualListModel<Role>(source, target);
    }
    //setter and getter for roles

    public void onTransfer(TransferEvent event)
    {
        StringBuilder builder = new StringBuilder();
        for(Object item : event.getItems()) {
            builder.append(((Role)
                item).getRoleName()).append("<br />");
        }
        String msg = null;
        if(event.isAdd()){
            msg = "Assigned Roles:<br/>"+builder.toString();
        } else {
            msg = "Revoked Roles:<br/>"+builder.toString();
        }
        FacesContext.getCurrentInstance().addMessage(null, new
            FacesMessage(msg));
    }
}
```

What just happened?

We have used `DualListModel<Role>` for populating the PickList data by loading roles details from the database and registering `RoleConverter` using `converter=#{roleConverter}`. Also we have displayed the options using nested `<p:column>` elements. The advantage of using nested `<p:column>` elements is that we can display custom content, such as images, as options:

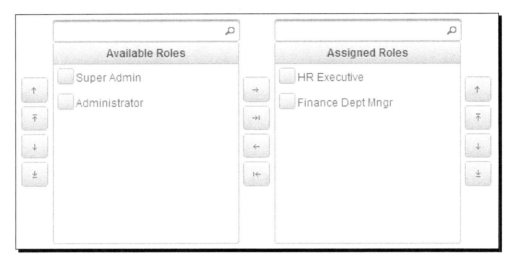

We have used the `showSourceControls` and `showTargetControls` attributes to display the Move Up, Move Top, Move Down, and Move Bottom buttons for source and target lists. We have used the `showSourceFilter` and `showTargetFilter` attributes to provide filtering options on both the lists. As we have set `showCheckbox="true"`, a checkbox is displayed with each option so that you can select multiple options and add them all at one go.

As of now, PickList component supports only the `transfer` event, which is the only available AJAX event and default event too. We have registered an event listener method, `pickListController.onTransfer(TransferEvent event)`, for the `transfer` event, which gets triggered whenever you transfer an option between source and target lists. You can use `event.isAdd()` or `event.isRemove()` to determine whether the move is from source to target or target to source.

Introducing the MultiSelectListbox component

MultiSelectListbox is a selection component that can be used to select an item from a collection of items with the parent-child hierarchical relationship.

For example, in e-commerce applications, we can display various types of categories and associated subcategories using MultiSelectListbox.

For the MultiSelectListbox component, we need to give a list of `SelectItem` instances, where each item can be a `SelectItemGroup` instance with its associated child `SelectItem` instances.

Time for action – using the MultiSelectListbox component

Let us see how to create a MultiSelectListbox component to display categories and its subcategories based on the selected category, by performing the following steps:

1. Instantiate `List<SelectItem>` instances with details of categories and subcategories:

```
public class CatalogController
{
    private List<SelectItem> categories;
    private String selectedCategory;

    public CatalogController()
    {
        categories = new ArrayList<SelectItem>();

        SelectItemGroup homeAppliancesGrp = new
        SelectItemGroup("Home Appliances");
        SelectItemGroup homeDecorGrp = new
            SelectItemGroup("Home & Decor");
        SelectItem clocks = new SelectItem("Wall Clocks");
        SelectItem candleHolders = new SelectItem("Candle
            Holders");
        SelectItem artPrints = new SelectItem("Art Prints");
        homeDecorGrp.setSelectItems(new SelectItem[] { clocks,
            candleHolders,artPrints });
        SelectItem indoorLighting = new SelectItem("Indoor
            Lighting");
        homeAppliancesGrp.setSelectItems(new SelectItem[] {
            homeDecorGrp,indoorLighting });

        SelectItemGroup electronicsGrp = new
            SelectItemGroup("Electronics");
        SelectItemGroup mobilesGrp = new
            SelectItemGroup("Mobiles");
        SelectItem android = new SelectItem("Android Phones");
        SelectItem windows = new SelectItem("Windows Phones");
        SelectItem dualSim = new SelectItem("Dual SIM Phones");
        mobilesGrp.setSelectItems(new SelectItem[] { android,
            windows, dualSim });
```

```
    SelectItemGroup laptopsGrp = new
        SelectItemGroup("Laptops");
    SelectItem apple = new SelectItem("Apple");
    SelectItem dell = new SelectItem("Dell");
    laptopsGrp.setSelectItems(new SelectItem[] { apple, dell
        });
    SelectItemGroup camerasGrp = new
        SelectItemGroup("Cameras");
    SelectItem canon = new SelectItem("Canon");
    SelectItem nikon = new SelectItem("Nikon");
    camerasGrp.setSelectItems(new SelectItem[] { canon,
        nikon });
    electronicsGrp.setSelectItems(new SelectItem[] {
        mobilesGrp, laptopsGrp, camerasGrp });

    SelectItemGroup booksGrp = new
        SelectItemGroup("Books");
    SelectItem literature = new SelectItem("Literature");
    SelectItem fiction = new SelectItem("Fiction");
    booksGrp.setSelectItems(new SelectItem[] { literature,
        fiction });
    categories.add(homeAppliancesGrp);
    categories.add(electronicsGrp);
    categories.add(booksGrp);
    }
    // setters and getters
}
```

2. Create the MultiSelectListbox component backing with the
   List<SelectItem> instance:

```
<h:form>
    <p:multiSelectListbox
        value="#{multiSelectListboxBean.selectedCategory}"
        effect="slide">
    <f:selectItems value="#{multiSelectListboxBean.categories}"
        />
    </p:multiSelectListbox>
    <p:commandButton value="Show Products"
        update="selectedCategory/>
    <h:outputText id="selectedCategory" value="Selected
        Category: #{catalogController.selection}"/>
</h:form>
```

What just happened?

We have created `List<SelectItem>` instances with the `SelectItemGroup` and `SelectItem` objects with the parent-child hierarchical relationship:

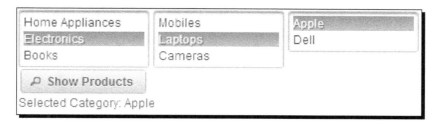

In MultiSelectListbox, when you click on a category group, associated subcategories and options will be displayed in an adjacent Listbox. We can select the desired category by clicking on any of the leaf (`SelectItem`) nodes.

Summary

In this chapter, we have learned how to use various PrimeFaces selection input components such as SelectManyCheckbox, SelectOneRadio, SelectOneMenu, SelectOneListbox, SelectManyMenu, PickList, and so on. In the next chapter, we will learn about PrimeFaces advanced input components such as Calendar, Rating, Spinner, Slider, File Upload, and so on.

7
Introducing Advanced Input Components

PrimeFaces provides several advanced input components such as Calendar, Spinner, Slider, Rating, and so on, which can be used to build rich user interfaces. Also, PrimeFaces provides the FileUpload and FileDownload components that simplify the process of uploading and downloading of files and provide an enhanced HTML5-powered FileUpload editor. In addition to these, PrimeFaces provides the CAPTCHA validation component that can be used to prevent spam and bots from crawling into our system.

Calendar is a very commonly-used component. PrimeFaces provides the Calendar component with lots of features and customization options such as inline/pop-up calendar, year/month navigation, customizable locale/date format support, and many more.

The Spinner component comes in very handy when getting input with increment and decrement features with a configurable step value.

In e-commerce applications we can use the Slider component to select a range of prices to filter the products display. And, we can use the Rating component to rate the product based on a rating scale.

In this chapter we will cover:

- Introducing the Calendar component
- Star-based rating using the Rating component
- Introducing the Spinner component

- Getting input on a scale using Slider
- Preventing spam and bots using CAPTCHA validation
- Uploading files using the FileUpload component
- Downloading files using the FileDownload component

Introducing the Calendar component

Calendar is a date and time picker component that provides the following list of features:

- Pop-up and inline display modes
- Localization support
- Month and year navigator
- Date and time range restriction
- Multiple pages calendar
- Customizable date formats
- AJAX event support for the `dateSelect` event
- Advanced customization for enabling/disabling dates and applying custom styles for dates

A basic Calendar component can be displayed using `<p:calendar>` as follows:

```
<p:calendar value="#{userController.registerUser.dob}"/>
```

The `<p:calendar>` component provides the following attributes to customize its behavior:

- `mindate`: This sets the calendar's minimum visible date.
- `maxdate`: This sets the calendar's maximum visible date.
- `pages`: This enables multiple page rendering. The default value is `1`.
- `disabled`: This disables the calendar when set to `true`. The default value is `false`.
- `mode`: This defines how the calendar will be displayed. The default value is `popup`. Valid values are `popup` and `inline`.
- `pattern`: The date format pattern for localization. The default value is `MM/dd/yyyy`.
- `locale`: This is the locale to be used for labels and conversion.
- `navigator`: This enables the month/year navigator. The default value is `false`.
- `timeZone`: `String` or a `java.util.TimeZone` instance to specify the timezone used for date conversion. This defaults to `TimeZone.getDefault()`.
- `readonly`: This makes both the input text and pop-up button of Calendar disabled. The default value is `false`.

- `readonlyInput`: This provides a read-only access to only the input text of a pop-up calendar. You can change the date using the datepicker button. The default value is `false`.

- `showButtonPanel`: This provides for the visibility of the button panel containing **Today** and **Done** buttons. The default value is `false`.

- `effect`: This specifies the effect to use when displaying and showing the pop-up calendar.

- `effectDuration`: This is the duration of the effect. The default value is `normal`.

- `showOn`: This is a client-side event that displays the pop-up calendar. The default value is `both`. Valid values are `focus`, `button`, and `both`.

- `showWeek`: This displays the week number next to each week. The default value is `false`.

- `disabledWeekends`: This disables weekend columns. The default value is `false`.

- `showOtherMonths`: This displays days belonging to other months. The default value is `false`.

- `selectOtherMonths`: This enables selection of days belonging to other months. The default value is `false`.

- `yearRange`: This provides the year range for the navigator, with the default being `c-10:c+10`.

- `timeOnly`: If set to `true`, this shows only the time picker without the date. The default value is `false`.

- `stepHour`: These are hour steps. The default value is `1`.

- `stepMinute`: These are minute steps. The default value is `1`.

- `stepSecond`: These are second steps. The default value is `1`.

- `minHour`: This specifies the minimum boundary for hour selection. The default value is `0`.

- `maxHour`: This specifies the maximum boundary for hour selection. The default value is `23`.

- `minMinute`: This specifies the minimum boundary for minute selection. The default value is `0`.

- `maxMinute`: This specifies the maximum boundary for minute selection. The default value is `59`.

- `minSecond`: This specifies the minimum boundary for second selection. The default value is `0`.

- `maxSecond`: This specifies maximum boundary for second selection. The default value is `59`.

- ◆ `pagedate`: This specifies the initial date to display if the value is null.
- ◆ `beforeShowDay`: This is the client-side callback to execute before displaying a date; used to customize the date display.

Time for action – displaying a pop-up Calendar with navigator

Let us see how we can display a pop-up Calendar component when a button is clicked with the custom date format and navigator features.

To do this, create the `<p:calendar>` component using the `navigator` and `pattern` attributes:

```
<p:calendar value="#{userController.registeredUser.dob}"
showOn="button" navigator="true" pattern="EEE, dd MMM, yyyy"/>
```

What just happened?

We have created a Calendar component and configured it to be displayed when a button icon is clicked on, using the `showOn` attribute. As we have set `navigator="true"`, year and month drop-down lists are displayed for easy navigation. Also, we have customized the date format to be displayed in the `EEE, dd MMM, yyyy` format using the `pattern` attribute. When a date is selected, it will be displayed as **Fri, 14 Feb, 2014**. This is shown in the following screenshot:

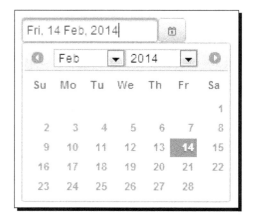

Understanding Internationalization (I18N) and Localization (L10N)

Before discussing how to localize the Calendar component, first let us understand what Internationalization (I18N) and Localization (L10N) is. Some web applications need to support multiple languages based on the user locale, which means that all the text on the screen should be displayed in the user-locale-specific locale.

For supporting Internationalization, we will store all the text, such as labels, messages, and so on, in externalized locale-specific properties files.

For example, we can store all messages in **properties files**, also known as **resource bundles**, with the base name `messages`.

For default, for the English language, we can store messages either in `messages.properties` or `messages_en.properties`. For the French locale, we can store messages in `messages_fr.properties`, and for the Spanish locale, we can store in `messages_es.properties`. Here `en`, `fr`, `es`, and so on are ISO 639 ISO language codes. These resource bundles should be placed in the classpath.

- **English (default)**: `messages.properties`

  ```
  label_password=Password
  invalid_login=Login failed. Please try again
  password_blank=Please enter password
  ```

- **French**: `messages_fr.properties`

  ```
  label_password=mot de passe
  invalid_login=Échec de la connexion. S'il vous plaît essayer de nouveau
  password_blank=S'il vous plaît entrer mot de passé
  ```

- **Spanish**: `messages_es.properties`

  ```
  label_password=contraseña
  invalid_login=Error de acceso. Por favor, inténtelo de nuevo
  password_blank=Por favor, introduzca la contraseña
  ```

Now, you need to register the resource bundles base name in `faces-config.xml` as follows:

```xml
<faces-config xmlns="http://java.sun.com/xml/ns/javaee"
  xmlns:xsi="http://www.w3.org/2001/XMLSchema-instance"
  xsi:schemaLocation="http://java.sun.com/xml/ns/javaee
  http://java.sun.com/xml/ns/javaee/web-facesconfig_2_0.xsd"
  version="2.0">
  <application>
    <resource-bundle>
      <base-name>messages</base-name>
      <var>msgs</var>
    </resource-bundle>
  </application>
</faces-config>
```

With the preceding `<resource-bundle>` configuration, JSF picks the appropriate properties file based on the user locale. If no resource bundle exists for the user locale, the default resource bundle (`messages.properties`) will be used.

Once the messages are externalized into resource bundles, we can refer to them in our facelets pages as follows:

```
<h:outputLabel value="#{msgs.label_password}" />
```

While adding `FacesMessage` objects, we can obtain the current locale-specific message as follows:

```
FacesContext context = FacesContext.getCurrentInstance();
ResourceBundle bundle = context.getApplication().
getResourceBundle(context, "msgs");
String message = bundle.getString(str);
context.addMessage(null, new FacesMessage(message));
```

Localization (L10N) means rendering a view using a specific locale. By default, the locale information will be obtained from the view's locale. We can override the locale by using the `<f:view>` element as follows:

```
<f:view contentType="text/html" locale="fr">
...
</f:view>
```

The preceding facelets page renders using the French locale resource bundle, `messages_fr.properties`.

We can also resolve locale dynamically and render a view based on a user-preferred locale as follows:

```
<f:view contentType="text/html" locale="#{loginUser.locale}">
...
</f:view>
```

Here `#{loginUser.locale}` resolves to a user-preferred locale and picks the appropriate resource bundle to resolve messages.

The PrimeFaces Calendar component uses a shared `PrimeFaces.locales` property to display the labels. PrimeFaces only provides English translations, so in order to localize the calendar, we need to put corresponding locales into a JavaScript file and include the scripting file to the page, as follows:

```
<h:outputScript library="js" name="calendarLocales.js" />
```

For already translated locales of the calendar, see `http://code.google.com/p/primefaces/wiki/PrimeFacesLocales`.

Time for action – displaying a multipage calendar with Localization and the dateSelect event listener

Let us see how we can display an inline calendar with multiple months displayed in the French locale and register the `dateSelect` event listener.

1. Configure the locale-specific Calendar labels in the `calendarLocales.js` file and save it in the `resources/js` folder:

```
<script type="text/javascript">
  PrimeFaces.locales['tr'] = {
    closeText: 'kapat',
    prevText: 'geri',
    nextText: 'ileri',
    currentText: 'bugün',
    monthNames: ['Ocak','Subat','Mart','Nisan','Mayis','Haziran','Temmuz','Agustos','Eylül','Ekim','Kasim','Aralik'],
    monthNamesShort: ['Oca','Sub','Mar','Nis','May','Haz', 'Tem','Agu','Eyl','Eki','Kas','Ara'],
    dayNames: ['Pazar','Pazartesi','Sali','Çarsamba','Persembe','Cuma','Cumartesi'],
    dayNamesShort: ['Pz','Pt','Sa','Ça','Pe','Cu','Ct'],
    dayNamesMin: ['Pz','Pt','Sa','Ça','Pe','Cu','Ct'],
    weekHeader: 'Hf',
    firstDay: 1,
    isRTL: false,
    showMonthAfterYear: false,
    yearSuffix: '',
    timeOnlyTitle: 'Zaman Seçiniz',
    timeText: 'Zaman',
    hourText: 'Saat',
    minuteText: 'Dakika',
    secondText: 'Saniye',
    ampm: false,
    month: 'Ay',
    week: 'Hafta',
    day: 'Gün',
    allDayText : 'Tüm Gün'
  };
</script>
```

2. Include the `calendarLocales.js` script file in the facelets page:

```
<h:outputScript library="js" name="calendarLocales.js" />
```

3. Create the `<p:calendar>` component displaying labels in the French language using the `locale` attribute:

```
<p:calendar value="#{calendarController.dob}"
      mode="inline"
      locale="fr"
      pages="3">
  <p:ajax event="dateSelect"
      listener="#{calendarController.handleDobSelect}"
      update="growl"/>
</p:calendar>
```

4. Implement the `handleDobSelect()` event listener method as shown:

```
@ManagedBean
@RequestScoped
public class CalendarController
{
  public void handleDobSelect(SelectEvent se)
  {
    Date date = (Date) se.getObject();
    FacesContext.getCurrentInstance().addMessage(null, new
FacesMessage("DOB Selected :"+date));
  }
}
```

What just happened?

We have created a Calendar component with the `inline` display mode to display three months using `pages="3"`. We have configured the French locale Calendar labels and set `locale="fr"`, which displayed the Calendar labels in French. Also, we have registered an event listener for the `dateSelect` event using `<p:ajax>`. When you click on any date, the `handleDobSelect(org.primefaces.event.SelectEvent event)` method gets invoked and we can get the selected date using the `event.getObject()` method. In the pop-up mode, Calendar also supports regular AJAX behavior events such as `blur` and `keyup`. The resultant Calendar is shown as follows:

Juin 2013							Juillet 2013							Août 2013						
L	M	M	J	V	S	D	L	M	M	J	V	S	D	L	M	M	J	V	S	D
					1	2	1	2	3	4	5	6	7				1	2	3	4
3	4	5	6	7	8	9	8	9	10	11	12	13	14	5	6	7	8	9	10	11
10	11	12	13	14	15	16	15	16	17	18	19	20	21	12	13	14	15	16	17	18
17	18	19	20	21	22	23	22	23	24	25	26	27	28	19	20	21	22	23	24	25
24	25	26	27	28	29	30	29	30	31					26	27	28	29	30	31	

In earlier versions of PrimeFaces, Calendar's `dateSelect` event listener method receives an instance of `org.primefaces. event.DateSelectEvent`. But, since PrimeFaces 3.5, the `DateSelectEvent` class was removed and instead the `SelectEvent` instance is passed. For more information, see `http://forum.primefaces.org/viewtopic. php?f=3&t=27590` and `https://code.google.com/p/ primefaces/issues/detail?id=2937`.

Restricting the date selection within the date range

Let us see how we can create a Calendar with a minimum and maximum date selection restrictions.

We can specify the `mindate` and `maxdate` values as strings in the format specified with the `pattern` attribute:

```
<p:calendar value="#{userController.registeredUser.dob}" pattern="dd-
MM-yyyy" mindate="01-06-2013" maxdate="15-08-2013"/>
```

Time for action – using Calendar with a date range

Let us see how we can use the `mindate` and `maxdate` values from backing beans.

1. Create a Calendar component with a date selection range using the `mindate` and `maxdate` attributes:

```
<p:calendar value="#{userController.registeredUser.dob}"
        pattern="dd-MM-yyyy"
        mindate="#{userController.dobMinDate}"
        maxdate="#{userController.dobMaxDate}"
        showButtonPanel="true"
        showWeek="true"
        showOtherMonths="true"
        selectOtherMonths="false"
        effect="slideDown"
        />
```

2. Implement the `getMinDate()` and `getMaxDate()` methods to return minimum and maximum dates:

```
@ManagedBean
@RequestScoped
public class UserController
{
```

```java
public Date getDobMinDate() throws ParseException
{
  return new SimpleDateFormat("dd-MM-yyyy").parse("01-06-2013");
}

public Date getDobMaxDate() throws ParseException
{
  return new SimpleDateFormat("dd-MM-yyyy").parse("15-08-2013");
}
}
```

What just happened?

We have specified the date range, which allows selecting any date between the `mindate` and `maxdate` values only. Also, we have seen how to use other attributes such as `showButtonPanel`, `showWeek`, `effect`, and so on:

Using Calendar with advanced customization options

PrimeFaces Calendar components provide options to customize enabling/disabling dates and for applying custom styles for each date using the `beforeShowDay` JavaScript callback function. This callback function takes `date` as the input parameter and returns an array with two values, of which the first value represents the enable/disable flag, and the second value represents the style class to be applied.

Time for action – using Calendar's advanced customization options

Let us see how we can customize the Calendar component to disable Saturday and Sunday dates and apply a custom style.

1. Create the JavaScript function `disableSatSundays()` using the following code:

```
function disableSatSunDays(date)
{
  var day = date.getDay();
  return [(day != 0 && day != 6), 'myCalendar'];
}
Create a new custom style myCalendar.
<style type="text/css">
  .myCalendar
  {
    font-size: 15px;
    background-color: #D3D3D3;
  }
</style>
```

2. Create a Calendar component and configure the `beforeShowDay` attribute to invoke the `disableSatSundays()` callback function:

```
<p:calendar value="#{userController.registeredUser.dob}" beforeSho
wDay="disableSatSunDays"/>
```

What just happened?

We have customized the Calendar to disable all Saturday and Sunday dates using the `beforeShowDay` attribute and applying the `myCalendar` CSS style. Even though we restricted selecting Saturdays and Sundays, it is always advisable to perform validations on the server side because there could be other means of getting input data, such as files from batch jobs.

Using the Calendar component's time picker options

The PrimeFaces's Calendar component also provides a time picker option to select the hour, minutes, and seconds.

Time for action – Calendar with the time picker options

Let us see how we can use the Calendar component as the date and time picker.

Create a Calendar component with time picker options using the `pattern` attribute:

```
<p:calendar value="#{calendarController.meetingTime}"
    pattern="MM/dd/yyyy HH:mm:ss a"
    stepHour="2" stepMinute="5" stepSecond="10"
        minHour="9" maxHour="18"/>
```

What just happened?

We have used `pattern="MM/dd/yyyy HH:mm:ss a"`, which makes the Calendar component display the time selection options. Here `HH`, `mm`, `ss` and a represents the hour, minutes, seconds and A.M./P.M. respectively. We have also used other options such as `stepHour` and `stepMinute` to specify the step value while dragging the sliders. Similar to the date range, we can also mention the time range using the `minHour, maxHour, minMinute, maxMinute, minSecond,` and `maxSecond` attributes. We can also use the Calendar component to display only the time picker options by using the `timeOnly="true"` attribute.

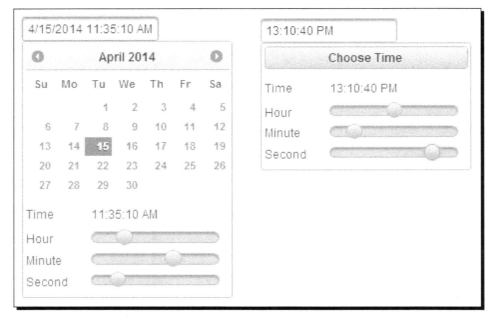

The Calendar component provides the following client-side API functions:

- `getDate()`: This returns the currently selected date
- `setDate(date)`: This sets the calendar display date
- `disable()`: This disables the calendar
- `enable()`: This enables the calendar

Star-based rating using the Rating component

The **Rating** component is a star-based rating input with AJAX callback support for the `rate` and `cancel` events:

```
<p:rating value="#{postController.selectedPost.rating}" />
```

By default, the Rating component displays five stars along with a cancel icon as follows:

The Rating component provides the following attributes to customize its behavior:

- `stars`: This specifies the number of stars to display. The default value is `5`.
- `cancel`: When enabled, this attribute displays a cancel icon to reset the ratings. The default value is `true`.
- `onRate`: This is a client-side callback, which is executed when a rating takes place.
- `disabled`: This disables user interaction. The default value is `false`.
- `readonly`: This disables user interaction without disabled visuals. The default value is `false`.

Time for action – using the Rating component

Let us see how we can use the Rating component with 10 stars and use the `rate` and `cancel` AJAX event listeners:

1. Create a Rating component and register the AJAX listeners for the `rate` and `cancel` events, using the following code:

```
<p:growl id="growl"/>
<p:rating value="#{postController.selectedPost.rating}"
stars="10">
  <p:ajax event="rate" listener="#{postController.
handlePostRating}" update="growl" />
```

```
        <p:ajax event="cancel" listener="#{postController.
handlePostRatingCancel}" update="growl" />
      </p:rating>
```

2. Implement the event listener methods:

```
@ManagedBean
@RequestScoped
public class PostController
{
  private Post selectedPost;
    //setters and getters

    public void handlePostRating(RateEvent rateEvent) {
      Integer rate = (Integer) rateEvent.getRating();
        JSFUtils.addInfoMessage("Post rated:" +rate);
    }

    public void handlePostRatingCancel() {
        JSFUtils.addInfoMessage("Post Rating Cancelled");
    }
}
```

What just happened?

We have used the `<p:rating>` component with `stars="10"` so that it will display a 10-stars-based Rating component. We have registered event listeners using the `<p:ajax>` element for the `rate` and `cancel` events. When you click on a star, the `handlePostRating()` method gets invoked, and if you click on the cancel icon, the `handlePostRatingCancel()` method gets invoked.

You can use the `onRate` attribute to register a client-side JavaScript callback function as follows:

```
<p:rating value="#{postController.selectedPost.rating}"
onRate="alert('Post rated :' + value)"/>
```

The `onRate` callback function is called when a star is selected with `value` as the only parameter.

Sometimes, we may need to display the Rating component in the read-only mode without the cancel icon. We can apply the read-only access to the Rating component using the following code snippet:

```
<p:rating value="#{postController.selectedPost.rating}"
readonly="true"/>
```

If you use `readonly="true"`, stars will be displayed as active but in the read-only mode, this prevents users from rating. Alternatively, you can use `disabled="true"`, which displays only the number of stars based on the rating value and the stars will be disabled. If you set `readonly="true"` or `disabled="true"`, the cancel icon will not be displayed automatically. These are shown in the following screenshot:

The Rating component provides the following client-side API functions:

◆ `getValue()`: This returns the current rating value

◆ `setValue(value)`: This sets the rating value

◆ `disable()`: This disables the Rating component

◆ `enable()`: This enables the Rating component

◆ `reset()`: This clears the rating value

Introducing the Spinner component

The Spinner component is used to provide an input with increment and decrement buttons on an input text. A basic Spinner component can be created as follows:

```
<p:spinner value="#{spinnerController.quantity}" />
```

The Spinner component provides the following attributes to customize its behavior:

◆ `stepFactor`: This specifies the stepping factor for each increment and decrement. The default value is 1.

◆ `min`: This is the minimum boundary value.

- max: This is the maximum boundary value.
- prefix: This is the prefix of the input.
- suffix: This is the suffix of the input.

By default, when you click on the increment/decrement buttons, the value will increment/decrement by 1. We can bind the Spinner component to decimal type properties and customize the increment/decrement value by setting the stepFactor attribute to the desired step value. Also, we can specify the minimum and maximum boundary values for the Spinner component and the prefix/suffix to be displayed with the Spinner component value.

Time for action – using the Spinner component

Let us see how we can use the Spinner component:

1. Create a Spinner component to hold a double value, say price, that steps by 0.25 with the $ prefix:

```
<p:spinner value="#{spinnerController.price}" prefix="$"
stepFactor="0.25" />
```

2. Create another Spinner component to hold a discount value with a % suffix and the discount value should be between 0 and 10:

```
<p:spinner value="#{spinnerController.discount}" suffix="%"
min="0" max="10" />
```

What just happened?

We have used the <p:spinner> component to create Spinner components with various features such as stepFactor, the min/max boundaries, and prefix/suffix.

However, even if you specify the min and max boundaries, the Spinner component will allow you to enter any value outside the boundaries directly in the text field. We can restrict entering the value in the Spinner input text field manually using the onkeydown event as follows:

```
<p:spinner value="#{spinnerController.discount}" suffix="%" min="0"
max="10" onkeydown="return false;"/>
```

However, doing server-side validations will be safe in case the data comes through other channels such as batch processes.

Getting input on a scale using the Slider component

The **Slider** component can be used to take input by using a slider bar. Slider requires an input component to hold the value selected by the slide bar.

The Slider component's `for` attribute is used to set the `id` value of the input component whose input will be provided by the slider.

A basic Slider component can be created as follows:

```
<p:inputText id="zoomlevelId" value="#{sliderController.zoomLevel}" />
<p:slider for="zoomlevelId"/>
```

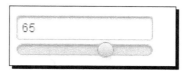

The Slider component provides the following attributes to customize its behavior:

- `for`: This is the ID of the input text that the slider will be used for.
- `display`: This is the ID of the component to display the slider value.
- `minValue`: This is the minimum value of the slider. The default value is `0`.
- `maxValue`: This is the maximum value of the slider. The default value is `100`.
- `animate`: This is the Boolean value to enable/disable the animated move when the background of slider is clicked. The default value is `true`.
- `type`: This sets the type of the slider, `horizontal` or `vertical`. This default value is `horizontal`.
- `step`: These are fixed pixel increments that the slider moves in. The default value is `1`.
- `disabled`: This disables or enables the slider. The default value is `false`.
- `onSlideStart`: This is the client-side callback to execute when sliding begins.
- `onSlide`: This is the client-side callback to execute during sliding.
- `onSlideEnd`: This is the client-side callback to execute when sliding ends.
- `range`: When enabled, two handles are provided for selecting a range. The default value is `false`.
- `displayTemplate`: This enables the string template to use when updating the display. Valid placeholders are `{value}`, `{min}`, and `{max}`.

Sometimes, we may want to display only Slider along with its value, without the input text field. To implement this, we can bind the slider to a hidden input component and use the `display` attribute to specify an `outputText` field ID to show the slider value:

```
<h:panelGrid columns="1" style="margin-bottom:10px">
  <h:outputText id="display" value="Value : #{sliderController.
zoomLevel}" />
  <h:inputHidden id="zoomLevelId" value="#{sliderController.
zoomLevel}"/>
  <p:slider for="zoomLevelId" display="display" style="width:150px"
displayTemplate="Value : {value}"/>
</h:panelGrid>
```

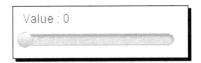

We can display the slider vertically using the `type="vertical"` attribute, by default `type` is set to `horizontal`. We can specify the value boundaries for the slider using the `minValue` and `maxValue` attributes. By default, the slider steps by 1, but we can customize it using the `step` attribute.

Let us see how we can use the Slider component's type, `minValue`, `maxValue`, and `step`:

```
<h:inputText id="zoomLevelId" value="#{sliderController. zoomLevel}"
/>
<p:slider for="zoomLevelId" type="vertical" minValue="0" maxValue="50"
step="10"/>
```

However, even if you specify the `min` and `max` boundaries, the Slider component allows entering any value outside the boundaries directly in the text field. We can restrict entering a value in the slider input text field manually as follows:

```
<h:inputText id="zoomLevelId" value="#{sliderController. zoomLevel}"
onfocus="this.readOnly=true;"/>
```

Or:

```
<h:inputText id="zoomLevelId" value="#{sliderController. zoomLevel}"
onkeydown="return false;"/>
```

The Slider component can also be used as a range selector. To use Slider as a range selector, set the `range` attribute to `true` and specify the comma-separated pair of input fields to bind the minimum and maximum values.

Time for action – using the Slider component

Let us see how to use Slider as a range selector.

Create a Slider component with the `range` attribute set to `true`:

```
<h:panelGrid columns="1" style="margin-bottom:10px">
  <h:outputText id="displayRange" value="Between #{sliderController.
minPrice} and #{sliderController.maxPrice}"/>
  <p:slider for="minPriceId1,maxPriceId2" display="displayRange"
style="width:300px" range="true" displayTemplate="Between {min} and
{max}"/>
  <h:inputHidden id="minPriceId1" value="#{sliderController.minPrice}"
/>
  <h:inputHidden id="maxPriceId2" value="#{sliderController.maxPrice}"
/>
</h:panelGrid>
```

What just happened?

We have used the `<p:slider>` component along with the `range="true"` attribute, which makes it as range selector. We bound the Slider's `min` and `max` values to two hidden input fields and displayed the selected range values using the `displayTemplate` attribute.

Slider supports the `slideEnd` AJAX event that is fired when the slide completes. You can register the event listener method, which can take the `org.primefaces.event.SlideEndEvent` argument:

```
<h:inputText id="zoomLevelId" value="#{sliderController.zoomLevel}" />
<p:slider for="zoomLevelId">
  <p:ajax event="slideEnd" listener="#{sliderController.onSlideEnd}"/>
</p:slider>

public void onSlideEnd(SlideEndEvent event) {
  int value = event.getValue();
  JSFUtils.addInfoMessage( "Value: " + value);
}
```

Preventing spam and bots using CAPTCHA validation

CAPTCHA is a form validation component based on the reCAPTCHA API. Generally, CAPTCHA validation is used to prevent spam and bots entering into the system.

To use the PrimeFaces CAPTCHA component, first we need to get the public key and private key from `http://recaptcha.net`. Once we have the public and private keys, we need to configure them as context parameters in `web.xml` as follows:

```xml
<context-param>
  <param-name>primefaces.PRIVATE_CAPTCHA_KEY</param-name>
  <param-value>REPLACE_YOUR_PRIVATE_KEY_HERE</param-value>
</context-param>
<context-param>
  <param-name>primefaces.PUBLIC_CAPTCHA_KEY</param-name>
  <param-value>REPLACE_YOUR_PUBLIC_KEY_HERE</param-value>
</context-param>
```

Time for action – using CAPTCHA for user registration

Now, let us see how to use the PrimeFaces Captcha component for user registration.

1. Create a user registration form with the Captcha component:

```xml
<h:form>
  <p:messages showDetail="true" autoUpdate="true"/>
  <h:panelGrid columns="2">
    <h:outputLabel value="EmailId" />
    <p:inputText value="#{userController.registerUser.emailId}"
required="true" label="EmailId"/>

    <h:outputLabel value="Password" />
    <p:password value="#{userController.registerUser.password}"
required="true" label="Password"/>

    <p:captcha label="Captcha" theme="red"/>
    <h:outputLabel value="" />

    <p:commandButton value="Register" ajax="false" actionListener=
"#{userController.doRegister}" />

  </h:panelGrid>
</h:form>
```

What just happened?

We have created the **User Registration Form** window using the Captcha component along with other required input fields such as **EmailId** and **Password**. When the user clicks on the **Register** button, the form will be submitted using a non-AJAX request. If the CAPTCHA validation failed, the form will be redisplayed with the following error message:

If you want to use an AJAX request to submit the form, you need to add `oncomplete="Recaptcha.reload()"` to `<p:commandButton>` to regenerate a new CAPTCHA image.

The Captcha component provides the following customization attributes:

- `theme`: This specifies the theme of the Captcha. The default is `red` and other possible values are `white`, `blackglass,` and `clean`.
- `language`: This specifies the key of the supported languages. The default value is `en`.
- `label`: This is the user presentable field name.
- `secure`: This enables HTTPS support. The default value is `false`.

By default, PrimeFaces displays the following error messages if the CAPTCHA validation failed:

```
primefaces.captcha.INVALID = {0}: Validation Error: Value is not
valid.
primefaces.captcha.INVALID_detail = {0}: ''{1}'' does not match the
displayed text.
```

You can customize these error messages by providing customized messages using message bundles. Add the following custom messages to the `validationmessages.properties` file:

```
primefaces.captcha.INVALID=Invalid Captcha value
primefaces.captcha.INVALID_detail={0}: ''{1}'' does not match the
captcha image text.
```

Now, configure `<message-bundle>` in the `faces-config.xml` file as shown in the following code:

```
<faces-config ...>
    <application>
        <message-bundle>validationmessages</message-bundle>
    </application>
</faces-config>
```

A couple of useful tips

- Use the label option to provide readable error messages in case validation fails
- Enable secure option to support HTTPS; otherwise, browsers will give warnings

Uploading files using the FileUpload component

The PrimeFaces **FileUpload** component provides a file upload mechanism with HTML5-powered UI with capabilities such as drag-and-drop, uploading multiple files, and progress tracking, and also supports graceful degradation for legacy browsers, such as IE8+.

PrimeFaces supports both `commons-fileupload` for JSF 2.1 and Servlet 3.0 Multipart for JSF 2.2 environments through its autodetection mechanism, and we can also explicitly configure the preferred method by configuring `primefaces.UPLOADER` `<context-param>` in `web.xml`, as shown in the following code snippet:

```
<context-param>
  <param-name>primefaces.UPLOADER</param-name>
  <param-value>auto</param-value>
</context-param>
```

The valid values for `primefaces.UPLOADER` are `auto`, `commons`, and `native`. A brief explanation for these is mentioned as follows:

- `auto`: This is the default mode and PrimeFaces determines the appropriate method by checking the JSF runtime environment. If the JSF runtime is at least 2.2, the `native` uploader is selected; otherwise, `commons`.

- `commons`: This mode uses `commons-fileupload` irrespective of the environment and works well on both Servlet 2.5 and 3.0 environments.

- `native`: This mode uses the Servlet 3.x MultiPart API to upload the files. If JSF runtime is less than 2.2, an exception will be thrown.

To be able to use the Commons FileUpload mechanism, either through the `auto` or `commons` mode, first we need to configure `FileUploadFilter`, which parses `MultiPartRequest`, in `web.xml` as follows:

```
<filter>
  <filter-name>PrimeFaces FileUpload Filter</filter-name>
  <filter-class> org.primefaces.webapp.filter.FileUploadFilter </
filter-class>
  <init-param>
    <param-name>thresholdSize</param-name>
    <param-value>51200</param-value>
  </init-param>
  <init-param>
    <param-name>uploadDirectory</param-name>
    <param-value>C:/primefaces/temp</param-value>
  </init-param>
</filter>

<filter-mapping>
  <filter-name>PrimeFaces FileUpload Filter</filter-name>
  <servlet-name>Faces Servlet</servlet-name>
</filter-mapping>
```

Here, `thresholdSize` and `uploadDirectory` are optional init parameters:

- `thresholdSize`: This parameter bears the maximum file size in bytes to keep uploaded files in memory. If a file exceeds this limit, it'll be temporarily written to disk.

- `uploadDirectory`: This parameter bears the directory path, where the temporary files that exceeds the threshold size will be placed. By default, it is `System.getProperty("java.io.tmpdir")`.

The PrimeFaces FileUpload component in the `commons` mode uses `commons-fileupload.jar` and `commons-io.jar`. So, add the following dependencies in the Maven file, `pom.xml`, to add these two JARs to the classpath:

```
<dependency>
  <groupId>commons-fileupload</groupId>
  <artifactId>commons-fileupload</artifactId>
  <version>1.2.1</version>
</dependency>
```

```
<dependency>
  <groupId>commons-io</groupId>
  <artifactId>commons-io</artifactId>
  <version>1.4</version>
</dependency>
```

We can create a FileUpload component as follows:

```
<h:form enctype="multipart/form-data">
    <p:fileUpload fileUploadListener="#{userController.
handleUserPicUpload}"/>
</h:form>
```

This FileUpload component, which by default works in the advanced mode, allows uploading one or more files and invokes the fileUploadListener method, once for each of the selected files with FileUploadEvent as the parameter, from which we can get the file data. This is shown in the following code:

```
@ManagedBean
@RequestScoped
public class UserController
{
  public void handleUserPicUpload(FileUploadEvent event) throws
IOException
  {
    UploadedFile uploadedFile = event.getFile();
    String fileName = uploadedFile.getFileName();
    String contentType = uploadedFile.getContentType();
    byte[] contents = uploadedFile.getContents();
    InputStream inputstream = uploadedFile.getInputstream();

JSFUtils.addInfoMessage("User Picture uploaded successfully");
    }
}
```

The following screenshot shows the result:

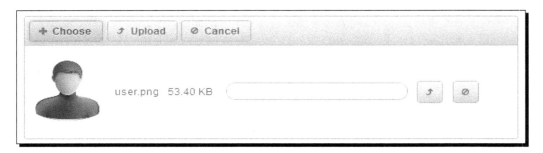

The FileUpload component provides the following attributes for customization:

- `fileUploadListener`: This method is invoked when a file is uploaded.

- `multiple`: This allows multifile selection when `true`. The default value is `false`.

- `auto`: This enables auto file uploads. The default value is `false`.

- `label`: This specifies the label of the browse button. The default value is `Choose`.

- `allowTypes`: This specifies the regular expression to restrict uploadable files.

- `sizeLimit`: This specifies the maximum file size limit in bytes.

- `fileLimit`: This specifies the maximum number of files that can be uploaded.

- `showButtons`: This determines the visibility of the **Upload** and **Cancel** buttons in the button bar. The default value is `true`.

- `mode`: This specifies the mode of the file upload. This can be `simple` or `advanced`. The default value is `advanced`.

- `uploadLabel`: This is the label of the **Upload** button. The default value is `Upload`.

- `cancelLabel`: This is the label of the **Cancel** button. The default value is `Cancel`.

- `invalidSizeMessage`: This specifies the message to be displayed when the size limit exceeds the particular given value.

- `invalidFileMessage`: This specifies the message to be displayed when the file is not accepted.

- `dragDropSupport`: This helps determine whether or not to enable drag-and-drop from the filesystem. The default value is `true`.

- `onstart`: This is the client-side callback to be executed when the upload begins.

- `oncomplete`: This is the client-side callback to be executed when the upload ends.

- `disabled`: This disables the component when set to `true`. The default value is `false`.

If you want a simple file upload functionality, similar to the traditional `<input type="file">`, you can use `<p:fileUpload>` with `mode="simple"`:

```
<h:form enctype="multipart/form-data">
    <p:fileUpload value="#{userController.userPic}" mode="simple"/>
    <p:commandButton value="Submit" ajax="false"/>
</h:form>
```

Then, perform the following code:

```
@ManagedBean
@RequestScoped
public class UserController
{
    private org.primefaces.model.UploadedFile userPic;
    //setter and getter
}
```

By default, the `<p:fileUpload>` component works in a single file selection mode (`multiple="false"`), which means you can select only one file through the file browser at a time. But still, it will allow you to select multiple files, one at a time, and you can upload all of them at once. You can set the attribute, `multiple="true"`, to be able to select multiple files at a time through the file browser. Also, you can set `auto="true"` to trigger the uploading process as soon as you select a file without requiring to click on the **Upload** button.

You can restrict the type of files to be uploaded using the `allowTypes` attribute:

```
<p:fileUpload fileUploadListener="#{userController.
handleUserPicUpload}" allowTypes="/(\.|\/)(gif|jpe?g|png)$/"/>
```

Here, we restricted the files to be uploaded only of the type `.gif`, `.jpg`, `.jpeg`, or `.png`, using the regular expression. If you select any other type of file, the **Invalid file type** error message will be displayed. You can customize this message using the `invalidFileMessage` attribute.

You can restrict the file size using the `sizeLimit` attribute, specifying the maximum limit in bytes. For example, if you want to restrict the file size to be a maximum of 10 Kilobytes, you can set `sizeLimit="10240"`, shown as follows:

```
<p:fileUpload fileUploadListener="#{userController.
handleUserPicUpload}" sizeLimit="10240"/>
```

Time for action – using the FileUpload component

Let us see how we can use the FileUpload component to upload the user profile image of type `.jpg`, `.jpeg`, `.gif`, or `.png`, which should be a maximum of 1 MB:

1. Create a user account form to upload the user image:
    ```
    <h:form enctype="multipart/form-data">
      <p:fileUpload
        fileUploadListener="#{userController.handleUserPicUpload}"
        allowTypes="/(\.|\/)(gif|jpe?g|png)$/"
        invalidFileMessage="Only gif, jpg or png type images are
    allowed"
    ```

```
        sizeLimit="1048576"
        invalidSizeMessage="File size should not exceed 1MB"/>
</h:form>
```

2. Implement the `actionListener` method to save the uploaded image:

```
public void handleUserPicUpload(FileUploadEvent event)
{
  UploadedFile uploadedFile = event.getFile();
  String fileName = uploadedFile.getFileName();
  byte[] contents = uploadedFile.getContents();
  //logic to save byte[]
  FacesMessage msg = new FacesMessage("Succesful", uploadedFile.
getFileName()+ " is uploaded.");
  FacesContext.getCurrentInstance().addMessage(null, msg);
JSFUtils.addInfoMessage("User picture uploaded successfully");
}
```

What just happened?

We have used the `<p:fileUpload>` component to upload the image of type `.gif`, `.jpg`, `.jpeg`, or `png`. We have restricted the file size to be a maximum of 1 MB using `sizeLimit="1048576"`. We have also customized the error messages for an invalid file type and invalid size errors using the `invalidFileMessage` and `invalidSizeMessage` attributes.

Downloading files using the FileDownload component

The **FileDownload** component is used to stream binary data such as images, PDFs, spreadsheets, or any other types of files. The FileDownload component is used with any JSF command components, such as `commanButton` or `commanLink`, to trigger the downloading action:

```
<h:commandLink value="Download">
  <p:fileDownload value="#{userController.userPic}" />
</h:commandLink>
```

The `value` attribute of FileDownload must be an `org.primefaces.model.StreamedContent` instance. We can use the built-in `org.primefaces.model.DefaultStreamedContent` class that implements the `StreamedContent` interfaces or we, ourselves, can implement the `StreamedContent` interface to suit our needs better.

By default, the PrimeFaces `<p:fileDownload>` component dispatches content as an `attachment`. You can set the `contentDisposition` attribute to `inline` to let the browser open the file internally without a prompt.

> As FileDownload needs a full page refresh, if you are using
> `<p:commandButton>` or `<p:commandLink>` to trigger the download
> action, you must set `ajax="false"` on the command components:
>
> ```
> <p:commandButton value="Download" ajax="false">
>   <p:fileDownload value="#{userController.userPic}" />
> </p:commandButton>
> ```

As FileDownload is a non-AJAX process we can't use `<p:ajaxStatus>` to monitor the progress. PrimeFaces provides the `PrimeFaces.monitorDownload(startFunction, endFunction)` utility method to bind JavaScript callback functions to trigger on start and end of the download process.

Time for action – using the FileDownload component

Let us see how we can use the FileDownload component:

1. Create the FileDownload component:

```
<p:dialog modal="true" widgetVar="statusDialog" header="File
Download Status" draggable="false" closable="false"
resizable="false">
  <p:graphicImage value="/resources/images/ajax-loader.gif" />
</p:dialog>

<h:form>
```

```
<p:commandButton id="downloadBtn" value="Download" ajax="false"
onclick="PrimeFaces.monitorDownload(onDownloadStart,
onDownloadStop)" icon="ui-icon-arrowthick-1-s">
  <p:fileDownload value="#{userController.userPic}" />
</p:commandButton>

</h:form>
```

2. Implement the JavaScript callback methods to show the dialog box when the download starts and close the dialog when the download completes:

```
<script type="text/javascript">
      function onDownloadStart()
      {
            statusDialog.show();
      }
      function onDownloadStop()
      {
            statusDialog.hide();
      }
</script>
```

3. Implement the managed beans `getUserPic()` method to return an instance of `StreamedContent`:

```
@ManagedBean
@RequestScoped
public class UserController
{
   public StreamedContent getUserPic()
   {
     InputStream stream = this.getClass().
getResourceAsStream("sample_report.pdf");
       StreamedContent file = new DefaultStreamedContent(stream,
"application/pdf", "sample_report.pdf");
         return file;
     }
}
```

What just happened?

We have used the `<p:fileDownload>` component along with `<p:commandButton>` to trigger the download process and set `ajax="false"` to disable the AJAX mode. We have read `sample_report.pdf`, which is there in the classpath and created the `DefaultStreamedContent` instance. We used the `PrimeFaces.monitorDownload()` utility method to monitor the download process, the `onDownloadStart()` function gets triggered when the download starts, which displays the modal dialog with the in-progress icon, and once the downloading is completed, the `onDownloadStop()` function gets triggered, which hides the modal dialog.

Summary

In this chapter, we have learned how to use various PrimeFaces advanced input components such as Calendar, Slider, Spinner, Rating, FileUpload, and FileDownload.

In the next chapter, we will learn about data components such as DataList, DataGrid, DataTable, and exporting data into PDF/Excel using DataExporter.

8
Working with Data Components

PrimeFaces provides several data iteration components, which include DataList, DataTable, DataGrid, and so on. These can be used to display data in a tabular format. Also, PrimeFaces provides the DataExporter component to export data into PDF, Excel, CSV, or XML formats.

In this chapter we will cover:

- ◆ Displaying data in a list layout using DataList
- ◆ Displaying data in a tabular format using DataTable
- ◆ Displaying data in a grid layout using the DataGrid component
- ◆ Exporting data into PDF, XLS, CSV, and XML formats using DataExporter

Introducing the DataList component

The DataList component displays a collection of data in the list layout with several display types and supports AJAX pagination. The DataList component iterates through a collection of data and renders its child components for each item.

Let us see how to use `<p:dataList>` to display a list of tag names as an unordered list:

```
<p:dataList value="#{tagController.tags}" var="tag" type="unordered"
itemType="disc">

  #{tag.label}

</p:dataList>
```

The preceding <p:dataList> component displays tag names as an unordered list of elements marked with disc type bullets. The valid type options are unordered, ordered, definition, and none.

We can use type="unordered" to display items as an unordered collection along with various itemType options such as disc, circle, and square. By default, type is set to unordered and itemType is set to disc.

We can set type="ordered" to display items as an ordered list with various itemType options such as decimal, A, a, and i representing numbers, uppercase letters, lowercase letters, and roman numbers respectively.

Time for action – displaying unordered and ordered data using DataList

Let us see how to display tag names as unordered and ordered lists with various itemType options.

1. Create <p:dataList> components to display items as unordered and ordered lists using the following code:

```
<h:form>
  <p:panel header="Unordered DataList">

    <h:panelGrid columns="3">
      <h:outputText value="Disc"/>
      <h:outputText value="Circle" />
      <h:outputText value="Square" />

      <p:dataList value="#{tagController.tags}" var="tag"
itemType="disc">
          #{tag.label}
      </p:dataList>
      <p:dataList value="#{tagController.tags}" var="tag"
itemType="circle">
          #{tag.label}
      </p:dataList>
      <p:dataList value="#{tagController.tags}" var="tag"
itemType="square">
          #{tag.label}
      </p:dataList>
    </h:panelGrid>
  </p:panel>
```

```
<p:panel header="Ordered DataList">
  <h:panelGrid columns="4">
    <h:outputText value="Number"/>
    <h:outputText value="Uppercase Letter" />
    <h:outputText value="Lowercase Letter" />
    <h:outputText value="Roman Letter" />


    <p:dataList value="#{tagController.tags}" var="tag"
type="ordered">
        #{tag.label}
    </p:dataList>
    <p:dataList value="#{tagController.tags}" var="tag"
type="ordered" itemType="A">
        #{tag.label}
    </p:dataList>
    <p:dataList value="#{tagController.tags}" var="tag"
type="ordered" itemType="a">
        #{tag.label}
    </p:dataList>
    <p:dataList value="#{tagController.tags}" var="tag"
type="ordered" itemType="i">
        #{tag.label}
    </p:dataList>
  </h:panelGrid>
</p:panel>

</h:form>
```

2. Implement the `TagController.getTags()` method to return a collection of tag objects:

```
public class TagController
{
  private List<Tag> tags = null;
  public TagController()
  {
    tags = loadTagsFromDB();
  }
  public List<Tag> getTags()
  {
    return tags;
  }
}
```

What just happened?

We have created DataList components to display tag names as an unordered list using `type="unordered"` and as an ordered list using `type="ordered"` with various supported `itemTypes` values. This is shown in the following screenshot:

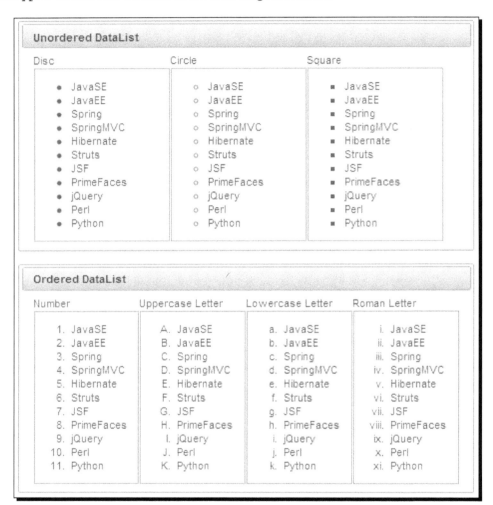

Using DataList with pagination support

DataList has built-in pagination support that can be enabled by setting `paginator="true"`. By enabling pagination, the various page navigation options will be displayed using the default paginator template. We can customize the paginator template to display only the desired options.

The paginator can be customized using the `paginatorTemplate` option that accepts the following keys of UI controls:

- `FirstPageLink`
- `LastPageLink`
- `PreviousPageLink`
- `NextPageLink`
- `PageLinks`
- `CurrentPageReport`
- `RowsPerPageDropdown`

Note that `{RowsPerPageDropdown}` has its own template, and options to display is provided via the `rowsPerPageTemplate` attribute (for example, `rowsPerPageTemplate="5,10,15"`). Also, `{CurrentPageReport}` has its own template defined with the `currentPageReportTemplate` option. You can use the `{currentPage}`, `{totalPages}`, `{totalRecords}`, `{startRecord}`, and `{endRecord}` keywords within the `currentPageReport` template. The default is `"{currentPage} of {totalPages}"`.

The default paginator template is `"{FirstPageLink} {PreviousPageLink} {PageLinks} {NextPageLink} {LastPageLink}"`.

We can customize the paginator template to display only the desired options.

For example:

```
{CurrentPageReport} {FirstPageLink} {PreviousPageLink} {PageLinks}
{NextPageLink} {LastPageLink} {RowsPerPageDropdown}
```

The paginator can be positioned using the `paginatorPosition` attribute in three different locations: `top`, `bottom`, or `both` (default).

The DataList component provides the following attributes for customization:

- `rows`: This is the number of rows to be displayed per page.
- `first`: This specifies the index of the first row to be displayed. The default is `0`.
- `paginator`: This enables pagination. The default is `false`.
- `paginatorTemplate`: This is the template of the paginator.
- `rowsPerPageTemplate`: This is the template of the `rowsPerPage` dropdown.
- `currentPageReportTemplate`: This is the template of the `currentPageReport` UI.
- `pageLinks`: This specifies the maximum number of page links to display. The default value is `10`.

◆ paginatorPosition: This specifies the position of the paginator. Valid values are top, bottom, or both. The default is both.

◆ paginatorAlwaysVisible: This defines whether the paginator should be hidden when the total data count is less than the number of rows per page. The default is true.

◆ rowIndexVar: This specifies the name of the iterator to refer to for each row index.

◆ varStatus: This specifies the name of the exported request scoped variable to represent the state of the iteration, the same as in the <ui:repeat> attribute varStatus.

Time for action – using DataList with pagination

Let us see how we can use the DataList component's pagination support to display five tags per page.

Create a DataList component with pagination support along with a custom paginatorTemplate:

```
<p:panel header="DataList Pagination">
  <p:dataList value="#{tagController.tags}" var="tag" id="tags"
type="none"
    paginator="true" rows="5"
    paginatorTemplate="{CurrentPageReport} {FirstPageLink}
{PreviousPageLink} {PageLinks} {NextPageLink} {LastPageLink}
{RowsPerPageDropdown}"
    rowsPerPageTemplate="5,10,15">
      <f:facet name="header">
        Tags
      </f:facet>
      <h:outputText value="#{tag.id} - #{tag.label}" style="margin-
left:10px" />
      <br/>
  </p:dataList>
</p:panel>
```

What just happened?

We have created a DataList component along with pagination support by setting paginator="true". We have customized the paginator template to display additional information such as CurrentPageReport and RowsPerPageDropdown. Also, we have used the rowsPerPageTemplate attribute to specify the values for RowsPerPageDropdown. The following screenshot displays the result:

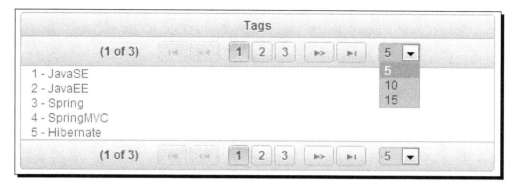

Displaying tabular data using the DataTable component

DataTable is an enhanced version of the standard DataTable that provides various additional features such as:

◆ Pagination

◆ Lazy loading

◆ Sorting

◆ Filtering

◆ Row selection

◆ Inline row/cell editing

◆ Conditional styling

◆ Expandable rows

◆ Grouping and SubTable, and many more

In our **TechBuzz** application, the administrator can view a list of users and enable/disable user accounts. First, let us see how we can display a list of users using basic DataTable as follows:

```
<p:dataTable id="usersTbl" var="user" value="#{adminController.
users}">
  <f:facet name="header">
    List of Users
  </f:facet>
  <p:column headerText="Id">
    <h:outputText value="#{user.id}" />
  </p:column>

  <p:column headerText="Email">
    <h:outputText value="#{user.emailId}" />
  </p:column>
```

```
<p:column headerText="FirstName">
  <h:outputText value="#{user.firstName}" />
</p:column>

<p:column headerText="Disabled">
  <h:outputText value="#{user.disabled}" />
</p:column>
<f:facet name="footer">
  Total no. of Users: #{fn:length(adminController.users)}.
</f:facet>
</p:dataTable>
```

◆ The following screenshot shows us the result:

List of Users			
Id	Email	FirstName	Disabled
1	admin@gmail.com	Mr	false
2	test@gmail.com	Mr	true
3	guest@gmail.com	Mr	false
4	essie@vaill.com	Essie	false
5	cruz@roudabush.com	Cruz	false
Total no. of Users: 5.			

PrimeFaces 4.0 introduced the Sticky component and provides out-of-the-box support for DataTable to make the header sticky, while scrolling using the stickyHeader attribute:

```
<p:dataTable var="user" value="#{adminController.users}"
stickyHeader="true">
...
</p:dataTable>
```

Using pagination support

If there are a large number of users, we may want to display users in a page-by-page style. DataTable has in-built support for pagination and works the same as described in the *Using DataList with pagination support* section.

Time for action – using DataTable with pagination

Let us see how we can display five users per page using pagination.

Create a DataTable component using pagination to display five records per page, using the following code:

```
<p:dataTable id="usersTbl" var="user" value="#{adminController.users}"
  paginator="true" rows="5"
  paginatorTemplate="{CurrentPageReport} {FirstPageLink}
{PreviousPageLink} {PageLinks} {NextPageLink} {LastPageLink}
{RowsPerPageDropdown}"
  currentPageReportTemplate="( {startRecord} - {endRecord}) of
{totalRecords} Records."
  rowsPerPageTemplate="5,10,15">

  <p:column headerText="Id">
    <h:outputText value="#{user.id}" />
  </p:column>
  <p:column headerText="Email">
    <h:outputText value="#{user.emailId}" />
  </p:column>
  <p:column headerText="FirstName">
    <h:outputText value="#{user.firstName}" />
  </p:column>
  <p:column headerText="Disabled">
    <h:outputText value="#{user.disabled}" />
  </p:column>
</p:dataTable>
```

What just happened?

We have created a DataTable component with the pagination feature to display five rows per page. Also, we have customized the paginator template and provided an option to change the page size dynamically using the rowsPerPageTemplate attribute.

Using columns sorting support

DataTable comes with built-in support for sorting on a single column or multiple columns. You can define a column as sortable using the `sortBy` attribute as follows:

```
<p:column headerText="FirstName" sortBy="#{user.firstName}">
    <h:outputText value="#{user.firstName}" />
</p:column>
```

You can specify the default sort column and sort order using the `sortBy` and `sortOrder` attributes on the `<p:dataTable>` element:

```
<p:dataTable id="usersTbl2" var="user" value="#{adminController.
users}" sortBy="#{user.firstName}" sortOrder="descending">
</p:dataTable>
```

The `<p:dataTable>` component's default sorting algorithm uses a Java comparator, you can use your own customized sort method as well:

```
<p:column headerText="FirstName" sortBy="#{user.firstName}"
sortFunction="#{adminController.sortByFirstName}">
  <h:outputText value="#{user.firstName}" />
</p:column>

public int sortByFirstName(Object firstName1, Object firstName2)
{
  //return -1, 0 , 1 if firstName1 is less than, equal to or greater
than firstName2 respectively
  return ((String)firstName1).compareToIgnoreCase(((String)
firstName2));
}
```

By default, DataTable's `sortMode` is set to `single`. To enable sorting on multiple columns, set `sortMode` to `multiple`. In multicolumns' sort mode, you can click on a column while the metakey (*Ctrl* or *command*) adds the column to the order group:

```
<p:dataTable id="usersTbl" var="user" value="#{adminController.users}"
sortMode="multiple">


</p:dataTable>
```

Using column filtering support

DataTable provides support for column-level filtering as well as global filtering (on all columns) and provides an option to hold the list of filtered records. In addition to the default match mode `startsWith`, we can use various other match modes such as `endsWith`, `exact`, and `contains`.

Time for action – using DataTable with filtering

Let us see how we can use filters with the users' DataTable.

1. Create a DataTable component and apply column-level filters and a global filter to apply filters on all columns:

```
<p:dataTable widgetVar="userTable" var="user"
value="#{adminController.users}"
    filteredValue="#{adminController.filteredUsers}"
    emptyMessage="No Users found for the given Filters">
  <f:facet name="header">
    <p:outputPanel>
      <h:outputText value="Search all Columns:" />
      <p:inputText id="globalFilter" onkeyup="userTable.filter()"
style="width:150px" />
    </p:outputPanel>
  </f:facet>

  <p:column headerText="Id">
    <h:outputText value="#{user.id}" />
  </p:column>

  <p:column headerText="Email" filterBy="#{user.emailId}"
      footerText="contains" filterMatchMode="contains">
    <h:outputText value="#{user.emailId}" />
  </p:column>

  <p:column headerText="FirstName" filterBy="#{user.firstName}"
footerText="startsWith">
    <h:outputText value="#{user.firstName}" />
  </p:column>

  <p:column headerText="LastName" filterBy="#{user.lastName}"
      filterMatchMode="endsWith" footerText="endsWith">
    <h:outputText value="#{user.lastName}" />
  </p:column>

  <p:column headerText="Disabled" filterBy="#{user.disabled}"
      filterOptions="#{adminController.userStatusOptions}"
      filterMatchMode="exact" footerText="exact">
    <h:outputText value="#{user.disabled}" />
  </p:column>

</p:dataTable>
```

2. Initialize `userStatusOptions` in `AdminController` managed bean:

```
@ManagedBean
@ViewScoped
public class AdminController
{
  private List<User> users = null;
  private List<User> filteredUsers = null;
  private SelectItem[] userStatusOptions;

  public AdminController()
  {
    users = loadAllUsersFromDB();
    this.userStatusOptions = new SelectItem[3];
    this.userStatusOptions[0] = new SelectItem("", "Select");
    this.userStatusOptions[1] = new SelectItem("true", "True");
    this.userStatusOptions[2] = new SelectItem("false", "False");
  }
  //setters and getters
}
```

What just happened?

We have used various `filterMatchMode` instances, such as `startsWith`, `endsWith`, and `contains`, while applying column-level filters. We have used the `filterOptions` attribute to specify the predefined filter values, which is displayed as a select drop-down list. As we have specified `filteredValue="#{adminController.filteredUsers}"`, once the filters are applied, the filtered users' list will be populated into the `filteredUsers` property. This following is the resultant screenshot:

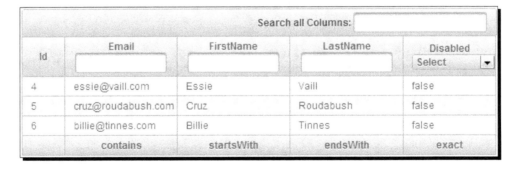

Since PrimeFaces Version 4.0, we can specify the `sortBy` and `filterBy` properties as `sortBy="emailId"` and `filterBy="emailId"` instead of `sortBy="#{user.emailId}"` and `filterBy="#{user.emailId}"`.

A couple of important tips

- ◆ It is suggested to use a scope longer than the request, such as the view scope, to keep the `filteredValue` attribute so that the filtered list is still accessible after filtering.
- ◆ The filter located at the header is a global one applying to all fields; this is implemented by calling the client-side API method called `filter()`. The important part is to specify the ID of the input text as `globalFilter`, which is a reserved identifier for DataTable.

Selecting DataTable rows

Selecting one or more rows from a table and performing operations such as editing or deleting them is a very common requirement. The DataTable component provides several ways to select one or more row(s).

Selecting a single row

We can use a PrimeFaces Command component, such as `commandButton` or `commandLink`, and bind the selected row to a server-side property using `<f:setPropertyActionListener>`, shown as follows:

```
<p:dataTable id="usersTbl" var="user" value="#{adminController.
users}">
  <!-- Column definitions -->

  <p:column style="width:20px;">
    <p:commandButton id="selectButton" update=":form:userDetails"
icon="ui-icon-search" title="View">
      <f:setPropertyActionListener value="#{user}"
target="#{adminController.selectedUser}" />
    </p:commandButton>
  </p:column>
</p:dataTable>

<h:panelGrid id="userDetails" columns="2" >
  <h:outputText value="Id:" />
  <h:outputText value="#{adminController.selectedUser.id}"/>

  <h:outputText value="Email:" />
  <h:outputText value="#{adminController.selectedUser.emailId}"/>
</h:panelGrid>
```

Selecting rows using a row click

Instead of having a separate button to trigger binding of a selected row to a server-side property, PrimeFaces provides another simpler way to bind the selected row by using `selectionMode`, `selection`, and `rowKey` attributes. Also, we can use the `rowSelect` and `rowUnselect` events to update other components based on the selected row, shown as follows:

```
<p:dataTable var="user" value="#{adminController.users}"
    selectionMode="single" selection="#{adminController.selectedUser}"
rowKey="#{user.id}">
    <p:ajax event="rowSelect" listener="#{adminController.
onRowSelect}" update=":form:userDetails"/>
    <p:ajax event="rowUnselect" listener="#{adminController.
onRowUnselect}" update=":form:userDetails"/>

  <!-- Column definitions -->

</p:dataTable>

<h:panelGrid id="userDetails" columns="2" >
  <h:outputText value="Id:" />
  <h:outputText value="#{adminController.selectedUser.id}"/>
  <h:outputText value="Email:" />
  <h:outputText value="#{adminController.selectedUser.emailId}"/>
</h:panelGrid>
```

Similarly, we can select multiple rows using `selectionMode="multiple"` and bind the `selection` attribute to an array or list of user objects:

```
<p:dataTable var="user" value="#{adminController.users}"
    selectionMode="multiple" selection="#{adminController.
selectedUsers}" rowKey="#{user.id}">
  <!-- Column definitions -->
</p:dataTable>
```

> rowKey should be a unique identifier from your data model and should be used by DataTable to find the selected rows. You can either define this key by using the `rowKey` attribute or by binding a data model that implements `org.primefaces.model.SelectableDataModel`.

When the `multiple` selection mode is enabled, we need to hold the *Ctrl* or *command* key and click on the rows to select multiple rows. If we don't hold on to the *Ctrl* or *command* key and click on a row the previous selection will be cleared with only the last clicked row selected. We can customize this behavior using the `rowSelectMode` attribute. If you set `rowSelectMode="add"`, when you click on a row, it will keep the previous selection and add the current selected row even if you don't hold the *Ctrl* or *command* key. The default `rowSelectMode` value is `new`. We can disable the row selection feature altogether by setting `disabledSelection="true"`.

Selecting rows using a radio button / checkbox

Another very common scenario is having a radio button or checkbox for each row, and the user can select one or more rows and then perform actions such as edit or delete.

The DataTable component provides a radio-button-based, single row selection using a nested `<p:column>` element with `selectionMode="single"`:

```
<p:dataTable var="user" value="#{adminController.users}"
selection="#{adminController.selectedUser}" rowKey="#{user.id}">
  <p:column selectionMode="single"/>
  <!-- Column definitions -->
</p:dataTable>
```

The DataTable component also provides checkbox-based, multiple row selection using a nested `<p:column>` element with `selectionMode="multiple"`:

```
<p:dataTable var="user" value="#{adminController.users}"
selection="#{adminController.selectedUsers}" rowKey="#{user.id}">
  <p:column selectionMode="multiple"/>
  <!-- Column definitions -->
</p:dataTable>
```

In our **TechBuzz** application, the administrator would like to have a facility to be able to select multiple users and disable them all in one go. Let us see how we can implement this using the checkbox-based, multiple rows selection.

Time for action – using DataTable with multiple row selection support

In this section we will demonstrate how to select multiple user rows and disable the selected users.

Create a DataTable component with the multiple row selection mode enabled, using the following code:

```
<p:dataTable var="user" value="#{adminController.users}"
    selection="#{adminController.selectedUsers}" rowKey="#{user.id}">

  <p:column selectionMode="multiple"/>

  <p:column headerText="Id" width="20px;">
    <h:outputText value="#{user.id}" />
  </p:column>

  <p:column headerText="Email" >
    <h:outputText value="#{user.emailId}" />
  </p:column>
  <f:facet name="footer">
    <p:commandButton value="Disable" actionListener="#{adminControll
er.disableSelectedUsers}"/>
  </f:facet>
</p:dataTable>
```

What just happened?

We have created a DataTable component with multiple row selection support by using a nested `<p:column>` with `selectionMode="multiple"`, which displays a checkbox for each row to select.

Using the row expansion feature

A row can be expanded to display detailed content using a row expansion column and the expansion facet. The `<p:rowToggler>` component places an expand/collapse icon. Clicking on a collapsed row loads expanded content with AJAX.

Let us see how to use the row expansion feature of DataTable:

```
<p:dataTable var="user" value="#{adminController.users}">
  <p:column style="width:15px;">
    <p:rowToggler />
  </p:column>
  <p:column headerText="Email" >
    <h:outputText value="#{user.emailId}" />
  </p:column>
  <p:rowExpansion>
    <h:panelGrid columns="2">
      <h:outputText  value="FirstName: " />
      <h:outputText value="#{user.firstName}" />
      <h:outputText  value="Disabled: " />
      <h:outputText value="#{user.disabled}" />
    </h:panelGrid>
  </p:rowExpansion>
</p:dataTable>
```

The preceding code renders a DataTable component with the row expansion feature as follows:

We can make the rows expanded by default by setting the expandedRow attribute to true.

It is a very common mistake that many developers forget to add `<p:rowToggler>`. Without `<p:rowToggler>`, the DataTable row toggling doesn't work.

Using the inline row editing feature

The DataTable component supports inline editing of data in row- and cell-based editing modes. Row-based editing is the default mode. For inline row/cell editing, the `input` and `output` facets are used to display data as labels in the `output` mode and as input components in the `input` mode. For the row-based editing mode, DataTable provides the `rowEdit` and `rowEditCancel` AJAX events to handle the save and cancel actions on the edited row data.

Time for action – using DataTable with row editing support

Let us see how to use the DataTable component row editing feature:

1. Create a DataTable component with the editable mode enabled by setting `editable` to `true`:

```
<p:dataTable id="usersTbl" var="user" value="#{adminController.
users}" editable="true">
  <p:ajax event="rowEdit" listener="#{adminController.onEdit}"/>
  <p:ajax event="rowEditCancel" listener="#{adminController.
onCancel}"/>

<p:column headerText="Email">
  <h:outputText value="#{user.emailId}" />
</p:column>

<p:column headerText="FirstName">
    <p:cellEditor>
      <f:facet name="output">
        <h:outputText value="#{user.firstName}" />
      </f:facet>
      <f:facet name="input">
        <p:inputText value="#{user.firstName}"/>
      </f:facet>
    </p:cellEditor>
  </p:column>

<p:column headerText="Disabled">
    <p:cellEditor>
      <f:facet name="output">
        <h:outputText value="#{user.disabled}" />
      </f:facet>
      <f:facet name="input">
        <h:selectOneMenu value="#{user.disabled}" >
          <f:selectItem itemLabel="True" itemValue="true"/>
```

```
            <f:selectItem itemLabel="False" itemValue="false"/>
          </h:selectOneMenu>
        </f:facet>
      </p:cellEditor>
    </p:column>
    <p:column style="width:6%">
      <p:rowEditor />
    </p:column>
  </p:dataTable>
```

2. Implement the `rowEdit` and `rowEditCancel` events' listener methods:

```
public void onEdit(RowEditEvent event)
{
  User user = (User) event.getObject();
  FacesMessage msg = new FacesMessage("Edited User Id : "+ user.
getId());
  FacesContext.getCurrentInstance().addMessage(null, msg);
}

public void onCancel(RowEditEvent event)
{
  User user = (User) event.getObject();
  FacesMessage msg = new FacesMessage("Editing Cancelled for User
Id: "+ user.getId());
  FacesContext.getCurrentInstance().addMessage(null, msg);
}
```

What just happened?

We have created DataTable with row editing enabled by setting `editable="true"`. The columns that we want to edit were wrapped in `<p:cellEditor>` with the `output` facet to display as the label and the `input` facet to display as the input element. We have used the `<p:rowEditor>` component to display the row edit icon. When the edit icon is clicked, the row switches to the edit mode and it shows the save and cancel icons to save or cancel the changes made to that row. When the save icon is clicked on, the `rowEdit` event listener method, `onEdit()`, will be invoked and if you click on the cancel icon, the `rowEditCancel` event listener method, `onCancel()`, will be invoked. A screenshot of the functioning is shown as follows:

DataTable Row Editing				
Id	Email	FirstName	Disabled	
1	admin@gmail.com	Mr	False ▼	✓ ✗
2	test@gmail.com	Mr	true	✎

Using the cell editing feature

As mentioned earlier, DataTable also supports the cell-based editing mode. In this mode, a cell switches to the edit mode when it is clicked on; losing focus triggers the `cellEdit` AJAX event, which saves the change value.

Time for action – using DataTable with cell editing support

Let us see how to use the cell editing feature of DataTable:

1. Create a DataTable component with the editable mode enabled by setting `editable` to `true` and `editMode` to `cell`, as shown in the following code:

```
<p:dataTable id="usersTbl" var="user" value="#{adminController.
users}" editable="true" editMode="cell">
  <p:ajax event="cellEdit" listener="#{adminController.
onCellEdit}"/>
  <p:column headerText="FirstName">
    <p:cellEditor>
      <f:facet name="output">
        <h:outputText value="#{user.firstName}" />
      </f:facet>
      <f:facet name="input">
        <p:inputText value="#{user.firstName}"/>
      </f:facet>
    </p:cellEditor>
  </p:column>
</p:dataTable>
```

2. Implement the `cellEdit` AJAX event listener method, `onCellEdit()`:

```
public void onCellEdit(CellEditEvent event)
{
  Object oldValue = event.getOldValue();
  Object newValue = event.getNewValue();
  if(newValue != null && !newValue.equals(oldValue))
  {
    FacesMessage msg = new FacesMessage("Cell Changed :"+ "Old: "
+ oldValue + ", New:" + newValue);
    FacesContext.getCurrentInstance().addMessage(null, msg);
  }
}
```

What just happened?

We have created a DataTable component with the cell-based editing mode enabled by setting `editMode` to `cell`. When an editable cell is clicked on, it switches to the editable mode and on losing focus, it saves the edited value and invokes the `cellEdit` event listener method, `onCellEdit()`.

Loading data leisurely

At times we may need to work with huge volumes of data where you can't load the whole data into the memory and display it. In those cases, we might want to load a subset of data in a page-by-page manner lazily.

DataTable supports loading data lazily by using `org.primefaces.model.LazyDataModel` as the data provider and setting `lazy ="true"`. We need to implement a custom model object by extending `org.primefaces.model.LazyDataModel` and implement the `load()` method to fetch page data that satisfies the sorting and filtering criteria applied on the DataTable:

```
public List<User> load(int first, int pageSize, String sortField,
SortOrder sortOrder, Map<String,String> filters) {
// code to fetch data based on applied sorting/filters
}
```

Here, the `load()` method parameters represents:

- ♦ `first`: This specifies the index of the first row to display
- ♦ `pageSize`: This specifies the number of rows to load on the page
- ♦ `sortField`: This specifies the name of the sort field, for example, `"firstName"` for `sortBy="#{user.firstName}"`
- ♦ `sortOrder`: This is an enumeration of type `org.primefaces.model.SortOrder`; could be either `ASCENDING` or `DESCENDING`
- ♦ `filter`: A map with field names as keys (for example, `"id"` for `filterBy="#{user.id}"`) and their corresponding filter values

Time for action – loading the DataTable data leisurely

Let us see how to use DataTable with the lazy loading feature.

1. Create a DataTable component with the `LazyDataModel` binding and set the `lazy` attribute to `true`, as shown in the following code:

```
<p:dataTable id="usersTbl" var="user" value="#{adminController.
lazyUserModel}" paginator="true" rows="10" lazy="true">
  <p:column headerText="Id" sortBy="#{user.id}" >
```

```
        <h:outputText value="#{user.id}" />
    </p:column>

    <p:column headerText="FirstName" filterBy="#{user.firstName}"
sortBy="#{user.firstName}">
        <h:outputText value="#{user.firstName}" />
    </p:column>
</p:dataTable>
```

2. Implement `LazyUserModel` by extending `LazyDataModel` to load data lazily:

```
import org.primefaces.model.LazyDataModel;
import org.primefaces.model.SortOrder;
public class LazyUserModel extends LazyDataModel<User>
{
    public User getRowData(String rowKey) {
        return loadUserFromDBByUserId(rowKey);
    }

    public Object getRowKey(User user) {
        return user.getId();
    }

    public List<User> load(int first, int pageSize, String
sortField, SortOrder sortOrder, Map<String,String> filters)
    {
        //get the count of total no. of records with filters
applied
        int dataSize = getTotalRecordsCount();
    this.setRowCount(dataSize);
        //load pageSize rows starting from index first by applying
sorting and filters from datasource
    List<User> data = loadDataFromDB();
return data;
    }
}
```

What just happened?

We have created a DataTable component with a lazy loading feature by setting `lazy` to `true` and binding the property to the `LazyDataModel` object. In the `load()` method, we load only a subset (page) of data that satisfies the applied filters and sorting.

Using the column grouping support

Grouping is defined by the ColumnGroup component used to combine the DataTable header and footers.

In the TechBuzz application, the administrator would like to see the statistics of the tag-wise posts count, for last year and the current year. Let us see how we can use the DataTable Grouping feature to implement this screen.

Create a DataTable component and display a header and footer using ColumnGroups:

```
<p:dataTable var="tagStats" value="#{adminController.
tagStatisticsList}">
  <f:facet name="header">
    Tag Usage Statistics
  </f:facet>
  <p:columnGroup type="header">
    <p:row>
      <p:column rowspan="2" headerText="Tag" />
      <p:column colspan="2" headerText="Posts Associated with Tag" />
    </p:row>
    <p:row>
      <p:column headerText="Last Year" />
      <p:column headerText="This Year" />
    </p:row>
  </p:columnGroup>
  <p:column headerText="Tag">
    <h:outputText value="#{tagStats.tag}" />
  </p:column>
  <p:column headerText="Posts Count">
    <h:outputText value="#{tagStats.postsCountLastYear}" />
  </p:column>
  <p:column headerText="Posts Count">
    <h:outputText value="#{tagStats.postsCountThisYear}" />
  </p:column>
  <p:columnGroup type="footer">
    <p:row>
      <p:column style="text-align:right" footerText="Totals:"/>
      <p:column style="text-align:left" footerText="#{adminController.
lastYearPostsCount}" />
      <p:column style="text-align:left" footerText="#{adminController.
thisYearPostsCount}" />
    </p:row>
  </p:columnGroup>
</p:dataTable>
```

The result is shown in the following screenshot:

Tag Usage Statistics		
Tag	Posts Associated with Tag	
	Last Year	This Year
JSF	1005	1500
PrimeFaces	2005	2200
jQuery	1205	1800
JavaScript	4005	5000
Totals:	8220	10500

The DataTable component also provides various other features such as scrolling, frozen rows, conditional coloring, resizable columns, and column reordering.

Using the scrolling feature

DataTable supports client and live scrolling. In the client mode, whole data is rendered. By enabling the `liveScroll` option, the data is loaded during scrolling. To enable scrolling, we need to set `scrollable="true"` and use the `scrollHeight` and `scrollWidth` attributes to specify scroll viewport height and width:

```
<p:dataTable id="usersTbl" var="user" value="#{adminController.users}"
scrollable="true" scrollHeight="150" scrollWidth="400">
...
</p:dataTable>
```

By enabling `liveScroll`, the data will be loaded while scrolling using AJAX. We can specify the number of rows to load on a live scroll using the `scrollRows` attribute, as shown in the following code:

```
<p:dataTable var="user" value="#{adminController.users}"
scrollable="true" scrollHeight="150" liveScroll="true"
scrollRows="25">
...
</p:dataTable>
```

Using the frozenRows feature

Sometimes we may want some rows to be displayed as sticky rows while scrolling. We can specify the rows to be displayed as sticky using the `frozenRows` attribute:

```
<p:dataTable var="user" value="#{adminController.users}"
scrollable="true" scrollHeight="150" frozenRows="#{adminController.
frozenUsers}">
..
</p:dataTable>
```

Applying custom styles for rows

We can apply custom styles conditionally using the `rowStyleClass` attribute. Suppose we want to display users in red color if the user status is disabled:

```
<p:dataTable var="user" value="#{adminController.users}"
rowStyleClass="#{user.disabled eq true ? 'disabledUser' : null}">
</p:dataTable>

<style type="text/css">
  .disabledUser {
  background-color: #FF0000;
  color: #FFFFFF;
  }
</style>
```

Using the resizable and draggable columns feature

By default, DataTable columns are not resizable and columns can't be reordered. We can make columns resizable by setting the `resizableColumns` attribute to `true`. By setting `draggableColumns="true"`, we can rearrange the column order by dragging-and-dropping column headers:

```
<p:dataTable var="user" value="#{adminController.users}"
draggableColumns="true" resizableColumns="true">
</p:dataTable>
```

The column order is preserved in postbacks and the `colReorder` event is available as an AJAX event.

Displaying data in the grid layout using the DataGrid component

The DataGrid component can be used to display a collection of data in the grid layout along with pagination support.

Let us see how we can use the DataGrid component to display user details in a grid layout using pagination, displaying five users per page:

```
<p:dataGrid var="user" value="#{adminController.users}"
        columns="3" rows="5" paginator="true"
        rowsPerPageTemplate="5,10,15">

   <p:panel header="#{user.firstName} #{user.lastName}"
       style="text-align:center">
     <h:panelGrid columns="1">
       <h:outputText value="#{user.id} : #{user.emailId}" />
     </h:panelGrid>
   </p:panel>
</p:dataGrid>
```

The preceding code displays DataGrid as shown in the following screenshot:

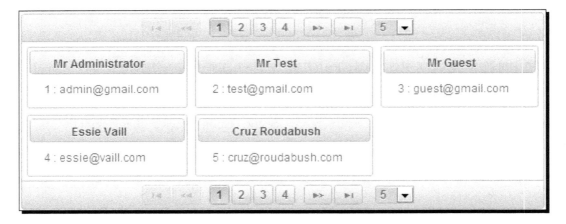

As we have specified `columns="3"` and `rows="5"`, DataGrid displayed five items arranged in three columns resulting in two rows. Here, `rows` represent the number of items to be displayed per page, not the actual number of rows in DataGrid.

Exporting data into PDF/XLS/XML/CSV formats using the DataExporter component

The **DataExporter** component provides the ability to export the DataTable data into various formats such as Excel, PDF, CSV, and XML. DataExporter provides options for:

◆ Exporting entire DataTable rows

◆ Exporting only current page rows

◆ Exporting only selected rows

◆ Excluding particular columns

◆ Customizing exporting data using pre- and post-processors

To export data into PDF and Excel formats, we need `itext.jar` and `apache-poi.jar` respectively to be added to the classpath:

```
<dependency>
  <groupId>org.apache.poi</groupId>
  <artifactId>poi</artifactId>
  <version>3.7</version>
</dependency>
<dependency>
  <groupId>com.lowagie</groupId>    <artifactId>itext</artifactId>
  <version>2.1.7</version>
</dependency>
```

The basic usage of DataExporter is as follows:

```
<p:dataTable id="usersTbl" var="user" value="#{adminController.
users}">
  //columns
</p:dataTable>
<p:commandButton value="Export to Excel" ajax="false">
  <p:dataExporter type="xls" target="usersTbl" fileName="users"/>
</p:commandButton>
```

The DataExporter component provides the following attributes to customize its behavior:

◆ `type`: This specifies the export type. Valid values are `xls`, `pdf`, `csv`, and `xml`.

◆ `target`: This is the ID of the DataTable whose data we want to export.

◆ `fileName`: This is the filename of the generated export file, defaults to the DataTable ID.

◆ `encoding`: This specifies the character encoding to use. The default is `UTF-8`.

- ◆ pageOnly: When set, it exports only the current page instead of the whole dataset. The default value is `false`.

- ◆ selectionOnly: When enabled, only the selection would be exported. The default value is `false`.

- ◆ preProcessor: This specifies the preprocessor method expression for the exported document.

- ◆ postProcessor: This specifies the postprocessor method expression for the exported document.

Time for action – using DataExporter to export data into XLS and PDF formats

Let us see how we can use various features of DataExporter, such as exporting a whole dataset, exporting the only current page, and excluding some columns:

1. Create a DataTable and a DataExporter component to export all the data, only page data, and register pre- and post-processors for XLS and PDF exporters:

```
<p:dataTable id="usersTbl" var="user" value="#{adminController.
users}" rowKey="#{user.id}"  paginator="true" rows="10">

  <p:column headerText="Id">
    <f:facet name="header">
      <h:outputText value="Id" />
    </f:facet>
    <h:outputText value="#{user.id}" />
  </p:column>

  <p:column>
    <f:facet name="header">
      <h:outputText value="Email" />
    </f:facet>
    <h:outputText value="#{user.emailId}" />
  </p:column>

  <p:column exportable="false">
    <f:facet name="header">
      <h:outputText value="Disabled" />
    </f:facet>
    <h:outputText value="#{user.disabled}" />
  </p:column>

</p:dataTable>

<h:panelGrid columns="2">
  <p:panel header="Export All Data">
```

```
      <h:commandLink>
        <p:graphicImage value="/resources/images/excel.png"/>
        <p:dataExporter type="xls" target="usersTbl"
fileName="users" postProcessor="#{adminController.postProcessXLS}"
/>
      </h:commandLink>
      <h:commandLink>
        <p:graphicImage value="/resources/images/pdf.png"/>
        <p:dataExporter type="pdf" target="usersTbl"
fileName="users" preProcessor="#{adminController.preProcessPDF}"/>
      </h:commandLink>
      <h:commandLink>
        <p:graphicImage value="/resources/images/csv.png"/>
        <p:dataExporter type="csv" target="usersTbl"
fileName="users" />
      </h:commandLink>
      <h:commandLink>
        <p:graphicImage value="/resources/images/xml.png"/>
        <p:dataExporter type="xml" target="usersTbl"
fileName="users"/>
      </h:commandLink>
    </p:panel>

    <p:panel header="Export Page Data">
      <h:commandLink>
        <p:graphicImage value="/resources/images/excel.png"/>
        <p:dataExporter type="xls" target="usersTbl"
fileName="users" pageOnly="true" />
      </h:commandLink>
      <h:commandLink>
        <p:graphicImage value="/resources/images/pdf.png"/>
        <p:dataExporter type="pdf" target="usersTbl"
fileName="users" pageOnly="true"/>
      </h:commandLink>
      <h:commandLink>
        <p:graphicImage value="/resources/images/csv.png"/>
        <p:dataExporter type="csv" target="usersTbl"
fileName="users" pageOnly="true"/>
      </h:commandLink>
      <h:commandLink>
        <p:graphicImage value="/resources/images/xml.png"/>
        <p:dataExporter type="xml" target="usersTbl"
fileName="users" pageOnly="true"/>
      </h:commandLink>
    </p:panel>

</h:panelGrid>
```

2. Implement pre- and post-processor methods using the following code:

```
public void postProcessXLS(Object document)
{
  HSSFWorkbook wb = (HSSFWorkbook) document;
  HSSFSheet sheet = wb.getSheetAt(0);
  HSSFRow header = sheet.getRow(0);
  //perform operations on sheet/header etc
}

public void preProcessPDF(Object document) throws IOException,
BadElementException, DocumentException
{
  Document pdf = (Document) document;
  pdf.open();
  pdf.setPageSize(PageSize.A4);
  //other operations on PDF
}
```

What just happened?

We have created a DataTable component with the `paginator` support to display 10 rows per page. We have created two sets of DataExporter components, one to export whole data and another to export only the current page data, into XLS, PDF, CSV, and XML formats. Note that we have used the `exportable="false"` attribute on the disabled `<p:column>` element and hence the disabled column data won't be exported. Also, we have registered `preProcessor` for PDF exporter and `postProcessor` for XLS exporter to manipulate the data before/after the exporting process.

A couple of important tips

- To be able to export the column name headings, you should use the `<f:facet name="header">` facets instead of `<p:column headerText="...">`.
- As of PrimeFaces Version 4.0, pre- and post-processor support is available only for XLS and PDF exporters, but not for CSV or XML.

Summary

In this chapter, we have learned about data components, such as DataList and DataTable, along with various features, such as pagination, sorting, filtering, lazy loading, and so on. Also, we have seen how to use DataExporter for exporting data into PDF, Excel, CSV, and XML formats. In the next chapter, we will look into advanced data visualization components such as Carousel, Tree, TagCloud, and so on.

9
Introducing Advanced Data Visualization Components

PrimeFaces provides various Data Visualization Components, such as Carousel, TagCloud, Tree, TreeTable, and Schedule, which can be used to display data in different formats.

In this chapter, we will cover:

- Displaying data with sliding effects using the **Carousel** component
- Introducing the **TagCloud** component
- Displaying hierarchical data in **Tree** and **TreeTable** formats
- Managing events using the **Schedule** component

Displaying data with sliding effects using the Carousel component

Carousel is a multipurpose component to display a set of data or general content with slide effects.

On many websites, a Company's information such as what they do, about their products and other types of services they provide, will be displayed in a slideshow style. We can use the Carousel component to implement this kind of feature.

Suppose we are building an e-commerce bookstore application and want to display all the latest books on the home page in a slideshow style. Let us see how we can use a `<p:carousel>` component to implement this.

```
<p:carousel value="#{carouselController.books}" var="book"
   headerText="Latest Books">
  <h:panelGrid columns="1" style="width:100%" cellpadding="5">
    <p:graphicImage value="/resources/images/books/#{book}"
width="180px" height="220px;"/>
  </h:panelGrid>
</p:carousel>
```

Here `CarouselController.books` is a `List<String>` containing the image names. The `<p:carousel>` component iterates through `List<String>` and displays each image. By default `<p:carousel>` displays three items and provides navigation icons to show other items. The following screenshot shows the same:

The Carousel component provides the following attributes to customize its behavior:

- ◆ **numVisible**: This is the number of visible items per page. The default value for it is 3.
- ◆ **firstVisible**: This is the index of the first element that is to be displayed. The default value for it is 0.
- ◆ **circular**: This enables the continuous scrolling. The default value for it is FALSE.
- ◆ **vertical**: This enables the vertical scrolling. The default value for it is FALSE.
- ◆ **autoPlayInterval**: This sets the time in milliseconds to have the Carousel component start scrolling automatically after being initialized. The default value for it is 0.

- ◆ **pageLinks**: This defines the number of page links of the paginator. The default value for it is 3.

- ◆ **effect**: This is the name of the animation, it could be `fade` or `slide`. The default value for it is `slide`.

- ◆ **easing**: This is the name of the easing animation. The default value for it is `easeInOutCirc`.

- ◆ **effectDuration:** This is the duration of the animation in milliseconds. The default value for it is 500.

- ◆ **dropdownTemplate:** This is the template string for the drop-down paginator. The default value for this is {page}.

- ◆ **itemStyle:** This is the inline style of each item.

- ◆ **itemStyleClass:** This is the style class of each item.

- ◆ **headerText:** This is the label for the header.

- ◆ **footerText:** This is the label for the footer.

Sometimes we might want to display the Carousel component with items containing static data only. For example, we might want to display a Carousel component in the header section of a company's website displaying About Us, Services, Products, and Contact Us slides. The information on these slides might be static and need not be fetched from the server. In these kinds of scenarios, we can use the Carousel component with nested `<p:tab>` components to display a specific number of items. The `<p:tab>` is a Layout component which we will discuss in *Chapter 10, Working with Layout Components*.

Time for action – creating Carousel using tabs

Let us see how we can create a Carousel component with the nested `<p:tab>` components, with each `<p:tab>` displaying one book's details.

Create a `<p:carousel>` component with nested `<p:tab>` components:

```
<p:carousel id="tabsCarousel" numVisible="1" itemStyle="height:220px;w
idth:600px;" effect="easeInStrong"
  headerText="Latest Books">

  <p:tab title="PrimeFaces Beginners Guide">
     <h:panelGrid columns="2" cellpadding="10">
       <p:graphicImage value="/resources/images/books/PFBG_Raw.jpg"
width="150px" height="200px;"/>
       <h:outputText
         value="Description about PrimeFaces Beginners Guide." />
```

```
        </h:panelGrid>
    </p:tab>

    <p:tab title="PrimeFaces Cookbook">
      <h:panelGrid columns="2" cellpadding="10">
        <p:graphicImage value="/resources/images/books/PF_Cookbook.jpg"
width="150px" height="200px;"/>
        <h:outputText
          value=" Description about PrimeFaces Cookbook." />
      </h:panelGrid>
    </p:tab>

    <p:tab title="JSF 2.0 Cookbook">
      <h:panelGrid columns="2" cellpadding="10">
        <p:graphicImage value="/resources/images/books/JSF2_Cookbook.
jpg" width="150px" height="200px;"/>
        <h:outputText
          value=" Description about JSF2 Cookbook." />
      </h:panelGrid>
    </p:tab>

    <p:tab title="Instant PrimeFaces Starter">
      <h:panelGrid columns="2" cellpadding="10">
        <p:graphicImage value="/resources/images/books/PF_Starter.jpg"
width="150px" height="200px;"/>
        <h:outputText
          value=" Description about Instant PrimeFaces Starter." />
      </h:panelGrid>
    </p:tab>

</p:carousel>
```

What just happened?

We have created a Carousel component with nested `<p:tab>` components instead of iterating through a collection of items. We have set `numVisible="1"` so that one tab will be visible at a time. As the default value for `pageLinks` is 3 and we have four tabs to display in Carousel, a dropdown will be displayed with the page numbers. The following screenshot shows the same:

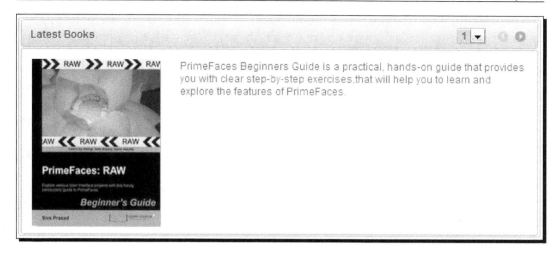

The Carousel component also provides an automatic slideshow feature using the `autoPlayInterval` attribute, which takes time in milliseconds to start scrolling automatically. Also we can set the `circular` attribute to `true` so that the items will be scrolled in a circular fashion. By default, Carousel scrolls horizontally, we can set `vertical="true"` to scroll vertically. The following code and screenshot will explain how it's done:

```
<p:carousel id="tabsCarouselSlideshow" numVisible="1"
  itemStyle="height:220px;width:600px;"
  effect="easeInStrong" pageLinks="4" vertical="true"
autoPlayInterval="4000" circular="true" headerText="Latest Books">

  ...
</p:carousel>
```

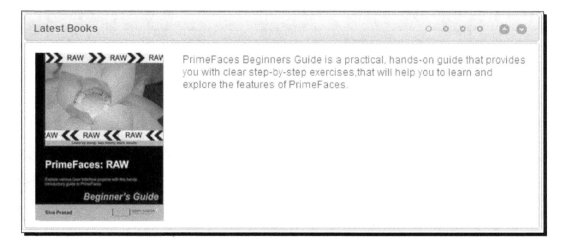

The preceding Carousel component slides the items vertically every four seconds, and after the fourth item, it will again start displaying the first item circularly. Also note that the Up and Down icons are displayed instead of the Previous and Next icons because it is vertically scrolling Carousel.

The JSF components which implement the interface `javax. faces.component.NamingContainer` are called the NamingContainer components. Many of the PrimeFaces components, such as AccordianPanel, Carousel, DataGrid, DataList, DataTable, TabView, Tree, TreeTable, and so on are NamingContainer components. While referencing components in other NamingContainer components, we should give the absolute componentId path something such as `:formId:compId:elementId`.

Introducing the TagCloud component

TagCloud displays a collection of Tags with different zoom levels using strengths associated with each Tag.

To use the TagCloud component we need to create an object of type `org.primefaces. model.tagcloud.TagCloudModel`. Each Tag will be represented by an instance of `org.primefaces.model.tagcloud.TagCloudItem` interface. PrimeFaces provides default implementations of `DefaultTagCloudModel`, `DefaultTagCloudItem` for `TagCloudModel`, and `TagCloudItem` respectively. Each `TagCloudItem` contains `label`, `url`, and `strength` properties. The tag `strength` can be between one and five.

Time for action – displaying tags as TagCloud

Let us see how we can create a TagCloud component and initialize it with some sample Tag data.

1. Create the `TagCloud` component using `<p:tagCloud>`:

```
<p:tagCloud model="#{tagController.model}"/>
```

2. Create the `TagCloudModel` object and populate `TagCloudItem`:

```
public class TagController
{
    private TagCloudModel model;
    public TagController()
    {
        model = new DefaultTagCloudModel();
```

```
model.addTag(new DefaultTagCloudItem("PrimeFaces",
    "/posts.jsf?tag=primefaces",5);
model.addTag(new DefaultTagCloudItem("JSF", "#",3);
model.addTag(new DefaultTagCloudItem("jQuery",2);
    }
}
```

What just happened?

We have created a `TagCloudModel` object using `DefaultTagCloudModel` and populated `TagCloudItem` with various `labels`, `urls`, and `strengths`. For the `"PrimeFaces"` tag we provided the URL relative to our application path `"/posts.jsf?tag=primefaces"`. The URL is optional; its default value is `"#"`.

TagCloud supports the `select` AJAX event. Only tags where URL equals `"#"` can trigger the `select` event. In the preceding code, we haven't specified any URL for the jQuery tag and hence the default value # will be used. So when you click on the jQuery tag, the `select` event will be fired.

In our TechBuzz application, we will display the available tags as TagCloud and users can click on any tag to display posts associated with that tag.

Time for action – choosing a tag in TagCloud with the select Event

In this section we will create a TagCloud component and display posts based on the selected tag.

1. Create a `TagCloud` component to display tags and a `DataList` component to display posts associated with that selected tag:

```
<p:tagCloud model="#{tagController.model}">
  <p:ajax event="select" update="posts"
    listener="#{tagController.onSelect}" />
</p:tagCloud>
<p:panel header="Posts by Tag">
  <p:dataList value="#{tagController.posts}" var="post" id="posts"
    type="none">
    <h:outputText value="#{post.title}"/><br/>
    <h:outputText value="#{post.description}"/><br/>
    <p:separator/>
  </p:dataList>
</p:panel>
```

2. Implement methods to get tags and posts by a selected tag.

```
public class TagController
{
  private BuzzService buzzService;
  private static Random random = new Random();
  private TagCloudModel model;
  private List<Post> posts;

  public TagController()
  {
      model = new DefaultTagCloudModel();
      posts = buzzService.findAllPosts();
      List<Tag> tags = buzzService.findAllTags();
      for (Tag tag : tags)
    {
      model.addTag(new DefaultTagCloudItem(tag.getLabel(),
        getStrength(1, 5)));
    }
  }
  public void onSelect(SelectEvent event)
  {
    TagCloudItem item = (TagCloudItem) event.getObject();
    String label = item.getLabel();
    FacesMessage msg = new FacesMessage("Selected Tag: "+
      item.getLabel());
    FacesContext.getCurrentInstance().addMessage(null, msg);
    posts = buzzService.findPostsByTag(label);
  }
  private int getStrength(int low, int high)
  {
    return random.nextInt(high-low) + low;
  }
//setters & getters for model, posts
}
```

What just happened?

We have created a `TagCloud` and registered the `select` event listener to invoke the `TagController.onSelect(SelectEvent)` method. We have obtained the selected tag label and fetched posts associated with that Tag, and updated the posts `DataList` component.

JavaSE JavaEE Spring
SpringMVC Hibernate Struts
JSF PrimeFaces jQuery Perl
Python

Displaying hierarchical data using the Tree component

The Tree component can be used to represent hierarchical data in a tree structure.

A Tree component can be created using the `org.primefaces.model.TreeNode` instance as the root of the tree. PrimeFaces provides a default implementation of the `TreeNode` interface `org.primefaces.model.DefaultTreeNode.DefaultTreeNode`.

In our TechBuzz application, we would like to display PostTitle in the tree structure using the Year/Month/PostTitle hierarchy.

Time for action – creating a Tree component

Let us see how we can use a Tree component to display PostTitle in a tree structure.

1. Initialize the root `TreeNode` component and add child nodes.

```
public class TreeController
{
  private TreeNode root;

  public TreeController()
  {
    root = new DefaultTreeNode("Root", null);

    TreeNode node2013 = new DefaultTreeNode("2013", root);
    TreeNode node2012 = new DefaultTreeNode("2012", root);
    TreeNode node2011 = new DefaultTreeNode("2011", root);

    TreeNode jan2013 = new DefaultTreeNode("Jan", node2013);
    TreeNode feb2013 = new DefaultTreeNode("Feb", node2013);

    TreeNode aug2012 = new DefaultTreeNode("Aug", node2012);
    TreeNode sep2012 = new DefaultTreeNode("Sep", node2012);

    TreeNode nov2011 = new DefaultTreeNode("Nov", node2011);


    TreeNode jan2013Post1 = new DefaultTreeNode("PrimeFaces Elite
      3.5.5 Released", jan2013);
    TreeNode jan2013Post2 = new DefaultTreeNode("PrimeFaces
      Extensions 0.7 Released", jan2013);
    TreeNode feb2013Post1 = new DefaultTreeNode("Spring Framework
4.0
      M1: WebSocket Support", feb2013);
```

```
TreeNode aug2012Post1 = new DefaultTreeNode("EclipseLink 2.5
   Release Available for Download", aug2012);
TreeNode sep2012Post1 = new DefaultTreeNode("Building REST-ful
   services with Spring", sep2012);

TreeNode nov2011Post1 = new DefaultTreeNode("PrimeUI 0.9
   Released", nov2011);
   }
}
```

2. Create the Tree component using the `<p:tree>` component.

```
<p:tree value="#{treeController.root}" var="node">
  <p:treeNode>
    <h:outputText value="#{node}"/>
  </p:treeNode>
</p:tree>
```

What just happened?

We have created a `TreeNode` instance as the root of the tree and added 2011, 2012, and 2013 year child nodes. For each year we have added Month child nodes and added PostTitle child nodes to the Month nodes. The following figure shows the same:

The `TreeNode` interface provides the following methods to obtain its data, type, parent node, child nodes, and also selecting or expanding nodes programmatically, and so on.

```
public interface TreeNode
{
  public String getType();
  public Object getData();
  public List<TreeNode> getChildren();
```

```
    public TreeNode getParent();
    public void setParent(TreeNode treeNode);
    public boolean isExpanded();
    public void setExpanded(boolean expanded);
    public int getChildCount();
    public boolean isLeaf();
    public boolean isSelected();
    public void setSelected(boolean value);
    public boolean isSelectable();
    public void setSelectable(boolean selectable);
    public boolean isPartialSelected();
    public void setPartialSelected(boolean value);
    public void setRowKey(String rowKey);
    public String getRowKey();
}
```

These methods come in very handy when manipulating the Tree component from the server-side code.

Loading tree nodes dynamically using AJAX

By default, the Tree nodes get loaded eagerly and toggling happens on the client side. We can load nodes dynamically by setting the `dynamic` attribute to `true`. In dynamic mode, when a node is expanded, child nodes will be loaded dynamically using AJAX. We can also set the `cache` attribute to `true` to cache the loaded nodes instead of fetching every time from the server.

```
<p:tree value="#{treeController.root}" var="node" dynamic="true"
cache="true">
  <p:treeNode>
    <h:outputText value="#{node}"/>
  </p:treeNode>
</p:tree>
```

Selecting tree nodes

The Tree component also supports selecting a single node or multiple nodes using the selection modes `single`, `multiple`, and `checkbox`. By using `selectionMode=multiple`, we can select multiple nodes by holding down the *Ctrl* or *Command* key and clicking on **nodes**. When `selectionMode` is set to `checkbox`, a checkbox is displayed for each node and we can select multiple nodes by selecting checkboxes.

```
<p:tree value="#{treeController.root}" var="node"
selectionMode="single"  selection="#{treeController.selectedNode}">
  <p:treeNode>
    <h:outputText value="#{node}" />
  </p:treeNode>
</p:tree>
```

```
<p:tree value="#{treeController.root}" var="node"
selectionMode="multiple"  selection="#{treeController.selectedNodes}">
  <p:treeNode>
    <h:outputText value="#{node}" />
  </p:treeNode>
</p:tree>


<p:tree value="#{treeController.root}" var="node"
selectionMode="checkbox"  selection="#{treeController.selectedNodes}">
  <p:treeNode>
    <h:outputText value="#{node}" />
  </p:treeNode>
</p:tree>
```

Handling node expand, collapse, select and unselect events

The Tree component provides AJAX events for `select`, `unselect`, `expand`, and `collapse` events.

```
<p:growl id="messages" escape="false"/>
<p:tree value="#{treeController.root}" var="node"
selectionMode="checkbox"  selection="#{treeController.selectedNodes}">
  <p:ajax event="expand" update="messages" listener="#{treeController.
onNodeExpand}" />
  <p:ajax event="collapse" update="messages"
listener="#{treeController.onNodeCollapse}" />
  <p:ajax event="select" update="messages" listener="#{treeController.
onNodeSelect}" />
  <p:ajax event="unselect" update="messages"
listener="#{treeController.onNodeUnselect}" />

  <p:treeNode>
    <h:outputText value="#{node}" />
  </p:treeNode>
</p:tree>
```

Implement event listener methods.

```
public void onNodeExpand(NodeExpandEvent event) {
  FacesContext.getCurrentInstance().addMessage(null, new
    FacesMessage("Expanded : "+ event.getTreeNode()));
}


public void onNodeCollapse(NodeCollapseEvent event) {
  FacesContext.getCurrentInstance().addMessage(null, new
    FacesMessage("Collapsed : "+ event.getTreeNode()));
}
```

```java
public void onNodeSelect(NodeSelectEvent event) {
  FacesContext.getCurrentInstance().addMessage(null, new
    FacesMessage("Selected : "+ event.getTreeNode()));
}

public void onNodeUnselect(NodeUnselectEvent event) {
  FacesContext.getCurrentInstance().addMessage(null, new
    FacesMessage("Unselected : "+ event.getTreeNode()));
}
```

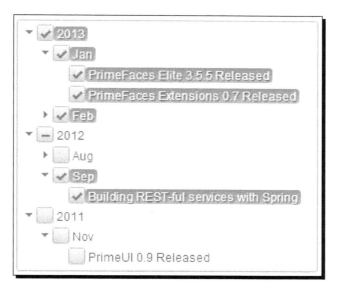

Rendering the tree horizontally

By default, the Tree component is displayed as a Vertical tree (orientation is vertical). We can display the Tree horizontally by setting the orientation attribute to horizontal, as shown in the following screenshot:

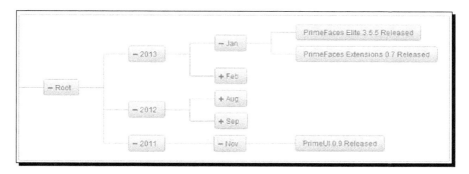

Displaying nodes with icons

The Tree component also supports displaying a specific icon for a specific type of node. For example, TechBuzz posts could be a text document, a picture or a video type post.

We can display a different icon based on the type of node using the nested `<p:treeNode>` element for each type.

We need to specify the type of the node as the first argument to the `DefaultTreeNode` objects.

```
TreeNode jan2013Post1 = new DefaultTreeNode("pic","PrimeFaces Elite
    3.5.5 Released", jan2013);
TreeNode jan2013Post2 = new DefaultTreeNode("pic","PrimeFaces
    Extensions 0.7 Released", jan2013);
TreeNode feb2013Post1 = new DefaultTreeNode("video","Spring Framework
    4.0 M1: WebSocket Support", feb2013);

TreeNode aug2012Post1 = new DefaultTreeNode("document","EclipseLink
    2.5 Release Available for Download", aug2012);
TreeNode sep2012Post1 = new DefaultTreeNode("document","Building
    REST-ful services with Spring", sep2012);

TreeNode nov2011Post1 = new DefaultTreeNode("video","PrimeUI 0.9
    Released", nov2011);
```

By using nested `<p:treeNode>` elements, specify the icon to be displayed using the `icon` attribute based on the `type` value. Also we can perform slide effects while expanding and collapsing nodes by setting the `animate` attribute to `true`.

```
<p:tree value="#{treeController.root}" var="node" animate="true">
    <p:treeNode expandedIcon="ui-icon-folder-open"
            collapsedIcon="ui-icon-folder-collapsed">
        <h:outputText value="#{node}"/>
    </p:treeNode>

    <p:treeNode type="document" icon="ui-icon-document">
        <h:outputText value="#{node}" />
    </p:treeNode>

    <p:treeNode type="pic" icon="ui-icon-image">
        <h:outputText value="#{node}" />
    </p:treeNode>

    <p:treeNode type="video" icon="ui-icon-video">
        <h:outputText value="#{node}" />
    </p:treeNode>
</p:tree>
```

We can attach a ContextMenu for the Tree component to provide context-specific actions. We will discuss how to use ContextMenu in detail in *Chapter 11, Introducing Navigation Components*.

Reordering Tree nodes using Drag and Drop

The Tree component supports reordering nodes by dragging-and-dropping them within the same tree and it also can be transferred to another tree component.

To enable the drag-and-drop feature, set draggable="true" and droppable="true" on the <p:tree> component.

```
<p:tree value="#{treeController.root}" var="node" draggable="true"
  droppable="true">
...
</p:tree>
```

The Tree component supports a dragdrop AJAX event that gets triggered when you drag and drop a node:

```
<p:tree id="tree1" value="#{treeController.root}" var="node"
  draggable="true" droppable="true">
  <p:ajax event="dragdrop" listener="#{treeController.handleDragDrop}"
/>
  <p:treeNode>
    <h:outputText value="#{node}" />
  </p:treeNode>
</p:tree>
```

```
public void handleDragDrop(TreeDragDropEvent event)
{
  TreeNode dragNode = event.getDragNode();
  TreeNode dropNode = event.getDropNode();
  int dropIndex = event.getDropIndex();
  String msg = "Dragged " + dragNode.getData()+ " and Dropped on " +
    dropNode.getData() + " at " + dropIndex;
  JSFUtils.addInfoMessage(msg);
}
```

In the preceding Tree component we can reorder nodes within the same tree. But if you want to transfer nodes into another tree, then we need to define the scope using the dragdropScope attribute. You can transfer a node from the source tree to the target tree if the source and target tree have the same dragdropScope.

```
<p:tree id="tree1" value="#{treeController.root}" var="node"
  draggable="true" droppable="false" dragdropScope="treeDnDScope">
  <p:treeNode>
    <h:outputText value="#{node}" />
  </p:treeNode>
</p:tree>

<p:tree id="tree2" value="#{treeController.root2}" var="node"
  draggable="true" droppable="true" dragdropScope="treeDnDScope">
  <p:ajax event="dragdrop"
    listener="#{treeController.handleDragDrop}" />
  <p:treeNode>
    <h:outputText value="#{node}" />
  </p:treeNode>
</p:tree>
```

In the preceding code, we have two Tree components which have the same dragdropScope value "treeDnDScope" so that we can transfer nodes from Tree1 to Tree2. We can also reorder nodes within Tree2 as both draggable and droppable are set to true. But we can't reorder nodes in Tree1 or transfer nodes from Tree2 to Tree1 because dropping is disabled in Tree1 by setting droppable="false".

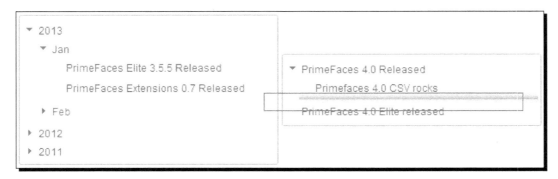

We can further customize the drag-and-drop feature by using the `dragMode` and `dropRestrict` attributes.

- ◆ **dragMode**: Represents the target node that would be dropped. Valid values are `self` (default), `parent` and `ancestor`.

- ◆ **dropRestrict**: By setting to `sibling` we can restrict the drop target to be a parent. Default value is `none`.

```
<p:tree id="tree1" value="#{treeController.root}" var="node"
    draggable="true" droppable="false" dragdropScope="treeDnDScope"
    dragMode="parent">
    . . .
</p:tree>

<p:tree id="tree2" value="#{treeController.root2}" var="node"
    draggable="true" droppable="true" dragdropScope="treeDnDScope"
    dropRestrict="sibling">
    . . .
</p:tree>
```

In the preceding code, we have set `dragMode="parent"` on Tree1. If we drag PrimeFaces Elite 3.5.5 Released node then the target node that would be dropped is Jan. If we have set `dragMode="ancestor"` then it would be 2013.

Also we have specified `dropRestrict="sibling"` on Tree2. With this, we can drag any node from Tree1 and drop it into Tree2 as the child of an existing node but not as a root node. The default value of `dropRestrict` is none which will allow you to drop a node as a root node.

Introducing the TreeTable component

The TreeTable component is used to display hierarchical data in a tabular format. The TreeTable component can be considered as a combo of the **Tree** and **DataTable** features.

Time for action – displaying posts using the TreeTable component

Let us see how we can display posts using the TreeTable component in the Year/Month/Posts hierarchy.

1. Create a root TreeNode and add Year, Month, and Posts child nodes:

```
public class TreeTableController
{
    private TreeNode root;
```

```
public TreeTableController() {

    root = new DefaultTreeNode("Root", null);

    TreeNode node2013 = new DefaultTreeNode(new
PostNode("2013",""),
        root);
    TreeNode node2012 = new DefaultTreeNode(new
PostNode("2012",""),
        root);
    TreeNode node2011 = new DefaultTreeNode(new
PostNode("2011",""),
        root);

    TreeNode jan2013 = new DefaultTreeNode(new PostNode("Jan",""),
        node2013);
    TreeNode feb2013 = new DefaultTreeNode(new PostNode("Feb",""),
        node2013);

    TreeNode aug2012 = new DefaultTreeNode(new PostNode("Aug",""),
        node2012);
    TreeNode sep2012 = new DefaultTreeNode(new PostNode("Sep",""),
        node2012);

    TreeNode nov2011 = new DefaultTreeNode(new PostNode("Nov",""),
        node2011);

    TreeNode jan2013Post1 = new DefaultTreeNode(new
        PostNode("PrimeFaces Elite 3.5.5 Released", "John"),
jan2013);
    TreeNode jan2013Post2 = new DefaultTreeNode(new
        PostNode("PrimeFaces Extensions 0.7 Released", "Mike"),
            jan2013);
    TreeNode feb2013Post1 = new DefaultTreeNode(new
PostNode("Spring
        Framework 4.0 M1: WebSocket Support", "James"), feb2013);

    TreeNode aug2012Post1 = new DefaultTreeNode(new
        PostNode("EclipseLink 2.5 Release Available for Download",
            "Roger"), aug2012);
    TreeNode sep2012Post1 = new DefaultTreeNode(new
        PostNode("Building REST-ful services with Spring", "Jenny"),
            sep2012);
```

```
        TreeNode nov2011Post1 = new DefaultTreeNode(new
    PostNode("PrimeUI
        0.9 Released", "Siva"), nov2011);
    }
    public TreeNode getRoot() {
      return root;
    }
  }
```

2. Create a TreeTable component using `<p:treeTable>` and define the columns to be displayed using nested `<p:column>` elements.

```
<p:treeTable value="#{treeTableController.root}" var="node">
  <p:column headerText="Title">
    <h:outputText value="#{node.title}" />
  </p:column>
  <p:column headerText="Title">
    <h:outputText value="#{node.createdBy}" />
  </p:column>
</p:treeTable>
```

What just happened?

We have created a TreeTable component similar to the Tree component. We have added `PostNode` objects as `TreeNode` data which takes `title` and `createdBy` values. For Year and Month nodes `createdBy` values are blank, and for post titles we have set the `createdBy` values. When the TreeTable component is rendered we can see the Year/Month/Post details in the tree structure as shown in the following screenshot:

Title	Created By
▾ 2013	
▾ Jan	
PrimeFaces Elite 3.5.5 Released	John
PrimeFaces Extensions 0.7 Released	Mike
▸ Feb	
▸ 2012	
▾ 2011	
▾ Nov	
PrimeUI 0.9 Released	Siva

Similar to the Tree component, the TreeTable component also supports node selection using `single`, `multiple`, and `checkbox` selectionModes, supports `select`, `unselect`, `expand`, `collapse` AJAX events and ContextMenu binding. Also similar to the DataTable component, TreeTable supports resizable columns, horizontal/vertical scrolling features, and so on.

Introducing the Schedule component

The Schedule component is an **Outlook/iCal**-like JSF component to manage events. The Schedule component supports Month, Week, and Day-based views, lazy loading of events, i18n support, and AJAX event listeners for the `dateSelect`, `eventSelect`, `eventMove`, and `eventResize` events.

To create the Schedule component we need to create an instance of `org.primefaces.model.ScheduleModel` and add events which are instances of `org.primefaces.model.ScheduleEvent`. The `DefaultScheduleModel` and `DefaultScheduleEvent` are default implementations for `ScheduleModel` and `ScheduleEvent` provided by PrimeFaces.

Time for action – creating the Schedule component

Let us see how to create a Schedule component and initialize some sample events.

1. Create the `ScheduleModel` instance and add the `ScheduleEvent` objects. Also implement the event listener methods for `dateSelect`, `eventSelect`, `eventMove`, and `eventResize` events.

```
@ManagedBean
@ViewScoped
public class ScheduleController implements Serializable
{
  private ScheduleModel eventModel;
  public ScheduleController()
  {
    eventModel = new DefaultScheduleModel();
    eventModel.addEvent(new DefaultScheduleEvent("John BirthDay",
      buildDate(2013,10,15,9,10), buildDate(2013,10,15,9,40)));
    eventModel.addEvent(new DefaultScheduleEvent("Meeting with ABC
      Corp", buildDate(2013,10,15,12,0),buildDa
te(2013,10,15,13,0)));
    eventModel.addEvent(new DefaultScheduleEvent("Product XYZ
Release
      Plan Meeting", buildDate(2013,10,16,8,0),
        buildDate(2013,10,16,9,0)));
  }
```

```
   private Date buildDate(int year, int month, int day, int hour,
int
      minute)
   {
      Calendar t = Calendar.getInstance();
      t.set(year, month, day);
      t.set(Calendar.HOUR, hour);
      t.set(Calendar.MINUTE, minute);
      t.set(Calendar.SECOND, 0);
      return t.getTime();
   }

   public void onEventSelect(SelectEvent selectEvent) {
      ScheduleEvent event = (ScheduleEvent) selectEvent.getObject();
      FacesContext.getCurrentInstance().addMessage(null, new
         FacesMessage("Selected Event :"+event.getTitle()));
   }

   public void onDateSelect(SelectEvent selectEvent) {
      Date date = (Date) selectEvent.getObject();
      FacesContext.getCurrentInstance().addMessage(null, new
         FacesMessage("Schedule Event at:"+date));
   }

   public void onEventMove(ScheduleEntryMoveEvent event) {
      String msg = "Event moved. Day delta:" + event.getDayDelta() +
",
      Minute delta:" + event.getMinuteDelta();
      FacesContext.getCurrentInstance().addMessage(null, new
         FacesMessage(msg));
   }

   public void onEventResize(ScheduleEntryResizeEvent event) {
      String msg = "Event resized. Day delta:" + event.getDayDelta()
+
      ", Minute delta:" + event.getMinuteDelta();
      FacesContext.getCurrentInstance().addMessage(null, new
         FacesMessage(msg));
   }
}
```

2. Create a Schedule component using `<p:schedule>` and register event listeners using nested `<p:ajax>` elements.

```
<p:growl id="messages" autoUpdate="true" />

<p:schedule value="#{scheduleController.eventModel}"
widgetVar="myschedule">
```

```
    <p:ajax event="dateSelect"
      listener="#{scheduleController.onDateSelect}" />
    <p:ajax event="eventSelect"
      listener="#{scheduleController.onEventSelect}"/>
    <p:ajax event="eventMove"
      listener="#{scheduleController.onEventMove}"/>
    <p:ajax event="eventResize"
      listener="#{scheduleController.onEventResize}"/>
  </p:schedule>
```

What just happened?

We have created a Schedule component with backing the `DefaultScheduleModel` instance. We have added a few `DefaultScheduleEvent` instances that represent events. Also we have registered event listeners for `dateSelect`, `eventSelect`, `eventMove`, and `eventResize` events.

To add a new event, we can use the `dateSelect` event listener to display a form to take event details, and on submit we can save the new event details in the database and add to `DefaultScheduleModel`.

When using the Schedule component backed by `DefaultScheduleModel` we need to load all the events eagerly. Instead we can use `org.primefaces.model.LazyScheduleModel` to load only the events that belong to the displayed timeframe lazily.

The `LazyScheduleModel` interface has a `loadEvents(Date start, Date end)` method to load events which will be called with new boundaries every time the displayed timeframe is changed.

```
class MyLazyScheduleModel extends LazyScheduleModel
{
  @Override
  public void loadEvents(Date start, Date end)
  {
    clear();
    //fetch events between start and end times
    addEvent(new DefaultScheduleEvent(event1Title, event1StartTime,
      event1EndTime));
    addEvent(new DefaultScheduleEvent(event2Title, event2StartTime,
      event2EndTime);
  }
}
```

Summary

In this chapter, we have learned about Data Visualization components, such as Carousel, TagCloud, Tree, TreeTable, and Schedule. In the next chapter, we will look into Layout components such as Panel, PanelGrid, ScrollPanel, Accordion, TabView, Wizard, and so on.

10
Working with Layout Components

One of the key aspects of developing web applications with rich user interfaces is creating content holder components with rich look and feel. But creating complex content holder components using plain HTML is tedious process and Java developers may not be good enough at web designing to create fancy user interfaces.

We may want to show data in tabbed panels or in accordion style. Similarly we might want to create Panels with various customizations such as minimizable, closable and with support for toolbar options.

Many of the web applications follow Border Layout style templates with a standard header on top, a navigation bar on left side and copyright information at the bottom.

Also, in many of the web applications, we may need to implement workflow kind of processes with a series of forms (also called Wizards) for collecting data step by step and complete the process once all the necessary information is provided.

To support these types of common needs, PrimeFaces provides various Layout Components such as Panel, PanelGrid, ScrollPanel, AccordionPanel, TabView, Wizard and various Layout styles.

In this chapter we will cover the following topics:

- Using Panel, PanelGrid, and ScrollPanel
- Creating stacked panels using AccordionPanel
- Creating tabbed panels using TabView
- Creating workflow style forms using Wizard
- Creating complex layouts using the Layout component
- Creating Portal like Layouts using Dashboard

Introducing the Panel component

Panel is a generic component that can be used to hold other JSF components. Panel component supports features such as, header, footer, toggling, closing, custom actions, and pop-up menus. Also, Panel component provides support for AJAX event listeners for toggle and close events.

Let us see how to create a basic panel component:

```
<p:panel header="About PrimeFaces" footer="PrimeFaces Rocks!!!">
  <p:outputLabel value="PrimeFaces is an open source JSF component
suite with 100+ Components."/>
</p:panel>
```

The preceding Panel component will be rendered as follows:

Panel component provides the following attributes to customize its appearance and behavior:

- `header`: Header text.
- `footer`: Footer text.
- `toggleable`: Makes panel toggleable. Default is false.
- `toggleSpeed`: Speed of toggling in milliseconds. Default is 1000.
- `collapsed`: Renders a toggleable panel as collapsed. Default is false.

- ◆ `closable`: Make panel closable. Default is false.
- ◆ `closeSpeed`: Speed of closing effect in milliseconds. Default is 1000.
- ◆ `visible`: Renders panel as visible. Default is true.
- ◆ `closeTitle`: Tooltip for the close button.
- ◆ `toggleTitle`: Tooltip for the toggle button.
- ◆ `menuTitle`: Tooltip for the menu button.
- ◆ `toggleOrientation`: Defines the orientation of the toggling, valid values are vertical and horizontal. Default is vertical.

We can enable toggling and closing of the panel by setting `toggleable` and `closable` attributes to `true`.

Time for action – using Panel with event listeners

Let us see how we can create a panel with close and toggle options and register AJAX event listeners for close and toggle events.

1. Create a Panel component and register event listeners for `close` and `toggle` events:

```
<p:panel id="AboutPrimeFacesPanel" closable="true"
toggleable="true">
  <p:ajax event="close" listener="#{sampleController.handleClose}"
/>
  <p:ajax event="toggle" listener="#{sampleController.
handleToggle}"/>
  <f:facet name="header">
    About PrimeFaces
  </f:facet>
  <f:facet name="footer">
    PrimeFaces Rocks!!!
  </f:facet>
  <p:outputLabel value="PrimeFaces is an open source JSF component
suite with 100+ Components."/>
</p:panel>
```

2. Implement event listener methods:

```
public class SampleController
{
  public void handleClose(CloseEvent event)
  {
      FacesMessage message = new FacesMessage("Closed Panel Id:"
+ event.getComponent().getId());
    FacesContext.getCurrentInstance().addMessage(null, message);
```

```
      }

      public void handleToggle(ToggleEvent event)
   {
         FacesMessage message = new FacesMessage("Toggled Panel
Id: "+ event.getComponent().getId() + " ,Status:" + event.
getVisibility().name());
         FacesContext.getCurrentInstance().addMessage(null,
message);
      }
   }
```

What just happened?

We have created a panel component and enabled close and toggle features by setting `toggleable` and `closable` attributes to `true`. We have used `header` and `footer` facets instead of attributes to specify header and footer values so that we can easily customize the header and footer text. We have registered AJAX event listeners for `close` and `toggle` events to invoke `handleClose(CloseEvent)` and `handleToggle(ToggleEvent)` methods respectively. We have obtained the panel ID from event object as `event.getComponent().getId()`. Also we can get the status of visibility from `ToggleEvent` using `event.getVisibility()` as `HIDDEN` or `VISIBLE`:

Using Panel with pop-up menu

A Panel component has built-in support for displaying a pop-up menu in the top-right corner using `options` facet as follows:

```
<p:panel widgetVar="panel" header="About PrimeFaces" closable="true"
toggleable="true">
  <f:facet name="options">
    <p:menu>
      <p:submenu label="Settings">
        <p:menuitem value="Toggle" url="#" icon="ui-icon-newwin"
          onclick="panel.toggle()"/>
        <p:menuitem value="Remove" url="#" icon="ui-icon-close"
          onclick="panel.close()"/>
      </p:submenu>
```

```
    </p:menu>
  </f:facet>
  <p:outputLabel value="PrimeFaces is an open source JSF component
suite with 100+ Components."/>
</p:panel>
```

Using Panel with custom actions

We can add custom actions to a panel title bar using the `actions` facet. Let us see how to add two custom actions to the title bar, one to display a Help dialog component and another to go to home page.

Time for action – creating Panel with custom actions

In this section we will look at creating a panel with two custom actions.

1. Create a panel component and add custom actions using the `actions` facet:

    ```
    <p:dialog widgetVar="helpWidget" header="PrimeFaces Help">
      <p>Forum: http://forum.primefaces.org/ </p>
    </p:dialog>

    <p:panel header="About PrimeFaces" footer="PrimeFaces Rocks!!!">

      <f:facet name="actions">
        <h:outputLink styleClass="ui-panel-titlebar-icon ui-corner-all
          ui-state-default"  value="javascript:void(0)"
          onclick="helpWidget.show()">
          <h:outputText styleClass="ui-icon ui-icon-help" />
        </h:outputLink>

        <h:outputLink styleClass="ui-panel-titlebar-icon ui-corner-all
          ui-state-default"  value="welcome.jsf?faces-redirect=true">
          <h:outputText styleClass="ui-icon ui-icon-home" />
        </h:outputLink>

      </f:facet>
      <p:outputLabel value="PrimeFaces is an open source JSF component
        suite with 100+ Components."/>
    </p:panel>
    ```

What just happened?

We have added two custom actions to panel title bar using `actions` facet. When you click on the **Help** icon we are showing the **Help** dialog component, and when you click on the **Home** icon we are navigating to welcome page.

In many scenarios we might want to have help icon to show some information about panel content. In these cases custom actions facet is very helpful.

◆ When panel is toggled only panel body will be toggled, but not footer

◆ In order to close or toggle a panel using client-side JavaScript functions `panel.close()` or `panel.toggle()`, the `closable` or `toggleable` features should be enabled respectively

◆ In legacy browsers like IE7/8 try to use `toggleSpeed="0"` and `closeSpeed="0"` to avoid style related issues

Introducing the PanelGrid component

The `panelGrid` component is an extension to a standard JSF `<h:panelGrid>` component supporting `rowspan` and `colspan` features along with theming support.

Let us see how to create a `PanelGrid` along with header and footer:

```
<p:panelGrid columns="2">
  <f:facet name="header">
    <h:outputLabel value="User Login Form" />
  </f:facet>
  <h:outputLabel value="UserName:" />
  <p:inputText value="#{userController.userName}"/>

  <h:outputLabel value="Password:" />
  <p:password value="#{userController.password}"/>

  <f:facet name="footer">
    <p:commandButton value="Login"/>
    <p:commandButton type="reset" value="Rest"/>
  </f:facet>
</p:panelGrid>
```

The preceding code renders a `panelGrid` component as follows:

By default PrimeFaces panelGrid generates an HTML table with borders. If you want to remove borders you can apply a custom style to remove borders as follows:

```
<p:panelGrid columns="2" styleClass="loginPanelGrid">
   ...
</p:panelGrid>

<style type="text/css">
  .loginPanelGrid tr, .loginPanelGrid td {
    border: none;
  }
</style>
```

Sometimes we need to display data that span across multiple columns and rows. The `panelGrid` component provides support for `rowspan` and `colspan` to hold data that span across rows and columns.

Time for action – using PanelGrid with rowspan and colspan features

Let us see how to use a `panelGrid` component's `rowspan` and `colspan` features.

1. Create a `panelGrid` component and use `rowspan` and `colspan` attributes of `<p:column>` to specify number of rows or columns to span across:

```
<p:panelGrid>
  <f:facet name="header">
    <p:row>
      <p:column colspan="5">
        Posts Statistics By Tag
      </p:column>
    </p:row>
    <p:row>
```

```
            <p:column >Tag</p:column>
            <p:column>Month</p:column>
            <p:column>Posts</p:column>
            <p:column>Total</p:column>
        </p:row>
    </f:facet>
    <p:row>
        <p:column rowspan="2">JSF</p:column>
        <p:column>JAN</p:column>
        <p:column>120</p:column>
        <p:column rowspan="2">270</p:column>
    </p:row>
    <p:row>
        <p:column>FEB</p:column>
        <p:column>150</p:column>
    </p:row>

    <p:row>
        <p:column rowspan="2">PrimeFaces</p:column>
        <p:column>JAN</p:column>
        <p:column>220</p:column>
        <p:column rowspan="2">570</p:column>
    </p:row>
    <p:row>
        <p:column>FEB</p:column>
        <p:column>350</p:column>
    </p:row>
    <f:facet name="footer">
        <p:row>
            <p:column colspan="3" style="text-align: right;">Grand
Total</p:column>
            <p:column>840</p:column>
        </p:row>
    </f:facet>
</p:panelGrid>
```

What just happened?

We have created a panelGrid component, and added rows using nested <p:row> elements. We have added columns for each row using <p:column> and specified the rows and columns to span using rowspan and colspan attributes respectively:

Posts Statistics By Tag			
Tag	Month	Posts	Total
JSF	JAN	120	270
	FEB	150	
PrimeFaces	JAN	220	570
	FEB	350	
		Grand Total	840

Displaying overflowed content using ScrollPanel

The ScrollPanel component can be used to display overflowed content with theme aware scrollbars as well as native browser scrollbars.

Time for action – using a ScrollPanel component

Let us see how we can use ScrollPanel to display overflowed content with scrollbars.

1. Create a ScrollPanel and set `height` and `width` using a `style` attribute:

```
<p:scrollPanel style="width:300px;height:250px">
  <p:dataTable var="user" value="#{adminController.users}">
    <f:facet name="header">
      List of Users
    </f:facet>
    <p:column headerText="Id">
      <h:outputText value="#{user.id}" />
    </p:column>
    <p:column headerText="Email">
      <h:outputText value="#{user.emailId}" />
    </p:column>
    <p:column headerText="FirstName">
      <h:outputText value="#{user.firstName}" />
    </p:column>
    <p:column headerText="Disabled">
      <h:outputText value="#{user.disabled}" />
    </p:column>
  </p:dataTable>
</p:scrollPanel>
```

What just happened?

We have created a ScrollPanel component and set its `width` and `height` using a `style` attribute. As the nested dataTable height and width exceeds the height and width of ScrollPanel, theme aware scrollbars are displayed. You can set the `mode` attribute to `native` if you want to display native browser scrollbars instead of theme aware scrollbars:

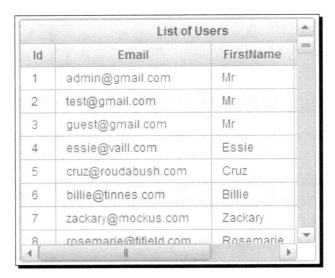

Creating workflows using a Wizard component

Often we may need to implement workflows which involve multiple steps to complete a task. For example, in e-commerce an application placing an order involves adding products to cart, entering shipping/billing address, entering payment information, and then submitting the order. At each step we may need to perform validations on the current page fields and move forward if no validation failures occur. A wizard component provides exactly this kind of functionality.

A Wizard component is a complex UI component to implement workflows in a single page. Each step in the workflow will be represented by a tab in a wizard component and displays **Next** and **Back** buttons to move across the steps. When you click on the **Next** button, it performs validations, and if any validation errors are found on the current page fields then current page will be redisplayed along with error. Note that when you navigate to previous steps by clicking on the **Back** button validations won't be executed. Optionally, we can use `flowListener` feature to execute server-side logic when moving between the steps and can alter the step navigation if required.

Let us take a simple example of creating a new contact in phonebook. Adding a new contact may involve entering personal details, address info, and contact details.

Time for action – using Wizard to implement workflows

Let us see how we can implement adding a new contact as a workflow using a Wizard component. In first step, we need to enter personal details such as, FirstName, LastName, and so on. In second step we enter details such as Address details and in third step Contact Information such as, e-mail and phone.

1. Create a Wizard component with three steps for entering personal details, address details, and contact details:

```
<p:wizard widgetVar="wiz" flowListener="#{wizardController.
onFlowProcess}">
  <!-- Personal Details Tab -->
  <p:tab id="personal" title="Personal">
    <p:panel header="Personal Details">
      <p:messages />
      <h:panelGrid columns="2">
        <h:outputLabel value="Firstname: *" />
        <p:inputText value="#{wizardController.user.firstName}"
          required="true" label="Firstname"/>
        <h:outputLabel value="Lastname: *" />
        <p:inputText value="#{wizardController.user.lastName}"
          required="true" label="Lastname"/>
        <h:outputLabel value="Skip to last: " />
        <h:selectBooleanCheckbox
          value="#{wizardController.skip}" />
      </h:panelGrid>
    </p:panel>
  </p:tab>
  <!-- Address Details Tab -->
  <p:tab id="address" title="Address">
    <p:panel header="Address Details">
      <p:messages />
      <h:panelGrid columns="2">
        <h:outputLabel value="Street: " />
        <p:inputText value=
          "#{wizardController.user.address.street}" />
        <h:outputLabel value="City: " />
        <p:inputText value=
          "#{wizardController.user.address.city}" />
        <h:outputLabel value="ZipCode: " />
        <p:inputText value=
          "#{wizardController.user.address.zip}" />
        <h:outputLabel value="Country: " />
        <p:inputText value=
          "#{wizardController.user.address.country}" />
        <h:outputLabel value="Skip to last: " />
```

```
            <h:selectBooleanCheckbox value=
                "#{wizardController.skip}" />
        </h:panelGrid>
    </p:panel>
</p:tab>
<!-- Contact Information  -->
<p:tab id="contact" title="Contact">
    <p:panel header="Contact Information">
        <p:messages />
        <h:panelGrid columns="2">
            <h:outputLabel value="Phone: *" />
            <p:inputText value="#{wizardController.user.phone}"
                required="true" label="Phone"/>
            <h:outputLabel value="EmailId: " />
            <p:inputText value="#{wizardController.user.emailId}"/>
            <h:outputLabel value="Skip to last: " />
            <h:selectBooleanCheckbox value=
                "#{wizardController.skip}" />
        </h:panelGrid>
    </p:panel>
</p:tab>
<!-- Confirmation Tab with all the details -->
<p:tab id="confirm" title="Confirmation">
    <p:panel header="Confirmation">
        <h:panelGrid id="confirmation" >
            <h:panelGrid columns="2">
                <h:outputLabel value="Firstname: " />
                <h:outputText value=
                    "#{wizardController.user.firstName}"/>
                <h:outputLabel value="Lastname: " />
                <h:outputText value=
                    "#{wizardController.user.lastName}"/>
            </h:panelGrid>
            <br/>
            <h:panelGrid columns="2">
                <h:outputLabel value="Street: " />
                <h:outputText value=
                    "#{wizardController.user.address.street}"/>
                <h:outputLabel value="City: " />
                <h:outputText value=
                    "#{wizardController.user.address.city}"/>
                <h:outputLabel value="State: " />
                <h:outputText value=
                    "#{wizardController.user.address.state}"/>
                <h:outputLabel value="ZipCode: " />
                <h:outputText value=
                    "#{wizardController.user.address.zip}"/>
```

```
        <h:outputLabel value="Country: " />
        <h:outputText value=
          "#{wizardController.user.address.country}"/>
      </h:panelGrid>
      <br/>
       <h:panelGrid columns="2">
        <h:outputLabel value="EmailId: " />
        <h:outputText value=
          "#{wizardController.user.emailId}"/>

        <h:outputLabel value="Phone: " />
        <h:outputText value=
          "#{wizardController.user.phone}"/>
      </h:panelGrid>
    </h:panelGrid>
    <p:commandButton value="Submit" actionListener=
      "#{wizardController.save}" process="@this"/>
  </p:panel>
</p:tab>
</p:wizard>
```

2. Implement `flowListener` and `save` methods.

```
@ManagedBean
@ViewScoped
public class WizardController implements Serializable
{
  private static Logger logger =
    Logger.getLogger(WizardController.class.getName());

  private boolean skip;
  private User user = new User();
    //setters and getters

    public String onFlowProcess(FlowEvent event) {
    String currentStep = event.getOldStep();
    String nextStep = event.getNewStep();
        logger.debug("Current Step:" + currentStep);
        logger.debug("Next Step:" + nextStep);
        if(skip)
    {
            skip = false;
            return "confirm";
        }
        else {
```

```
                        return event.getNewStep();
                }
        }

    public void save() {
      //logic to save User
            FacesMessage msg = new FacesMessage("Successfully saved
                User details.");
            FacesContext.getCurrentInstance().addMessage(null,
                msg);
        }
    }
```

What just happened?

We have created a wizard component containing four steps, first three steps to get personal details, address, contact details; and fourth step to display all these details to confirm before saving.

When you click on the **Back** or **Next** button, the flowListener method WizardController.onFlowProcess(FlowEvent) will be invoked. We can get the current step and next step details from FlowEvent using event.getOldStep() and event.getNewStep() methods. From the flowListener method we will return the id of the next tab to be displayed. Here we are maintaining a Boolean skip flag in each step so that user can skip to the **Confirmation** page directly if the current page validations succeed. In the flowListener method we are checking for skip flag, and if it is checked we are taking the user to confirmation page directly by returning confirmation tab ID confirm:

Also a Wizard component provides the following client-side callback methods to navigate through steps and **Show/Hide** navigation buttons:

- `next()`: Proceeds to next step
- `back()`: Goes back in flow
- `getStepIndex()`: Returns the index of current step
- `showNextNav()`: Shows **Next** button
- `hideNextNav()`: Hides **Next** button
- `showBackNav()`: Shows **Back** button
- `hideBackNav()`: Hides **Back** button

If you want to customize the navigation of a wizard component, you can set the `showNavBar` attribute to `false`, and use `next()` and `back()` JavaScript functions on `widgetVar` value for navigation.

> We should use a wizard component with `ManagedBean` of scope greater than `RequestScoped` such as `ViewScoped` or `SessionScoped`, because the backing bean should retain the data across multiple requests.

Creating stacked panels using the AccordionPanel component

The AccordionPanel component is a container component with vertically stacked panels.

A basic AccordionPanel can be created as follows:

```
<p:accordionPanel>
  <p:tab title="PrimeFaces">
    <h:outputText value="PrimeFaces is an open source JSF component
      library with 100+ Rich UI Components support. It has built-in
      Ajax support based on standard JSF 2.0 Ajax APIs." />
  </p:tab>
  <p:tab title="JSF">
    <h:outputText value="JavaServer Faces is a Java specification for
      building component-based user interfaces for web
      applications. It was formalized as a standard through the Java
      Community Process and is part of the Java Platform, Enterprise
      Edition." />
  </p:tab>
  <p:tab title="JavaEE">
```

```
    <h:outputText value="Java Platform, Enterprise Edition (Java EE)
        is the standard in community-driven enterprise software. Java
        EE is developed using the Java Community Process, with
        contributions from industry experts, commercial and open source
        organizations, Java User Groups, and countless individuals." />
    </p:tab>
</p:accordionPanel>
```

The preceding code displays a AccordionPanel component as follows:

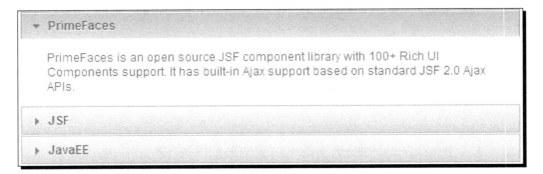

AccordionPanel component supports the following attributes to customize its behavior:

- `activeIndex`: Index of the active tab or a comma separated string of indexes when multiple mode is on. Default is 0.

- `onTabChange`: Client-side callback to invoke when an inactive tab is clicked.

- `onTabShow`: Client-side callback to invoke when a tab gets activated.

- `dynamic`: When enabled loads data lazily. Default is false.

- `cache`: Defines if activating a dynamic tab should load the contents from server again. Default is true.

- `value`: List to iterate to display a dynamic number of tabs.

- `var`: Name of iterator to use in a dynamic number of tabs.

- `multiple`: Controls multiple selection. Default is false.

By default, only one tab can be expanded, when you click on the other tab, then current tab gets collapsed and the new tab will be expanded. You can set the `multiple` attribute to `true` to enable multiple tab selection:

```
<p:accordionPanel multiple="true">
    . . .
</p:accordionPanel>
```

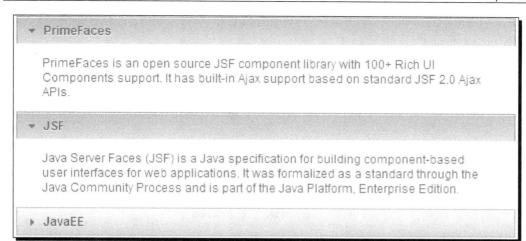

Loading tabs content dynamically

By default, AccordionPanel loads all the tabs content eagerly. We can set the `dynamic` attribute to `true` to enable lazy loading of tabs content. When dynamic loading is enabled, only active tabs content will be loaded lazily using AJAX. We can also enable caching of loaded tabs content by setting the `cache` attribute to `true`. When caching is enabled, toggling on an already loaded tab doesn't initiate AJAX request.

```
<p:accordionPanel dynamic="true" cache="true">
  <p:tab title="PrimeFaces">
    <h:outputText value="#{sampleController.tab1Content}" />
  </p:tab>
  <p:tab title="JSF">
    <h:outputText value="#{sampleController.tab2Content}" />
  </p:tab>
  <p:tab title="JavaEE">
    <h:outputText value="#{sampleController.tab3Content}" />
  </p:tab>
</p:accordionPanel>
```

Creating a dynamic number of tabs

In the preceding code snippet, we have created an AccordionPanel component using static tab definitions. Sometimes we may have to create an AccordionPanel component with a dynamic number of tabs using data loading from the server.

We can create AccordionPanel backed by a collection of objects, and create tabs dynamically as follows:

```
<p:accordionPanel value="#{tagController.tags}" var="tag">
  <p:tab title="#{tag.label}">
    <h:outputText value="#{tag.description}" />
  </p:tab>
</p:accordionPanel>
```

Here we have created AccordionPanel backed by `tagController.tags`, which is `List<Tag>` objects. It will create a tab for each `Tag` in the collection.

Handling tabChange and tabClose events

The AccordionPanel component supports tab change and tab close event listeners on both client and server side. We can create a server-side `tabChange` and `tabClose` event listeners as follows:

```
<p:accordionPanel value="#{tagController.tags}" var="tag">
  <p:ajax event="tabChange" listener="#{tagController.onTabChange}"/>
    <p:ajax event="tabClose" listener="#{tagController.onTabClose}"/>
  <p:tab title="#{tag.label}">
    <h:outputText value="#{tag.description}" />
  </p:tab>
</p:accordionPanel>
```

When you click on any inactive tab, `tabChange` event gets triggered and event listener method `onTabChange()` will be invoked with `TabChangeEvent` as a parameter. When you collapse an active tab then the `tabClose` event gets triggered with `TabCloseEvent` as parameter:

```
public void onTabChange(TabChangeEvent event)
{
  String activeTabId = event.getTab().getId();
    JSFUtils.addInfoMsg("Active Tab:" + activeTabId);
}
public void onTabClose(TabCloseEvent event)
{
  String tabId = event.getTab().getId();
    JSFUtils.addInfoMsg("Closed Tab:" + tabId);
}
```

Similarly, we can attach client-side JavaScript callback functions for `tabChange` and `tabShow` events using the `onTabChange` and `onTabShow` attributes. The `onTabChange` callback is called before a tab is shown and the `onTabShow` callback is called after a tab is shown. Both callback functions receive container element of the tab to show as the parameter.

```
<p:accordionPanel value="#{tagController.tags}" var="tag"
onTabChange="tabChanged(panel)" onTabShow="tabShowed(panel)>
  <p:tab title="#{tag.label}">
    <h:outputText value="#{tag.description}" />
  </p:tab>
</p:accordionPanel>

<script type="text/javascript">
  function tabChanged(panel)
  {
    alert("Tab Changed");
  }

  function tabShowed(panel)
  {
    $(panel).effect( "highlight", {color:"#669966"}, 3000 );
  }
</script>
```

Let us see how we can use AccordionPanel to display each tag details in a tab and disable the tabs, which are not associated with any posts.

Time for action – creating AccordionPanel with dynamic tabs and event listener

Create AccordionPanel and specify to disable a tab if no posts are associated with the tag using the `disabled` attribute of the `<p:tag>` element:

```
<p:accordionPanel value="#{tagController.tags}" var="tag"
activeIndex="2">
  <p:ajax event="tabChange" listener="#{tagController.onTabChange}"/>
  <p:tab title="#{tag.label}" disabled="#{empty tag.posts}">
    <h:outputText value="#{tag.description}" />
  </p:tab>
</p:accordionPanel>
```

What just happened?

We have created an AccordionPanel backed by the `List<Tag>` collection. We have specified `disabled="#{empty tag.posts}"` to disable a tab if there are no posts associated with that tag. As there are no posts associated with struts and hibernate tags, these two tabs are disabled. Also, we have specified `activeIndex="2"` to expand the third tab by default, instead of first tab:

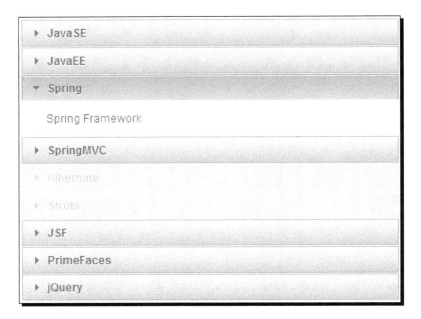

Creating a tabbed panel using a TabView component

A TabView component is a tabbed panel component, similar to AccordionPanel, providing features such as dynamic tabs, lazy loading of tabs, and server/client-side event listeners for `tabChange`, `tabShow` events. Usage of the TabView component is very similar to AccordionPanel.

In our TechBuzz application we will use a TabView component to show the **User Account** screen to display user-specific information in multiple tabs, such as **My Profile**, **Change Password**, and **My Buzz**.

Let us see how to create a **User Account** page using a TabView component:

```
<p:tabView>
  <p:tab title="My Profile">
    <p:panel header="Personal Info">
    <h:panelGrid columns="2" columnClasses="label">
```

```
        <h:outputLabel value="First Name:" />
        <h:outputText value=" #{userController.loginUser.firstName}"/>
        <h:outputLabel value="Last Name:" />
        <h:outputText value=" #{userController.loginUser.lastName}"/>
        <h:outputLabel value="Email:"/>
        <h:outputText value=" #{userController.loginUser.emailId}"/>
        <h:outputLabel value="Phone: " />
        <h:outputText value=" #{userController.loginUser.phone}"/>
      </h:panelGrid>
      </p:panel>
  </p:tab>

  <p:tab title="Change Password">
    <h:form id="changePwdForm">
      <p:messages id="messages" severity="error" showDetail="true"
        autoUpdate="true"/>
<p:panel header="Change Password">
  <h:panelGrid columns="2">

<p:outputLabel for="oldPwd" value="Current Password"/>
<p:password id="oldPwd" value=
  "#{userController.changePwd.currentPwd}"  required="true"/>

  <p:outputLabel for="newPwd" value="New Password"/>
  <p:password id="newPwd" value="#{userController.changePwd.newPwd}"
      feedback="true"
      promptLabel="Enter New Password"
      weakLabel="Weak Password"
      goodLabel="Good Password"
      strongLabel="Strong Password"
      match="confPwd"  required="true"/>

<p:outputLabel for="confPwd" value="Confirm Password"/>
<p:password id="confPwd" value="#{userController.changePwd.newPwd}"
  required="true"/>

<p:commandButton value="Submit" actionListener=
  "#{userController.changePassword}" update="@form"/>
      </h:panelGrid>
      </p:panel>
    </h:form>
  </p:tab>

  <p:tab title="My Buzz">
```

```
    <p:dataList value="#{postController.posts}" var="post" id="posts"
      paginator="true" rows="10" type="none">
      <h:outputText value="#{post.title}" style="margin-left:10px;
        font-size:7; font-weight:bold" /><br />
      <h:outputText value="#{post.description}" style="margin-
        left:10px" escape="false"/><br /><br />
      <p:separator/>
    </p:dataList>
  </p:tab>
</p:tabView>
```

The preceding code renders a TabView component as follows:

Loading tabs content dynamically

We can load tabs content lazily using AJAX by setting the dynamic attribute to true. Also
we can enable caching of loaded tab content by setting the cache attribute to true:

```
<p:tabView dynamic="true" cache="false">
  <p:tab title="My Profile">
    . . .
  </p:tab>
  <p:tab title="Change Password">
    . . .
  </p:tab>
  <p:tab title="My Buzz">
    . . .
  </p:tab>
</p:tabView>
```

Creating TabView with closable tabs

The TabView component also supports `closable` tabs, and you can register a server-side AJAX listener for the `tabClose` event.

```
<p:tabView>
  <p:ajax event="tabClose" listener=
    "#{sampleController.onTabClose}"/>
  <p:tab title="My Profile" closable="true">
    . . .
  </p:tab>
  <p:tab title="Change Password" closable="true">
    . . .
  </p:tab>
  <p:tab title="My Buzz" closable="true">
    . . .
  </p:tab>
</p:tabView>

public void onTabClose(TabCloseEvent event)
{
  FacesMessage msg = new FacesMessage("Closed Tab: " +
    event.getTab().getTitle());
  FacesContext.getCurrentInstance().addMessage(null, msg);
}
```

The preceding TabView component renders closable tabs as follows:

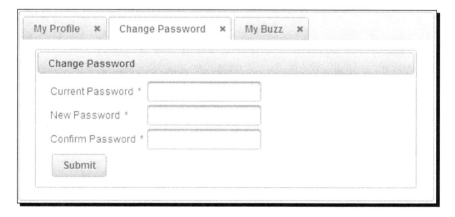

When you click on tab's close icon, tab will be closed and the `tabClose` event listener method will be invoked.

Tab headers with different orientations

By default, the TabView component display tab headers at the top. You can change the position of tab headers using the `orientation` attribute. The valid `orientation` values are `top`, `bottom`, `left`, and `right`:

```
<p:tabView orientation="bottom">
  <p:tab title="My Profile">
    ...
  </p:tab>
  <p:tab title="Change Password">
    ...
  </p:tab>
  <p:tab title="My Buzz">
    ...
  </p:tab>
</p:tabView>
```

Creating TabView with a dynamic number of tabs

Instead of static tab definitions, we can also create a TabView component with dynamic number of tabs using data backed by a server-side collection of objects:

```
<p:tabView value="#{tagController.tags}" var="tag">
  <p:tab title="#{tag.label}">
    <h:outputText value="#{tag.description}" />
  </p:tab>
</p:tabView>
```

Creating TabView with scrollable tabs

We can create a TabView component with scrollable tabs to deal with more number of tabs by setting `scrollable` attribute to `true`.

```
<p:tabView value="#{tagController.tags}" var="tag" scrollable="true">
  <p:tab title="#{tag.label}">
    <h:outputText value="#{tag.description}" />
  </p:tab>
</p:tabView>
```

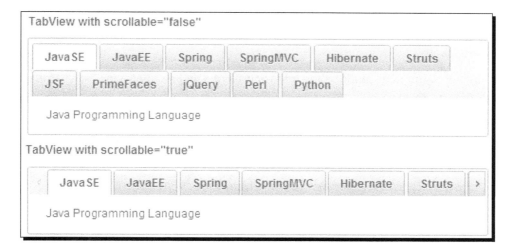

When scrollable feature enabled TabView will get scroll buttons to scroll across the tabs.

Handling TabView component's events

The TabView component supports `onTabChange` and `onTabShow` client-side callbacks. The `onTabChange` callback is executed when an inactive tab is clicked and the `onTabShow` callback is executed when an inactive tab becomes active to be shown. These callbacks receive an argument `index`, which represents the index of the tab clicked:

```
<p:tabView onTabChange="tabChanged(index)"
onTabShow="tabShowed(index)">
  <p:tab title="My Profile">
    ...
  </p:tab>
  <p:tab title="Change Password">
    ...
  </p:tab>
  <p:tab title="My Buzz">
    ...
```

```
    </p:tab>
  </p:tabView>

  <script type="text/javascript">
    function tabChanged(index)
    {
      alert("Tab Changed:"+index);
    }
    function tabShowed(index)
    {
      alert("Tab Show:"+index);
    }
  </script>
```

The TabView component supports the following client-side functions, which can be invoked on `widgetVar` value:

◆ `select(index)`: Activates tab with given index

◆ `disable(index)`: Disables tab with given index

◆ `enable(index)`: Enables tab with given index

◆ `remove(index)`: Removes tab with given index

◆ `getLength()`: Returns the number of tabs

◆ `getActiveIndex()`: Returns index of current tab

Let us see how we can use TabView with dynamic data from server side and register event listeners for `tabChange` and `tabClose` event listeners.

Time for action – using TabView with dynamic tabs and event listeners support

Let us look at how we can create a TabView component with dynamic number of tabs that are loaded lazily and handle `tabChange` and `tabClose` events:

1. Create a TabView component backed by server-side data and register `tabChange` and `tabClose` event listeners:

```
<p:tabView value="#{tagController.tags}" var="tag"
  dynamic="true" cache="false" activeIndex="2">
  <p:ajax event="tabChange" listener=
    "#{sampleController.onTabChange}"/>
  <p:ajax event="tabClose" listener=
    "#{sampleController.onTabClose}"/>
```

```
    <p:tab title="#{tag.label}" closable="true" disabled="#{empty
       tag.posts}">
       <h:outputText value="#{tag.description}" />
    </p:tab>
  </p:tabView>
```

What just happened?

We have created a TabView component backed by the `List<Tag>` collection. We have specified `disabled="#{empty tag.posts}"` to disable the tab if there are no posts associated with that tag. Also, we have specified `activeIndex="2"` to expand the third tab by default instead of first tab. When an inactive tab is activated then the `tabChange` event listener gets invoked. When a tab is closed then the `tabClose` event listener gets invoked. Also we can apply transition effect and its duration using `effect` and `effectDuration` attributes.

Creating complex layouts using the Layout component

Many of the web applications use a standard border layout model, where it has five regions (north, south, west, east, and center) to present data. To support this common usecase PrimeFaces provides layout component which provides border layout component with various customization features such as full page layout, toggling, closing, resizing of regions, and ability to create complex layouts using nested layouts.

The following diagram depicts how border layout look like:

Layout can be applied for full page or for a specific region in a page. You can set fullPage="true" to create full page layout, by default fullPage="false". Each region is created by using a <p:layoutUnit> subcomponent. You can enable toggling, closing, and resizing of the units by setting collapsible, closable, resizable attributes to true on the <p:layoutUnit> elements.

Time for action – creating FullPage layout

Let us see how to create a FullPage layout component with five regions:

1. Create a Layout component using <p:layout fullPage="true">.

```
<p:layout fullPage="true">

  <p:layoutUnit position="north" size="100" resizable="true"
    closable="true" collapsible="true">
    <center><font size="6">TechBuzz</font></center>
  </p:layoutUnit>

  <p:layoutUnit position="south" size="100" header="Footer"
    resizable="true" closable="true" collapsible="true">
    <h:outputText value="Copyright @ 2013" />
  </p:layoutUnit>

  <p:layoutUnit position="west" size="200"
    header="NavigationBar" resizable="true" closable="true"
    collapsible="true">
    <h:form>
      <h:link value="User Management" /><br/>
      <h:link value="Tag Config" /><br/>
      <h:link value="System Admin"/>
    </h:form>
  </p:layoutUnit>

  <p:layoutUnit position="east" size="200" header="Latest Buzz"
    resizable="true" closable="true" collapsible="true"
    effect="drop">
    <h:outputText value="PrimeFaces forum reached 98,000
      posts." />
  </p:layoutUnit>

  <p:layoutUnit id="centerUnit" position="center">
      <h:outputText value="FullPage Layout using PrimeFaves
        Layout Component." />
  </p:layoutUnit>

</p:layout>
```

What just happened?

We have created a FullPage layout with five regions, which will display as follows:

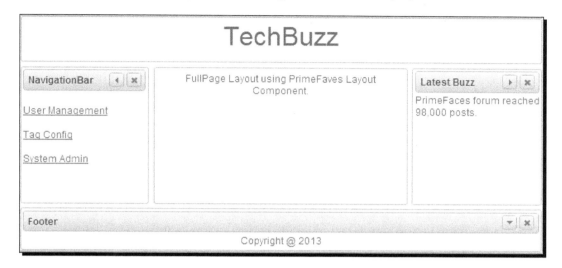

As we have enabled toggling and closing features of layout units, we can minimize or close the individual units.

Creating an element-based layout

We can also use Layout component to create a border layout container within a specific region in page by setting `fullPage="false"`, which is default.

Let us see how we can create element-based layout:

```
<p:layout style="min-width:250px;min-height:220px;" id="layout">
  <p:layoutUnit position="west" resizable="true" size="100">
    West
  </p:layoutUnit>
  <p:layoutUnit position="north">
    North
  </p:layoutUnit>
  <p:layoutUnit position="south" >
    South
  </p:layoutUnit>
  <p:layoutUnit position="center">
    <center>Center</center>
  </p:layoutUnit>
</p:layout>
```

Creating nested layouts

We can also create complex layout containers using nested layouts.

Let us see how we can create a nested layout with a main outer layout, which contains a nested layout with `north` and `center` `layoutUnits` in its `center` `layoutUnit`.

```
<p:layout fullPage="true">

  <p:layoutUnit position="north" size="80" resizable="true">
    <center><font size="6">TechBuzz</font></center>
  </p:layoutUnit>
  <p:layoutUnit position="south" size="50" header="Footer"
    resizable="true">
    <center><h:outputText value="Copyright @ 2013" /></center>
  </p:layoutUnit>
  <p:layoutUnit position="east" size="200" header="Latest Buzz"
    resizable="true">
    <h:outputText value="PrimeFaces forum reached 98,000 posts." />
  </p:layoutUnit>
  <p:layoutUnit position="west" size="150" header="NavigationBar"
    resizable="true">
    <h:form>
      <h:link value="User Management" /><br/>
      <h:link value="Tag Config" /><br/>
      <h:link value="System Admin"/>
    </h:form>
  </p:layoutUnit>

  <p:layoutUnit position="center">
    <p:layout>
      <p:layoutUnit position="north" size="50" resizable="true">
        <font size="4">Tag Configuration</font>
      </p:layoutUnit>
      <p:layoutUnit position="center">
        <h:outputText value="List of Tags:" />
        <p:dataList value="#{tagController.tags}" var="tag">
         <h:outputText value="#{tag}" />
        </p:dataList>
      </p:layoutUnit>
    </p:layout>
  </p:layoutUnit>
</p:layout>
```

The preceding code renders a nested layout as follows:

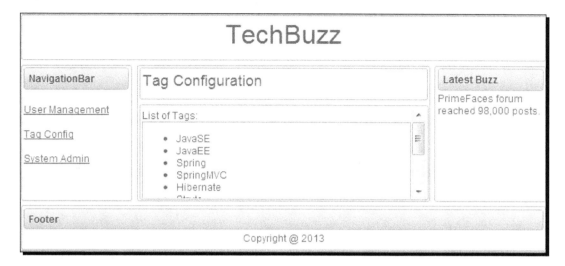

Handling layout events

Layout component supports AJAX event listeners for toggle, close, and resize events.

```
<p:layout fullPage="true">
  <p:ajax event="toggle" listener=
    "#{sampleController.handleLayoutToggle}"  />
  <p:ajax event="close" listener=
    "#{sampleController.handleLayoutClose}" />
  <p:ajax event="resize" listener=
    "#{sampleController.handleLayoutResize}" />
  ...
</p:layout>

public void handleLayoutClose(org.primefaces.event.CloseEvent event)
{
  String msg = "Position: "+((LayoutUnit)event.getComponent()).
getPosition();
  FacesMessage message = new FacesMessage(FacesMessage.SEVERITY_INFO,
    "LayoutUnit Closed", msg);
  FacesContext.getCurrentInstance().addMessage(null, message);
}

public void handleLayoutToggle(org.primefaces.event.ToggleEvent
  event)
{
```

```
    String msg =  "Position: "+((LayoutUnit)event.getComponent()).
getPosition() + " , Status:" +
    event.getVisibility().name();
    FacesMessage message = new FacesMessage
      (FacesMessage.SEVERITY_INFO,"LayoutUnit Toggled",msg);
    FacesContext.getCurrentInstance().addMessage(null, message);
}

public void handleLayoutResize(org.primefaces.event.ResizeEvent
    event)
{
    String msg =  "Position:
      "+((LayoutUnit)event.getComponent()).getPosition();
    FacesMessage message = new FacesMessage(FacesMessage.SEVERITY_INFO,
      "LayoutUnit Resized", msg);
    FacesContext.getCurrentInstance().addMessage(null, message);
}
```

- ◆ If you are working with forms and full page layout, avoid using a form that contains `layoutUnits`, as generated DOM may not be the same. Instead create forms within `layoutUnits`.
- ◆ Update `layoutUnit` contents instead of updating `layoutUnits` itself.
- ◆ Except center `layoutUnit`, other layout units must have dimensions defined using size option.

Creating portal like layout using a Dashboard component

Dashboard is layout component that provides portal like layout with drag-and-drop feature to rearrange its UI widgets as per user choice.

To create a Dashboard layout we need to create a custom model object of type `org.primefaces.model.DashboardModel`. We can create multiple panel widgets and group them by adding to `org.primefaces.model.DashboardColumn`, which in turn should be added to `DashboardModel`.

Time for action – creating a Dashboard layout

Let us see how to create a Dashboard layout component:

1. Create a Dashboard Layout using `<p:dashboard>`.

```
<p:dashboard id="board" model="#{dashboardController.model}">
  <p:panel id="twitter" header="Twitter">
    <h:outputText value="Twitter feed" />
```

```
    </p:panel>
    <p:panel id="facebook" header="Facebook">
      <h:outputText value="Facebook feed" />
    </p:panel>
    <p:panel id="youtube" header="YouTube">
      <h:outputText value="YouTube Videos"  />
    </p:panel>
    <p:panel id="dzone" header="DZone">
      <h:outputText value="DZone Posts" />
    </p:panel>
    <p:panel id="jcg" header="Java Code Geeks">
      <h:outputText value="JavaCodeGeeks Posts" />
    </p:panel>
    <p:panel id="linkedIn" header="LinkedIn">
      <h:outputText value="LinkedIn Content" />
    </p:panel>
  </p:dashboard>
```

2. Create and initialize `org.primefaces.model.DashboardModel` backing model object:

```
public DashboardController()
{
  model = new DefaultDashboardModel();
  DashboardColumn column1 = new DefaultDashboardColumn();
  DashboardColumn column2 = new DefaultDashboardColumn();
  DashboardColumn column3 = new DefaultDashboardColumn();

  column1.addWidget("twitter");
  column1.addWidget("facebook");
  column1.addWidget("youtube");

  column2.addWidget("linkedIn");
  column3.addWidget("dzone");
  column3.addWidget("jcg");

  model.addColumn(column1);
  model.addColumn(column2);
  model.addColumn(column3);
}
```

What just happened?

We have created a portal kind of Dashboard with six panel widgets fitted into three columns. We can drag-and-drop any panel into other widget positions as per our preference. If you want to disable drag-and-drop feature set `disabled="false"`.

You can programmatically move panel widget from one location to another location using the `transferWidget()` method on the `DashboardModel` instance:

```
void transferWidget(DashboardColumn from, DashboardColumn to, String
widgetId, int index)
```

This method will relocate the widget identified with widget id to the given index of the new column from old column.

By default, if you move all the panels from one column to another and the column is empty then you can't fill that column again by dragging panels back.

To have columns of a fixed size you need to define `ui-dashboard-column` style with the preferred `width`.

```
<style type="text/css">
  .ui-dashboard-column {
    width:200px;
  }
</style>
```

The Dashboard component supports the reorder AJAX event and invokes the event listener method with `org.primefaces.event.DashboardReorderEvent` type parameter:

```
<p:dashboard id="board" model="#{dashboardController.model}"
disabled="false">
  <p:ajax event="reorder" listener="#{dashboardController.
handleReorder}" />
  ...
</p:dashboard>

public void handleReorder(DashboardReorderEvent event)
{
  FacesMessage message = new FacesMessage();
  message.setSummary("Reordered: " + event.getWidgetId());
  message.setDetail("Item index: " + event.getItemIndex()
    + ", Column index: " + event.getColumnIndex()
    + ", Sender index: " + event.getSenderColumnIndex());
  FacesContext.getCurrentInstance().addMessage(null, message);
}
```

Summary

In this chapter, we have learned how to create and use complex user interface layouts using various layout components such as Panel, PanelGrid, ScrollPanel, AccordionPanel, and TabView. We have learned how to create workflows using a Wizard component. We have created complex border layout-style full page layout using layout component. Also we have created a sample portal kind of layout using a dashboard component with drag-and-drop capabilities.

In the next chapter, we will learn about navigation components such as Menus, BreadCrumb, Toolbar, and so on.

11
Introducing Navigation Components

Typically, web applications have many screens and users navigate through the screens using various types of navigation menus. HTML has a very basic support for navigating through screens using hyperlinks or form submissions. Various JavaScript libraries provide a rich set of navigation components such as drop-down menus, pop-up menus, tabbed menus, and so on. PrimeFaces brings support for most of the rich navigation menu components to JSF-based applications.

PrimeFaces provides various navigation components such as Menu, TieredMenu, Menubar, MegaMenu, TabMenu, ContextMenu, Breadcrumb menu, and so on.

In this chapter we will cover:

- Understanding MenuModel
- Introducing the Menu component
- Introducing the MenuButton component
- Displaying multilevel nested menus using TieredMenu
- Creating nested menus with SlideMenu
- Creating a horizontal navigation menu using Menubar
- Creating the multicolumn menu using MegaMenu
- Creating tab-based menus using TabMenu
- Introducing the PanelMenu Component
- Introducing ContextMenu
- Introducing the Breadcrumb navigation menu

Understanding MenuModel

Many of the PrimeFaces menu components such as Menu, TieredMenu, SlideMenu, MegaMenu, MenuBar, TabMenu, PanelMenu, and Breadcrumb are backed by the `org.primefaces.model.MenuModel` instance, and can also be created in a declarative way using the same `<p:menuitem>` and `<p:submenu>` elements.

Building menus declaratively

We can create menus declaratively using the `<p:menuitem>` and `<p:submenu>` elements. The `<p:submenu>` element can be used to group menu options, and submenus can be nested inside other submenus.

The `<p:menuitem>` element provides the following options to customize its behavior:

- `value`: Label of the MenuItem.
- `icon`: Path of the MenuItem image.
- `title`: Advisory tooltip information.
- `disabled`: Disables the MenuItem component. Default is `false`.
- `target`: Target type of the URL navigation.
- `url`: URL to be navigated when MenuItem is clicked.
- `outcome`: Navigation case outcome.
- `action`: Action to be invoked when MenuItem is clicked.
- `actionListener`: Action listener to be invoked when MenuItem is clicked.
- `immediate`: When `true`, action of this MenuItem is processed after the Apply Request phase. Default is `false`.
- `partialSubmit`: Enables serialization of values belonging to the partially processed components only. Default is `false`.
- `ajax`: Specifies submit mode. Default is `true`.
- `async`: When set to `true`, AJAX requests are not queued. Default is `false`.
- `process`: Component ID(s) to process partially instead of whole view.
- `update`: Client-side ID of the component(s) to be updated after the `async` partial submit request.
- `includeViewParams`: Defines whether page parameters should be in the target URI. Default is `false`.
- `fragment`: Identifier of the target page element to scroll to.
- `global`: Global AJAX requests are listened to by the ajaxStatus component, setting global to false will not trigger ajaxStatus. Default is `true`.

- ◆ `onclick`: JavaScript event handler for the click event.

- ◆ `onstart`: JavaScript handler to execute before the AJAX request begins.

- ◆ `oncomplete`: JavaScript handler to execute when the AJAX request is completed.

- ◆ `onsuccess`: JavaScript handler to execute when the AJAX request succeeds.

- ◆ `onerror`: JavaScript handler to execute when the AJAX request fails.

Let us examine the following TieredMenu definition:

```
<p:tieredMenu style="width:180px">
    <p:submenu label="User Management" icon="ui-icon-person">
        <p:submenu label="View Users">
            <p:menuitem value="Moderators" url="tieredMenu.jsf"/>
            <p:menuitem value="Normal Users"
                action="#{menuController.showUserManagement()}"/>
        </p:submenu>
        <p:menuitem value="Monitor User Activity"
            actionListener="#{menuController.showUserActivity()}"
            ajax="false"/>
    </p:submenu>
    <p:submenu label="Tag Management" icon="ui-icon-tag">
        <p:menuitem value="View Tags" url="tieredMenu.jsf"/>
        <p:menuitem value="Tag Stistics" outcome="tieredMenu"/>
    </p:submenu>
    <p:menuitem value="System Config" icon="ui-icon-gear"
        outcome="tieredMenu"/>
</p:tieredMenu>
```

The preceding code renders a TieredMenu component, which we are going to discuss in the later section of this chapter, with multiple submenus and nested submenus. When you mouse over any MenuItem, it will display Submenu options if it has any, as shown in the following screenshot:

The `<p:submenu>` element can contain child `<p:submenu>` elements to display nested submenus. We can display an icon for MenuItem and Submenu headings using the `icon` attribute.

We can specify GET type navigations using the `url` or `outcome` attributes, as shown in the following code snippet:

```
<p:menuitem value="View Configuration" outcome="tieredMenu"/>
<p:menuitem value="View Tags" url="tieredMenu.jsf"/>
```

We can send a POST request using the `action` or `actionListener` attributes. By default, the POST request is issued using AJAX, we can alter this behavior using the `ajax` attribute, shown as follows:

```
<p:menuitem value="Normal Users"
    action="#{menuController.showUserManagement()}"/>
<p:menuitem value="Monitor User Activity"
    actionListener="#{menuController.showUserActivity()}"
ajax="false"/>
```

Building menus programmatically

We can create menus dynamically by creating an instance of MenuModel programmatically and adding the `org.primefaces.model.menu.DefaultMenuItem` and `org.primefaces.model.menu.DefaultSubMenu` instances, representing menuitems and submenus, respectively.

Let us see how to create the same Menu component that we created declaratively in the previous section in a programmatic way:

```
void initMenuModel()
{
    menuModel = new DefaultMenuModel();

    DefaultSubMenu sm1 = new DefaultSubMenu();
    sm1.setLabel("User Management");
    sm1.setIcon("ui-icon-person");
        DefaultSubMenu sm1Menu1 = new DefaultSubMenu();
        sm1Menu1.setLabel("View Users");
            DefaultMenuItem sm1Menu1Ite1 = new DefaultMenuItem();
            sm1Menu1Ite1.setValue("Moderators");
            sm1Menu1Ite1.setUrl("tieredMenu.jsf");
            DefaultMenuItem sm1Menu1Ite2 = new DefaultMenuItem();
            sm1Menu1Ite2.setValue("Normal Users");
            sm1Menu1Ite2.setCommand("#{menuController
                .showUserManagement()}");
            sm1Menu1Ite2.setAjax(false);
        sm1Menu1.addElement(sm1Menu1Ite1);
        sm1Menu1.addElement(sm1Menu1Ite2);
```

```
        DefaultMenuItem sm1Item2 = new DefaultMenuItem();
        sm1Item2.setValue("Monitor User Activity");
        sm1Item2.setCommand("#{menuController.
            showUserActivity()}");
        sm1Item2.setAjax(false);
    sm1.addElement(sm1Menu1);
    sm1.addElement(sm1Item2);
    menuModel.addElement(sm1);

    DefaultSubMenu sm2 = new DefaultSubMenu();
    sm2.setLabel("Tag Management");
    sm2.setIcon("ui-icon-tag");
        DefaultMenuItem sm2Item1 = new DefaultMenuItem();
        sm2Item1.setValue("View Tags");
        sm2Item1.setOutcome("menu");
        DefaultMenuItem sm2Item2 = new DefaultMenuItem();
        sm2Item2.setValue("Tag Stistics");
        sm2Item2.setUrl("menu.jsf");
    sm2.addElement(sm2Item1);
    sm2.addElement(sm2Item2);
    menuModel.addElement(sm2);

    DefaultMenuItem sm3 = new DefaultMenuItem();
    sm3.setValue("System Config");
    sm3.setIcon("ui-icon-gear");
    menuModel.addElement(sm3);
}
```

Here, we have created an instance of MenuModel and added the DefaultMenuItem and DefaultSubMenu type instances to MenuModel.

We have used the following methods to set various properties of the DefaultMenuItem and DefaultSubMenu components:

- menuItem.setValue(String) : Set the label of MenuItem.

- menuItem.setIcon(String): Set the icon name.

- menuItem.setOutcome(String): Set the outcome(facelets page) name.

- menuItem.setUrl(String): Set the target URL path.

- menuItem.setCommand(String): Binds the MethodExpression String to be invoked when MenuItem is clicked.

- menuItem.setAjax(Boolean): Enable or disable the AJAX submission mode.

- ◆ `submenu.setLabel(String)`: Set the Submenu header label.
- ◆ `submenu.setIcon(String)`: Set the icon name for the header.
- ◆ `submenu.addElement(Menuitem)`: Adds MenuItem or another nested Submenu to Submenu group.
- ◆ `menuModel.addElement(Menuitem)`: Adds a MenuItem or Submenu to MenuModel at root level.

Introducing the Menu component

Menu is a navigation component that can contain menuitems or submenus. We can create a Menu component either in declarative or programmatic way. In many of the web applications, there would be a left-hand side navigation bar that contains all the navigation links grouped according to related actions. To create such a navigation menu, we can use the `<p:menu>` component.

Time for action – creating a simple Menu

Let us see how to create a simple Menu in a declarative fashion, by performing the following step:

1. Create a Menu component using `<p:menu>` with `<p:menuitem>` and `<p:submenu>` to add menuitems and Submenu groups:

```
<p:menu>
    <p:menuitem value="System Config" outcome="menu"/>
    <p:submenu label="User Management" >
        <p:menuitem value="View Users"
            actionListener="#{menuController.
            showUserManagement()}"/>
        <p:menuitem value="Monitor User Activity"
            actionListener="#{menuController.
            showUserActivity()}" ajax="false"/>
    </p:submenu>
    <p:submenu label="Tag Management">
        <p:menuitem value="View Tags" url="menu.jsf"/>
        <p:menuitem value="Tag Statistics" outcome="menu"/>
    </p:submenu>
</p:menu>
```

What just happened?

In the preceding code snippet, we have created a menu using the `<p:menu>` component. We have added a MenuItem, `<p:menuitem>`, directly at the root level and added two Submenu `<p:submenu>` elements, which in turn contains `<p:menuitem>` elements. This menu component will be displayed as shown in the following screenshot:

As you can see, the first MenuItem is added to the menu at the root level without any header, and Submenu items are displayed with a header name that we have mentioned using the `label` attribute.

Instead of static menus created in declarative fashion, we can create dynamic menus programmatically by binding an instance of the `org.primefaces.model.MenuModel` type to the `model` attribute:

```
<p:menu model="#{menuController.menuModel}"></p:menu>
```

Displaying Menu based on trigger

By default, Menu will be displayed as an inline component on the page load. Instead of displaying as an inline menu, we can set the `overlay` attribute to `true` and define a trigger to show the menu. The position of the menu will be relative to the trigger component and specified using the `my` and `at` attributes:

- ◆ `my`: Corner of menu to align with the trigger element.
- ◆ `at`: Corner of trigger to align with the Menu element.

The valid values for my and at is a combination of:

- left
- right
- bottom
- top

Time for action – displaying an overlay menu with trigger

Let us see how we can create a menu that will be displayed on clicking a button, by performing the following step:

1. Create an overlay menu and define a trigger component to show it:

```
<p:commandButton id="overlayBtn" value="ShowMenu"
    type="button"/>
<p:menu overlay="true" trigger="overlayBtn" my="left top"
    at="right bottom">
    <p:menuitem value="System Config" outcome="menu"/>
    <p:submenu label="User Management" >
        <p:menuitem value="View Users"
            actionListener="#{menuController.
            showUserManagement()}"/>
        <p:menuitem value="Monitor User Activity"
            actionListener="#{menuController.
            showUserActivity()}" ajax="false"/>
    </p:submenu>
    <p:submenu label="Tag Management">
        <p:menuitem value="View Tags" url="menu.jsf"/>
        <p:menuitem value="Tag Statistics" outcome="menu"/>
    </p:submenu>
</p:menu>
```

What just happened?

We have created a menu and bound the trigger attribute to id of commandButton. Once the page is loaded, only the **ShowMenu** button will be displayed. When you click on the **ShowMenu** button, the menu will be displayed at the position as per the my and at attribute values.

By default, the `click` event on the trigger component displays the menu. You can change it using the `triggerEvent` attribute:

```
<p:menu overlay="true" trigger="overlayBtn" triggerEvent="mouseover"
    my="left top" at="left bottom">
...
</p:menu>
```

Introducing the MenuButton component

MenuButton is a menu component that will display one or more menuitems in a pop-up menu.

Time for action – creating MenuButton

Let us see how we can create MenuButton declaratively, by performing the following steps:

1. Create the MenuButton component using `<p:menuButton>`:

```
<p:menuButton value="Administration">
    <p:menuitem value="View Users"
        actionListener="#{menuController.
        showUserManagement()}"/>

    <p:menuitem value="Tag Management" outcome="menuButton"/>
    <p:menuitem value="System Config" url="menuButton.jsf"/>
</p:menuButton>
```

The preceding MenuButton component will be rendered as shown in the following screenshot:

2. We can also build the same the MenuButton component programmatically as follows:

```
<p:menuButton value="Administration" model="#{menuController.
menuButtonModel}"></p:menuButton>
```

3. Create menuButtonModel, which is an instance of type org.primefaces. model.MenuModel:

```
public MenuModel getMenuButtonModel()
{
    MenuModel menuButtonModel = new DefaultMenuModel();

    DefaultMenuItem item1 = new DefaultMenuItem();
    item1.setValue("View Users");
    item1.setCommand("#{menuController.showUserManagement()}");
    menuButtonModel.addElement(item1);

    DefaultMenuItem item2 = new DefaultMenuItem();
    item2.setValue("Tag Management");
    item2.setOutcome("menuButton");
    menuButtonModel.addElement(item2);

    DefaultMenuItem item3 = new DefaultMenuItem();
    item3.setValue("System Config");
    item3.setUrl("menuButton.jsf");
    menuButtonModel.addElement(item3);

    return menuButtonModel;
}
```

What just happened?

We have learned how to create the MenuButton component both declaratively and programmatically.

Displaying multilevel nested menus using TieredMenu

TieredMenu is a menu component that can be used to display nested submenus with overlays. Similar to the `<p:menu>` component, TieredMenu can be created programmatically and also supports the trigger-based menu display.

Time for action – displaying a multilevel menu using TieredMenu

Let us see how to create a TieredMenu with multilevel nested submenus, by performing the following step:

1. Create a TieredMenu component with multilevel menu options using nested `<p:submenu>` elements:

    ```
    <p:tieredMenu style="width:180px">
        <p:submenu label="User Management" icon="ui-icon-person">
            <p:submenu label="View Users">
                <p:menuitem value="Moderators"
                    url="tieredMenu.jsf"/>
                <p:menuitem value="Normal Users"
                    actionListener="#{menuController.
                    showUserManagement()}"/>
            </p:submenu>
            <p:menuitem value="Monitor User Activity"
                actionListener="#{menuController.
                showUserActivity()}" ajax="false"/>
        </p:submenu>
        <p:submenu label="Tag Management" icon="ui-icon-tag">
            <p:menuitem value="View Tags" url="tieredMenu.jsf"/>
            <p:menuitem value="Tag Stistics"
                outcome="tieredMenu"/>
        </p:submenu>
        <p:submenu label="System Config" icon="ui-icon-gear">
            <p:menuitem value="Email Server" icon="ui-icon-mail-
                closed" outcome="tieredMenu"/>
        </p:submenu>
    </p:tieredMenu>
    ```

What just happened?

We have created a TieredMenu component that displays multilevel submenu options as shown in the following screenshot:

The TieredMenu component can also be created programmatically and can be displayed using a trigger component:

```
<p:commandButton id="menuButton" value="ShowMenu" type="button"/>
<p:tieredMenu overlay="true" trigger="menuButton"
    model="#{menuController.menuModel}" my="left top" at="right
    bottom"/>
```

By default, Submenu options will be displayed when you hover the mouse over the Submenu header. We can set the attribute `autoDisplay="false"`, so that Submenu options will only be displayed when you click on the Submenu.

Creating nested menus with SlideMenu

SlideMenu is a menu component that can be used to display nested submenus with sliding animation. When you click on any Submenu, the menuitems will be displayed along with a **Back** button to navigate back to the parent-level menu.

Time for action – creating the SlideMenu component

Let us see how we can create a SlideMenu, by performing the following step:

1. Create SlideMenu with multilevel submenus using `<p:slideMenu>` declaratively:

```
<p:slideMenu style="width:180px">
    <p:submenu label="User Management" icon="ui-icon-person">
        <p:submenu label="View Users">
            <p:menuitem value="Moderators"
                outcome="slideMenu"/>
            <p:menuitem value="Normal Users"
                actionListener="#{menuController.
                showUserManagement()}"/>
        </p:submenu>
```

```
                <p:menuitem value="Monitor User Activity"
                    actionListener="#{menuController.
                    showUserActivity()}" ajax="false"/>
        </p:submenu>
        <p:submenu label="Tag Management" icon="tag-icon">
            <p:menuitem value="View Tags" url="slideMenu.jsf"/>
            <p:menuitem value="Tag Stistics" outcome="slideMenu"/>
        </p:submenu>
        <p:submenu label="System Config" icon="ui-icon-gear">
            <p:menuitem value="View Configuration"
                outcome="slideMenu"/>
        </p:submenu>
    </p:slideMenu>
```

What just happened?

The preceding code will display a SlideMenu as shown in the following screenshot:

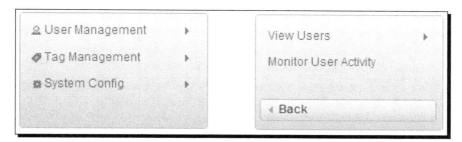

When you click on the **User Management** MenuItem, then Submenu items will be displayed along with a **Back** button to navigate back to the parent menu.

The SlideMenu component can also be created programmatically, can be displayed using a trigger component, and supports enabling or disabling the `autoDisplay` feature.

Creating a horizontal navigation menu using Menubar

Menubar is a horizontal navigation menu that can be used to display multilevel menuitems and submenus. We can use the same MenuModel used for previous menu components for the Menubar component as well.

Time for action – creating a Menubar component

Let us see how to create a Menubar component, by performing the following step:

1. Create a Menubar component using `<p:menubar>` declaratively:

```
<p:menubar autoDisplay="false">
    <p:submenu label="User Management" icon="ui-icon-person">
        <p:menuitem value="Disable/Enable Users"
            actionListener="#{menuController.
            showUserManagement()}"/>
        <p:menuitem value="View User Activity"
            actionListener="#{menuController.
            showUserActivity()}" ajax="false"/>
    </p:submenu>
    <p:submenu label="Tag Management" icon="ui-icon-tag">
        <p:menuitem value="View Tags" url="menubar.jsf"/>
        <p:menuitem value="Create Tag" outcome="menubar"/>
    </p:submenu>
    <p:submenu label="System Config" icon="ui-icon-gear">
        <p:submenu label="Global Settings">
            <p:menuitem value="Cache Settings"
                url="menubar.jsf"/>
            <p:menuitem value="User Lock Policy"
                outcome="menubar"/>
        </p:submenu>
        <p:submenu label="Email Service">
            <p:menuitem value="SMTP Settings"
                url="menubar.jsf"/>
        </p:submenu>
    </p:submenu>
</p:menubar>
```

What just happened?

We have created the Menubar component with three Submenu components at the root level using `<p:submenu>` and added menuitems for each Submenu using `<p:menuitem>`. We also added a nested Submenu for the **System Config** MenuItem. The preceding code renders a Menubar component as shown in the following screenshot:

Similar to other menu components, the Menubar component also supports creating menu options programmatically and enabling/disabling the `autoDisplay` feature.

Creating a multicolumn menu using MegaMenu

MegaMenu is a horizontal navigation menu that displays menu options in the grid layout and each MenuItem and Submenu should be defined inside a `<p:column>` element.

Generally, in e-commerce applications, there might be many subcategories in each category. In such scenarios, we can use MegaMenu to display all submenus at once, instead of letting the user navigate through multiple levels of tiered menus.

Time for action – creating MegaMenu with multiple columns

Let us see how to create a multicolumn menu using the MegaMenu component, by performing the following step:

1. Create the MegaMenu component with multiple columns using `<p:column>` to group the menu options into a column:

```
<p:megaMenu>
    <p:submenu label="Users">
        <p:column>
            <p:submenu label="Normal Users">
                <p:menuitem value="View Users" url="#"/>
                <p:menuitem value="User Activity" url="#"/>
            </p:submenu>
            <p:submenu label="Inactive Users">
                <p:menuitem value="View Inactive Users"
                    url="#"/>
                <p:menuitem value="Unlock Users" url="#"/>
            </p:submenu>
        </p:column>
        <p:column>
            <p:submenu label="Moderators">
                <p:menuitem value="View Moderators" url="#"/>
                <p:menuitem value="Deleted Buzz" url="#"/>
            </p:submenu>
        </p:column>
    </p:submenu>

    <p:submenu label="Tags">
        <p:column>
            <p:submenu label="Tag Management">
                <p:menuitem value="View Tags" url="#"/>
                <p:menuitem value="Create Tags" url="#"/>
            </p:submenu>
```

```
                </p:column>
                <p:column>
                    <p:submenu label="Tag Usage">
                        <p:menuitem value="Tags Statistics" url="#"/>
                        <p:menuitem value="Tags usage By User"
                            url="#"/>
                    </p:submenu>
                </p:column>
            </p:submenu>

            <p:submenu label="Configuration">
                <p:column>
                    <p:submenu label="Global Settings">
                        <p:menuitem value="Cache Settings" url="#"/>
                        <p:menuitem value="User Lock Policy" url="#"/>
                    </p:submenu>
                    <p:submenu label="Email Server Settings">
                        <p:menuitem value="SMTP Settings" url="#"/>
                        <p:menuitem value="POP3 Settings" url="#"/>
                    </p:submenu>
                </p:column>
            </p:submenu>

        </p:megaMenu>
```

What just happened?

We have created a MegaMenu component to display three root-level menus: **Users**, **Tags**, and **Configuration**. In each menu, we are displaying all the submenus and menuitems in multiple columns.

The preceding code displays a MegaMenu component as shown in the following screenshot:

Creating tab-based menus using TabMenu

TabMenu is a navigation component that displays menuitems as tabs. TabMenu takes a list of menuitems and displays each as a tab. Similar to other menu components, we can do GET requests to MenuItem using the `url` or `outcome` attributes and can send POST requests using the `action` or `actionListener` attributes.

In the TechBuzz application, we will be using the TabMenu component to display a top-level navigation bar to display the **Home**, **Post Buzz**, **Search**, and **My Account** screens as tabs.

Time for action – creating the TabMenu component

Let us see how to create a TabMenu component, by performing the following step:

1. Create the TabMenu component with four Menu options to show the **Home**, **Post Buzz**, **Search**, and **My Account** screens:

```
<p:tabMenu activeIndex="0">
    <p:menuitem value="Home" url="home.jsf" icon="ui-icon-
        home"/>
    <p:menuitem value="Post Buzz" outcome="newPost"    icon="ui-
        icon-document"/>
    <p:menuitem value="Search"
        action="#{menuController.showSearchPage}" ajax="false"
        icon="ui-icon-search" />
    <p:menuitem value="My Account"
        actionListener="#{menuController.showMyAccount()}"
        icon="ui-icon-person" />
</p:tabMenu>
```

What just happened?

The preceding code renders a TabMenu component as shown in the following screenshot:

Here, we have associated various types of requests for each MenuItem. For the **Home** tab, we have bound a GET request to `home.jsf` using the `url` attribute. For the **Post Buzz** tab, we associated a GET request using the `outcome` attribute to show the `newPost.xhtml` facelets page. For the **Search** tab, we bound a non-AJAX POST request to invoke the `menuController.showSearchPage()` method using the `action` attribute. For the **My Account** tab, we associated an AJAX POST request to invoke the `actionListener` attribute's method `menuController.showMyAccount()`.

Only one of the tabs of a TabMenu component will be displayed as an active tab, based on the `activeIndex` value. So, in the preceding TabMenu component, the **Home** tab will be displayed as active.

But in applications, we might need to keep track of `activeIndex` dynamically, based on the tab that the user clicked.

Time for action – tracking an active tab dynamically

Let us see how we can maintain the `activeIndex` value of the tab that the user clicked, so that we can display the user-clicked tab as an active tab, by performing the following steps:

1. To dynamically keep track of the active tab, we can create a template containing the TabMenu definition with `activeIndex` bound to a dynamic property:

```
<ui:composition xmlns="http://www.w3.org/1999/xhtml"
    xmlns:ui="http://java.sun.com/jsf/facelets"
    xmlns:p="http://primefaces.org/ui">

    <p:tabMenu activeIndex="#{activeIndex}">
        <p:menuitem value="Home" url="home.jsf" icon="ui-icon-
            home"/>
        <p:menuitem value="Post Buzz" outcome="tabMenu"
            icon="ui-icon-document"/>
        <p:menuitem value="Search"
            action="#{menuController.showSearchPage}"
            ajax="false" icon="ui-icon-search" />
        <p:menuitem value="My Account"
            actionListener="#{menuController.showMyAccount()}"
            icon="ui-icon-person" />
    </p:tabMenu>

</ui:composition>
```

2. In client pages, we can include that template using `<ui:insert>` and pass the `activeIndex` parameter value using `<ui:param>` as follows:

   To display the first tab as an active tab, pass the `activeIndex` parameter's value as 0.

```
<ui:include file="/tabMenuTemplate.xhtml">
    <ui:param name="activeIndex" value="0" />
</ui:include>
```

   To display the second tab as an active tab, pass the `activeIndex` parameter's value as 1.

```
<ui:include file="/tabMenuTemplate.xhtml">
    <ui:param name="activeIndex" value="1" />
</ui:include>
```

What just happened?

We have created a template for showing TabMenu with all the tabs definitions and we are including this template in each screen using `<ui:include>`. Instead of hard coding the TabView `activeIndex` value, we are getting the `activeIndex` value as a parameter from individual screens using `<ui:param>`.

Similar to other Menu components, we can build the TabMenu component's MenuModel programmatically and use the `model` attribute to bind Menu options.

Introducing the PanelMenu component

PanelMenu is a hybrid component of AccordionPanel and Tree components where the leaf nodes can be used as navigational menuitems to send GET or POST requests. First-level submenus will be rendered as AccordionPanels and descendant submenus rendered as Tree nodes.

Time for action – creating the PanelMenu component

Let us see how to create a PanelMenu component, by performing the following step:

1. Create the PanelMenu component using `<p:panelMenu>` and add menuitems and submenus using `<p:menuitem>` and `<p:submenu>`:

```
<p:panelMenu style="width:200px">
    <p:submenu label="User Management">
        <p:submenu label="View Users" icon="ui-icon-person">
            <p:menuitem value="Moderators" url="#"   />
            <p:menuitem value="Normal Users"
                actionListener="#{menuController.
                showUserManagement()}"/>
        </p:submenu>
    </p:submenu>
    <p:submenu label="Tag Management">
        <p:menuitem value="View Tags" url="panelMenu.jsf"
            icon="ui-icon-tag"/>
        <p:menuitem value="Tag Stistics" outcome="panelMenu"
            icon="ui-icon-image"/>
    </p:submenu>
    <p:submenu label="System Config" >
        <p:menuitem value="View Configuration"
            outcome="panelMenu" icon="ui-icon-gear"/>
    </p:submenu>
</p:panelMenu>
```

What just happened?

The preceding code renders a PanelMenu component as shown in the following screenshot:

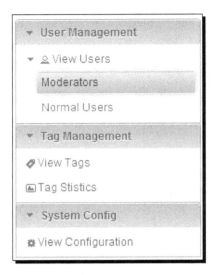

Here, top-level submenus **User Management**, **Tag Management**, and **System Config** are displayed as AccordionPanel headers and the nested submenus and menuitems are displayed as Tree nodes.

The PanelMenu component stores the submenus in open or close state in cookies and maintains that state across the web pages. The cookie name is `panelMenu-<id>`, where `<id>` is the client ID of `<p:panelMenu>`. When the user navigates to the same page again, PanelMenu will be displayed in the same state as it was in the previously viewed state. If you want to turn off this feature, you can either call the widget's `clearState()` method or clear the cookie from response on the server side.

Introducing ContextMenu

The ContextMenu component can be used to display an overlay menu on the mouse's right-click event. Optionally, we can attach ContextMenu to any JSF component and contain nested submenus and menuitems. If you don't specify any particular JSF component, ContextMenu will be attached to the entire page, meaning right-clicking anywhere on the page will display the same ContextMenu.

The ContextMenu component provides the following attributes to customize its behavior:

- ◆ `for`: ID of the component to attach to.
- ◆ `event`: Event to bind the ContextMenu display, default is `contextmenu`, which means right-click.
- ◆ `model`: The MenuModel instance to create menu programmatically.
- ◆ `nodeType`: Specific type of Tree nodes to attach to.
- ◆ `beforeShow`: Client-side callback to execute before showing.

Time for action – creating ContextMenu

Let us see how to create a page-level and component-level ContextMenu, by performing the following steps:

1. Create a ContextMenu component with menu options using `<p:menuitem>` and `<p:submenu>`:

```
<p:contextMenu>
    <p:submenu label="PrimeFaces">
    <p:menuitem value="Website"
        url="http://www.primefaces.org"/>
    <p:menuitem value="Showcase"
        url="http://www.primefaces.org/showcase/ui/home.jsf"/>
        <p:menuitem value="Forum"
            url="http://forum.primefaces.org/"/>
        <p:menuitem value="IssueTracker"
            url="http://www.primefaces.org/issuetracker.html"/>
    </p:submenu>
    <p:submenu label="jQuery">
        <p:menuitem value="jQuery" url="http://jquery.com/"/>
        <p:menuitem value="jQueryUI"
            url="http://jqueryui.com/"/>
    </p:submenu>
    <p:menuitem value="JSF"
        url="http://javaserverfaces.java.net/"/>
</p:contextMenu>
```

With the preceding ContextMenu component definition, if you right-click anywhere on the page, an overlay menu will be displayed with submenus and menuitems.

2. We can attach a ContextMenu component to many particular JSF components using the `for` attribute. Let us see how to attach the preceding ContextMenu to a Button component:

```
<p:button id="myButton" value="ShowMenu"/>
<p:contextMenu for="myButton">
```

```
    . . .
</p:contextMenu>
```

With the preceding code, ContextMenu will be displayed when you right-click on the
ShowMenu button.

What just happened?

We have learned how to create a page-level ContextMenu as well as bind a ContextMenu to
a particular JSF component. With the preceding code, if you right-click on the **ShowMenu**
button, ContextMenu will be displayed as shown in the following screenshot:

Integrating DataTable with ContextMenu

Data components such as DataTable, Tree, and TreeTable have special integration with
ContextMenu. Let us see how to attach a ContextMenu to a DataTable to display a menu
with the **View** and **Disable** options, when you right-click on table rows.

Time for action – creating ContextMenu for DataTable

In this section, we will take a look at how we can integrate ContextMenu with DataTable,
so that we will see a custom menu instead of a browser menu, when you right-click on any
DataTable row, by performing the following steps:

1. Create a DataTable component with the single row selection mode:

```
<p:dataTable id="usersTbl" var="user"
    value="#{adminController.users}" style="width: 300px;"
        paginator="true" rows="5" selectionMode="single"
            selection="#{adminController.selectedUser}"
            rowKey="#{user.id}" >
    <f:facet name="header">
        List of Users
    </f:facet>
```

```
<p:column headerText="Id" width="20px;">
    <h:outputText value="#{user.id}" />
</p:column>

<p:column headerText="Email" >
    <h:outputText value="#{user.emailId}" />
</p:column>
</p:dataTable>
```

2. Create a Dialog component to display the selected user details:

```
<p:dialog widgetVar="selectedUserDlg">
    <h:panelGrid id="userDetails" columns="2" >

        <h:outputText value="Id:" />
        <h:outputText
            value="#{adminController.selectedUser.id}" />

        <h:outputText value="Email:" />
        <h:outputText
        value="#{adminController.selectedUser.emailId}" />

        <h:outputText value="FirstName:" />
        <h:outputText
            value="#{adminController.selectedUser.firstName}"
            />

        <h:outputText value="LastName:" />
        <h:outputText value="#{adminController.selectedUser.
lastName}" />

    </h:panelGrid>
</p:dialog>
```

3. Create a ContextMenu component and attach it to DataTable with two menuitems for viewing and disabling the selected user record:

```
<p:contextMenu for="usersTbl">
    <p:menuitem value="View" update="userDetails" icon="ui-
        icon-search" oncomplete="selectedUserDlg.show()"/>
    <p:menuitem value="Disable" update="usersTbl" icon="ui-
        icon-close" actionListener="#{adminController.
        disableSelectedUser}"/>
</p:contextMenu>
```

What just happened?

We have created a DataTable component with the single row selection mode. We have created a ContextMenu with the **View** and **Disable** menuitems and attached it to the DataTable. When you right-click on any row, it will display a ContextMenu as shown in the following screenshot:

When the **View** MenuItem is clicked, we are displaying selected user details in a dialog box. When the **Disable** MenuItem is clicked, an AJAX POST request will be executed to invoke the `adminController.disableSelectedUser()` method.

Integrating Tree with ContextMenu

The Tree component has a finer integration with ContextMenu to display a separate context menu for different node types.

Let us see how we can attach a different ContextMenu for the `document` and `picture` type Tree nodes.

Time for action – creating ContextMenu for the Tree component

In this section, we will take a look at how we can integrate ContextMenu with Tree, so that we will see a custom menu instead of the browser menu, when you right-click on any Tree node, by performing the following steps:

1. Create a Tree component with single selection mode having different node types such as `document`, `picture`, and `video`:

```
<p:tree id="docTree" value="#{treeController.rootx}" var="node"
    animate="true" style="width: 350px;"
```

```
        selectionMode="single"
            selection="#{treeController.selectedNode}">
        <p:ajax event="select" update=":form:docNode,:form:picNode"
            />
        <p:treeNode expandedIcon="ui-icon-folder-open"
            collapsedIcon="ui-icon-folder-collapsed">
            <h:outputText value="#{node}"/>
        </p:treeNode>
        <p:treeNode type="document" icon="ui-icon-document">
            <h:outputText value="#{node}" />
        </p:treeNode>
        <p:treeNode type="picture" icon="ui-icon-image">
            <h:outputText value="#{node}" />
        </p:treeNode>
        <p:treeNode type="video" icon="ui-icon-video">
            <h:outputText value="#{node}" />
        </p:treeNode>
    </p:tree>
```

2. Create two dialog components to display the `document` and `picture` type selected nodes:

```
<p:dialog id="docNode" widgetVar="docNodeDlg" header="Selected
    Document Node">
    <h:outputText value="#{treeController.selectedNode.data}"
        />
</p:dialog>

<p:dialog id="picNode" widgetVar="picNodeDlg" header="Selected
    Picture Node">
    <h:outputText value="#{treeController.selectedNode.data}"
        />
</p:dialog>
```

3. Create two context menus and associate them to the Tree component's `document` and `picture` type nodes:

```
<p:contextMenu for="docTree" nodeType="document">
    <p:menuitem value="View Document" icon="ui-icon-search"
        oncomplete="docNodeDlg.show()"/>
</p:contextMenu>

<p:contextMenu for="docTree" nodeType="picture">
    <p:menuitem value="View Picture" icon="ui-icon-search"
        oncomplete="picNodeDlg.show()"/>
</p:contextMenu>
```

What just happened?

We have created a Tree component with the single selection mode and various node types such as document, picture, and video. We have created one ContextMenu and associated it with the document type Tree nodes and another ContextMenu attached to the picture type tree nodes. When you right-click on the document type nodes, we will see the ContextMenu associated with document nodes. Similarly, when you right-click on picture type nodes, we will see the ContextMenu associated with picture type nodes:

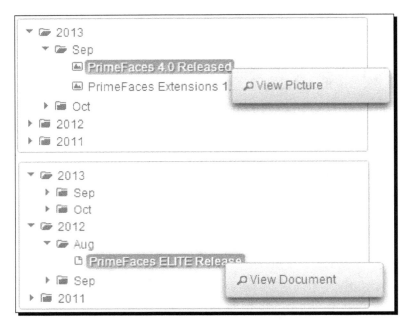

Introducing the Breadcrumb navigation menu

Breadcrumb is a navigation component that provides contextual information about the page hierarchy in the workflow. The Breadcrumb menu provide links back to each previous page the user navigated through, to get to the current page.

Time for action – creating the Breadcrumb menu

Let us see how to create a Breadcrumb menu, by performing the following step:

1. Create a Breadcrumb menu and provide navigation menu options using `<p:menuitem>`:

```
<p:breadCrumb>
    <p:menuitem value="PrimeFaces"
        url="http://www.primefaces.org/" />
    <p:menuitem value="Board index"
        url="http://forum.primefaces.org/index.php" />
    <p:menuitem value="JavaServer Faces"
        url="http://forum.primefaces.org/viewforum.php?f=19" />
    <p:menuitem value="General"
        url="http://forum.primefaces.org/viewforum.php?f=3" />
</p:breadCrumb>
```

What just happened?

The preceding code displays the Breadcrumb menu component as shown in the following screenshot:

The preceding Breadcrumb menu component is a static menu. But for many of the web applications, Breadcrumb menus should be dynamic, reflecting their current location in the page hierarchy.

Time for action – creating the Breadcrumb menu programmatically

We can create dynamic Breadcrumb menus by creating a MenuModel object programmatically and binding the `<p:breadcrumb>` component's `model` attribute to the MenuModel instance as follows:

```
<p:breadCrumb model="#{menuController.breadcrumbMenuModel}"/>
```

1. Create the MenuModel component and add menuitems:

```
public MenuController()
{
    breadcrumbMenuModel = new DefaultMenuModel();
    MenuItem item1 = new MenuItem();
    item1.setValue("PrimeFaces");
    item1.setUrl("http://www.primefaces.org/");
```

```
        breadcrumbMenuModel.addMenuItem(item1);

        MenuItem item2 = new MenuItem();
        item2.setValue("Board index");
        item2.setUrl("http://forum.primefaces.org/index.php");
        breadcrumbMenuModel.addMenuItem(item2);

        MenuItem item3 = new MenuItem();
        item3.setValue("JavaServer Faces");
        item3.setUrl("http://forum.primefaces.
            org/viewforum.php?f=19");
        breadcrumbMenuModel.addMenuItem(item3);

        MenuItem item4 = new MenuItem();
        item4.setValue("General");
        item4.setUrl("http://forum.primefaces.
            org/viewforum.php?f=3");
        breadcrumbMenuModel.addMenuItem(item4);
    }
```

What just happened?

Here, we have created a dynamic Breadcrumb menu by using instantiating MenuModel programmatically. For the menuitems, we have associated GET requests by setting the `url` property. We can also associate AJAX or non-AJAX POST requests by setting the `action` or `actionListener` attributes:

- ◆ The first MenuItem of the Breadcrumb menu will be displayed as the home icon
- ◆ In addition to GET requests using the `url` attribute, we can also send AJAX or non-AJAX POST requests using the `action` or `actionListener` attributes
- ◆ If you specify both the `url` and `action/actionListener` attributes, then `url` takes precedence and performs a GET request and will not invoke `action/actionListener` methods

Summary

In this chapter, we have learned how to create and use menus declaratively and programmatically. We have seen how to create simple menus using the Menu component, and multilevel menus using the TieredMenu and SlideMenu components. We also looked into creating horizontal navigation menus using the Menubar and MegaMenu components. We learned how to create ContextMenu and attach it to various other JSF components such as DataTable and Tree. Finally, we learned how to create Breadcrumb menus to display current contextual location of the page hierarchy.

In the next chapter, we will look into drawing various types of charts, such as Line, Bar, and Pie charts, and exporting them as images.

12

Drawing Charts

Businesses use various reporting tools to compare results and measure performance. Often businesses want reports in graphical representations such as charts so that it will be easy to compare the results and measure the overall performance of their business. PrimeFaces provides support for creating various types of charts, such as Line, Area, Bar, Pie, Donut, Bubble, MeterGauge, and Open High Low Close (OHLC). PrimeFaces also supports rendering charts generated by JFreeCharts.

In our TechBuzz application, administrators can see the statistics of the number of posts by tags, in each year, with graphical representation using various types of charts.

In this chapter, we will cover the following commonly used charts:

◆ Creating a Line chart
◆ Creating an Area chart
◆ Creating a Bar chart
◆ Creating a Pie chart
◆ Creating a Donut chart
◆ Exporting charts as images
◆ Rendering dynamic charts using the JFreeChart API
◆ Creating interactive charts using the ItemSelect AJAX event

Creating a Line chart

A Line chart represents a series of data points in a line graph. The Line chart data model should be an instance of `org.primefaces.model.chart.CartesianChartModel`.

Let us see how to visualize a number of posts for various tags in each year using the Line chart.

```
<p:lineChart value="#{chartController.chartModel}"
   legendPosition="se"/>
```

The `chartModel` can be created and initialized as follows:

```
public ChartController()
{
   CartesianChartModel chartModel = new CartesianChartModel();

   ChartSeries primefacesSeries = new ChartSeries();
   primefacesSeries.setLabel("PrimeFaces");
   primefacesSeries.set("2009", 150);
   primefacesSeries.set("2010", 250);
   primefacesSeries.set("2011", 300);
   primefacesSeries.set("2012", 240);
   primefacesSeries.set("2013", 400);

   ChartSeries jquerySeries = new ChartSeries();
   querySeries.setLabel("jQuery");
   jquerySeries.set("2009", 210);
   jquerySeries.set("2010", 150);
   jquerySeries.set("2011", 200);
   jquerySeries.set("2012", 280);
   jquerySeries.set("2013", 320);

   chartModel.addSeries(primefacesSeries);
   chartModel.addSeries(jquerySeries);
}
public CartesianChartModel getChartModel()
{
   return chartModel;
}
```

The preceding Line chart component renders as follows:

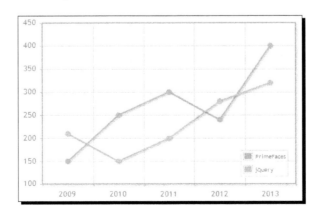

Here, we have created a Line chart with two series of data representing the number of posts with tags, PrimeFaces and jQuery from the year 2009 to 2013. We also mentioned displaying legends in the SouthEast position using `legendPosition="se"`. The other possible `legendPosition` values are nw, w, sw, ne, or e, representing NorthWest, West, SouthWest, NorthEast, East, and SouthEast respectively.

The Line chart component supports the following attributes to customize its representation and behavior:

◆ **title**: This is the title of the chart.

◆ **legendPosition**: This is the position of the legend.

◆ **minX**: This is the minimum X axis value.

◆ **maxX**: This is the maximum X axis value.

◆ **minY**: This is the minimum Y axis value.

◆ **maxY**: This is the maximum Y axis value.

◆ **xaxisLabel**: This is the label of the x-axis.

◆ **yaxisLabel**: This is the label of the y-axis.

◆ **xaxisAngle**: This is the angle of the x-axis ticks.

◆ **yaxisAngle**: This is the angle of the y-axis ticks.

◆ **breakOnNull**: This determines whether line segments should be broken at null value. False will join points on either side of the line. The default value of it is false.

◆ **seriesColors**: This is the comma-separated list of colors in hex format.

◆ **zoom**: This enables plot zooming. The default value for it is false.

◆ **animate**: This enables the animation on plot rendering. The default value for it is false.

◆ **shadow**: This shows the shadow effect or not. The default value for it is true.

◆ **fill**: This is set to true to fill under lines. The default value for it is false.

◆ **stacked**: This is set to true to stack series. The default value for it is false.

◆ **showMarkers**: If enabled, this shows markers at data points. The default value for it is true.

◆ **legendCols**: This is the column count of legend. The default value for it is 1.

◆ **legendRows**: This is the row count of legend.

◆ **showDataTip**: This defines the visibility of dataTip. The default for it is true.

◆ **datatipFormat**: This is the template for datatips.

◆ **extender**: This is the client-side JavaScript function to extend the chart with jqPlot options.

Let us see how we can create a Line chart with various customizations such as labels on X and Y axes, custom series colors, zooming, and animation.

Time for action – creating a Line chart

In this section, we will create a Line chart depicting the number of posts with PrimeFaces and jQuery tags from years 2009 to 2013.

1. Create a Line chart with custom labels, axis angles, series colors, and enable zooming and animation.

```
<p:lineChart value="#{chartController.chartModel}"
  style="width: 450px; height: 300px;"
  title="Linear Chart"
  legendPosition="nw"
  xaxisLabel="Year" yaxisLabel="No. of Posts"
  xaxisAngle="45" yaxisAngle="45"
  minY="0" maxY="1000"
  breakOnNull="true" zoom="true" animate="true"
  seriesColors="800000,006400"
  legendCols="2"/>
```

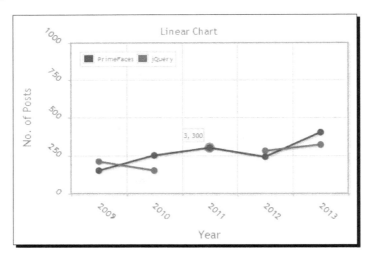

What just happened?

Here, we have specified the labels and angles for X-axis and Y-axis. We have also customized the series to display `#800000` and `#006400` colors instead of the default colors. As we have specified `breakOnNull="true"` the jQuery series disconnected at year 2011. If you set `breakOnNull="false"`, which is the default, the jQuery data point at year 2010 will be directly connected to the data point at year 2012.

We have enabled zooming by setting `zoom="true"` and hence we can zoom any region of the chart by selecting the region on the canvas plot.

 It seems some of the chart components such as Line and Bar charts missed the dependency of `jquery-plugins.js`. If the charts are not rendering and showing errors such as **TypeError: c.browser is undefined** then include the `jquery-plugins.js` manually. You can obtain the `jquery-plugins.js` file from `primefaces-4.0.jar/META-INF/resources/primefaces/jquery/jquery-plugins.js`.

When you move your mouse over any data point, a dataTip will be displayed showing **[index, value]**. We can customize the dataTip by setting a tip format using the `datatipFormat` attribute as follows:

```
<p:lineChart title="Line Chart" value="#{chartController.chartModel}"
    legendPosition="nw" style="width: 450px; height: 300px;"
    datatipFormat="#{chartController.datatipFormat}"
    />

public String getDatatipFormat()
{
    return "<span style=\"display:none;\">%s</span><span>No. of Posts:
    %s</span>";
}
```

 In the custom `dataTipFormat`, the first `%s` represents `index` and the second `%s` represents `value`.

The PrimeFaces chart components use the jqPlot charting library (`http://www.jqplot.com/`) which is a canvas-based charting engine. The PrimeFaces chart components provide support for many of the commonly used options. However jqPlot charts support many more customization options. To make those jqPlot options available, PrimeFaces provides an Extender feature to utilize and configure those advanced configuration options.

```
<p:pieChart value="#{chartController.pieChartModel}"
    style="width: 350px; height: 250px;"
    legendPosition="ne"
    extender="ext"/>

<script type="text/javascript">
    function ext()
    {
```

```
      //this = chart widget instance
      //this.cfg = options
      this.cfg.grid= {
        borderColor: '#A52A2A',
        borderWidth: 2,
        background: '#FAEBD7'
      };
    }
  </script>
```

For more jqPlot options see `http://www.jqplot.com/docs/files/optionsTutorial-txt.html`.

By default, markers will be displayed at data points as `filledCircles`. We can customize them by using `org.primefaces.model.chart.LineChartSeries` instead of `org.primefaces.model.chart.ChartSeries` and set marker styles using `lineChartSeries.setMarkerStyle("diamond")`. Valid values for marker styles are `circle`, `diamond`, `square`, `filledCircle`, `filledDiamond`, or `filledSquare`.

We can also set different marker styles using the `extender` feature as follows:

```
this.cfg.seriesDefaults.markerOptions = {
    style: 'square'
};
```

Creating an Area chart

We can create an Area chart using the Line chart component by setting `fill="true"` to fill under the lines from the X-axis, which visually looks like an Area chart. Also, we can set `stacked="true"` to display the series stacked on top of the other series by adding data sets.

Let us see how we can create Area charts using the `<p:lineChart>` component by using `fill` and `stacked` attributes.

```
<p:lineChart title="Area Chart" value="#{chartController.chartModel}"
   legendPosition="nw" style="width: 450px; height: 300px;"
   xaxisLabel="Year" yaxisLabel="No. of Posts" xaxisAngle="45"
     yaxisAngle="45"
   minY="0" maxY="1000"
   fill="true" stacked="true"/>
```

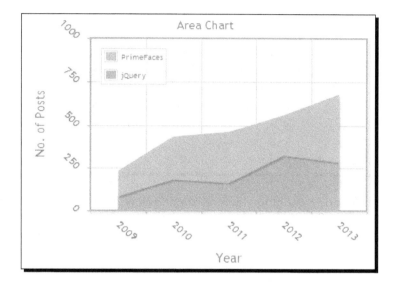

Here we have created a Stacked Area chart using the `<p:lineChart>` component by setting `fill="true"` and `stacked="true"`.

Creating a Bar chart

The Bar chart component visualizes a series of data points as bars. We can use the same `org.primefaces.model.chart.CartesianChartModel` type instance, which we used for the Line chart, to provide the data for the Bar chart.

Let us create a Bar chart representing tags usage statistics over recent years.

```
<p:barChart value="#{chartController.chartModel}" legendPosition="nw"
style="width: 400px; height: 250px;" />
```

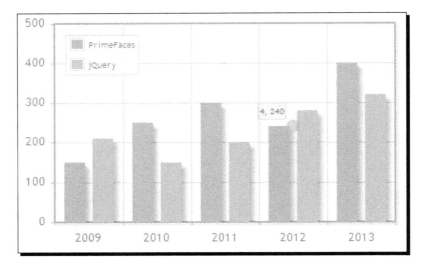

A Bar chart also supports most of the features supported by the Line chart, such as labels and angles for X and Y axis, various `legendPositions`, `seriesColors`, `stacked`, `zoom`, `animate`, custom `dataTipFormat`, and so on. In addition to these options, the Bar chart provides the following options to customize its behavior:

- **barPadding**: This is the padding of the bars. The default value for it is 8.
- **barMargin**: This is the margin of the bars. The default value for it is 10.
- **orientation**: This is the orientation of the bars, the valid values for it are **vertical** and **horizontal**. The default value for it is **vertical**.
- **min**: This is the minimum boundary value.
- **max**: This is the maximum boundary value.

Let us see how we can create a Bar chart with a `horizontal` orientation and custom `seriesColors`.

Time for action – creating a Bar chart

Let us look at creating a Bar chart with horizontal orientation displaying the number of posts with PrimeFaces and jQuery tags from years 2009 to 2013.

1. Create a Bar chart using horizontal orientation with custom `seriesColors` and `dataTipFormat`.

```
<p:barChart value="#{chartController.chartModel}"
  style="width: 400px; height: 250px;"
  xaxisLabel="No. of Posts" yaxisLabel="Year"
  xaxisAngle="45"
  datatipFormat="#{chartController.datatipFormat}"
  legendPosition="se" barMargin="5" barPadding="4"
  seriesColors="A52A2A, 1E90FF"
  orientation="horizontal" animate="true"
/>
```

2. Write a method to return the custom `dataTipFormat`.

```
public String getDatatipFormat()
{
  return "<span>No. of Posts: %s</span>";
}
```

What just happened?

We have created a horizontal Bar chart by setting `orientation="horizontal"`. We have customized the series colors by setting `seriesColors="A52A2A, 1E90FF"`.

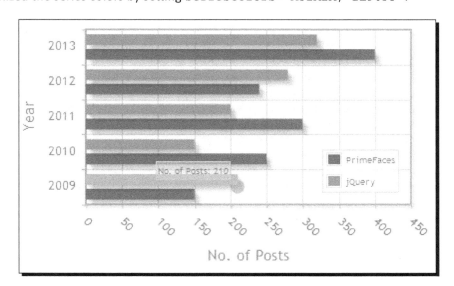

Also we have customized the datatip format using the `datatipFormat` attribute to display the tip as **No. of Posts: 210**.

 For Bar charts with a `vertical` orientation, the first `%s` represents `index` and the second `%s` represents `value`. For Bar charts with a `horizontal` orientation, the first `%s` represents `value` and the second `%s` represents `index`.

We can also create a Stacked Bar chart with bars stacked on top of each other by setting `stacked="true"`.

```
<p:barChart value="#{chartController.chartModel}"
    style="width: 400px; height: 250px;"
    legendPosition="nw" stacked="true"/>
```

Creating a Pie chart

The Pie chart component renders the category data as a Pie chart. The Pie chart uses the `org.primefaces.model.chart.PieChartModel` type instance as a backing bean model.

Let us see how we can create a Pie chart representing the percentage of posts being created with various tags:

```
<p:pieChart value="#{chartController.pieChartModel}"
    style="width: 350px; height: 250px;"
    showDataLabels="true" legendPosition="ne"/>


public class ChartController
{
  private PieChartModel pieChartModel;
  public ChartController()
  {
    pieChartModel = new PieChartModel();
    pieChartModel.set("JSF", 380);
    pieChartModel.set("PrimeFaces", 455);
    pieChartModel.set("jQuery", 202);
    pieChartModel.set("JPA", 180);
  }
  public PieChartModel getPieChartModel()
  {
    return pieChartModel;
  }
}
```

The preceding code renders a Pie chart as follows:

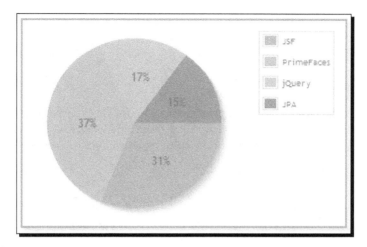

In addition to the `title`, `legendPosition`, `seriesColors`, `fill`, `shadow`, `legendCols`, `legendRows`, `extender` options, the Pie chart component also provides the following options to customize its behavior:

- **diameter**: This is the diameter of the pie, it is auto computed by default.
- **sliceMargin**: This is the gap between the slices. The default value for it is 0.
- **showDataLabels**: This displays data on each slice. The default value for it is false.
- **dataFormat**: This is the format of the data labels. The default value for it is `percent`. Other valid values for it are `label` and `value`.

Let us see how we can create a Pie chart with a custom `diameter`, `sliceMargin`, and `dataFormat` options.

Time for action – creating a Pie chart

In this section we are going to create a Pie chart with various customization options, such as `diameter`, `sliceMargin`, and `dataFormat` showing the total number of posts that are posted with each tag.

1. Create a Pie chart without filling the slices with colors, gaps between slices, and displaying the slice data value instead of the percentage.

```
<p:pieChart value="#{chartController.pieChartModel}"
    style="width: 350px; height: 250px;"
    title="Post Statistics By Tag"
    legendPosition="ne"
    legendCols="2"
```

```
showDataLabels="true"
diameter="150"
sliceMargin="5"
fill="false"
dataFormat="value"/>
```

What just happened?

We have created a Pie chart by disabling the color filling for slices by setting `fill= "false"`. By setting the `dataFormat= "value"`, the slice data value will be displayed instead of the percentage. Also we have specified the custom diameter value instead of using the computed value.

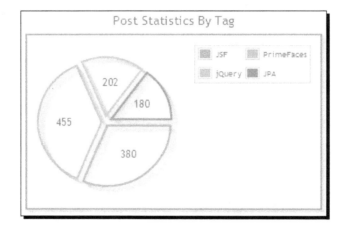

Creating a Donut chart

The Donut chart visualizes a multiseries Pie chart in a single plot. The Donut chart uses the `org.primefaces.model.chart.DonutChartModel` type instance as a backing bean model.

Let us see how we can create a Donut chart representing the number of posts being posted with various tags in years 2011, 2012, and 2013 years.

```
<p:donutChart value="#{chartController.donutChartModel}"
   style="width: 350px; height: 250px;"
   legendPosition="se"
   sliceMargin="5"
   dataFormat="value" />

public class ChartController
{
   private DonutChartModel donutChartModel;
```

```
public ChartController()
{
  donutChartModel = new DonutChartModel();
  Map<String, Number> year2011Circle = new HashMap<String,
    Number>();
  year2011Circle.put("PrimeFaces", 80);
  year2011Circle.put("jQuery", 350);
  year2011Circle.put("JSF", 50);
  donutChartModel.addCircle(year2011Circle);

  Map<String, Number> year2012Circle = new HashMap<String,
    Number>();
  year2012Circle.put("PrimeFaces", 380);
  year2012Circle.put("jQuery", 60);
  year2012Circle.put("JSF", 320);
  donutChartModel.addCircle(year2012Circle);

  Map<String, Number> year2013Circle = new HashMap<String,
    Number>();
  year2013Circle.put("PrimeFaces", 520);
  year2013Circle.put("jQuery", 230);
  year2013Circle.put("JSF", 180);
  donutChartModel.addCircle(year2013Circle);
}
public DonutChartModel getDonutChartModel()
{
  return donutChartModel;
}
}
```

The preceding code renders a Donut chart as follows:

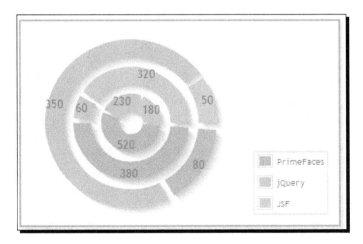

Similar to the Pie chart, a Donut chart also supports `fill`, `sliceMargin` options.

Exporting charts as images

PrimeFaces provides the ability to export charts generated by various chart components as images using the client-side API method `widgetVar.exportAsImage()`.

```
<h:form id="form1">
  <p:lineChart widgetVar="chartWgt"
    value="#{chartController.chartModel}"
      style="width:500px;height:300px"
      title="Linear Chart"
      legendPosition="e"
      minY="0" maxY="600"/>

  <p:commandButton type="button" value="Export"
    onclick="exportChart()"/>

  <p:dialog widgetVar="dlg" showEffect="fade" modal="true"
    header="Chart as an Image">
    <p:outputPanel id="output" layout="block"
      style="width:500px;height:300px"/>
  </p:dialog>
</h:form>


<script type="text/javascript">
  function exportChart()
  {
    $(PrimeFaces.escapeClientId('form1:output')).empty().
      append(chartWgt.exportAsImage());
    dlg.show();
  }
</script>
```

Here, we have created a Line chart with `widgetVar= "chartWgt"`. When you click on the Export button we are calling `chartWgt.exportAsImage()` and appending the generated image to `outputPanel` in the dialog.

 The chart export feature won't work in IE7/8 but it works fine on IE9 and other browsers.

Rendering dynamic charts using the JFreeChart API

PrimeFaces internally uses the jqPlot library, which is based on jQuery, to generate charts using a canvas element. We can also create charts on the server side using the JFreeChart library (http://www.jfree.org/jfreechart/) and render the chart images using the PrimeFaces <p:graphicImage> component.

To add the JFreeChart jar file to the classpath, add the following maven dependency.

```
<dependency>
  <groupId>jfree</groupId>
  <artifactId>jfreechart</artifactId>
  <version>1.0.13</version>
</dependency>
```

Let us see how we can create a Pie chart using the JFreeChart API and render it using the PrimeFaces <p:graphicImage>.

Time for action – creating a Pie chart using the JFreeChart API

In this section, we will demonstrate how to create a Pie chart using the JFreeChart API and rendering it using the <p:graphicImage> and StreamedContent API.

1. Create a Pie chart using the JFreeChart API and attach the PrimeFaces StreamedContent to a stream-generated chart image.

```
import java.io.File;
import java.io.FileInputStream;
import org.jfree.chart.ChartFactory;
import org.jfree.chart.ChartUtilities;
import org.jfree.chart.JFreeChart;
import org.jfree.data.general.DefaultPieDataset;
import org.jfree.data.general.PieDataset;
import org.primefaces.model.DefaultStreamedContent;
import org.primefaces.model.StreamedContent;
public StreamedContent getJfreeChart()
{
  StreamedContent content = null;
  try
  {
    DefaultPieDataset dataset = new DefaultPieDataset();
    dataset.setValue("PrimeFaces", 455);
    dataset.setValue("JSF", 380);
    dataset.setValue("jQuery", 202);
    dataset.setValue("JPA", 180);

    boolean legend=true, tooltip=true, urls =false;
```

```
      JFreeChart chart = ChartFactory.createPieChart("JFreeChart",
        dataset, legend, tooltip, urls);

      File chartFile = new File("jfreechart");
      int width=375, height=300;
      ChartUtilities.saveChartAsPNG(chartFile, chart, width,
height);

      content = new DefaultStreamedContent(new
        FileInputStream(chartFile), "image/png");
    } catch (Exception e)
    {
      e.printStackTrace();
      throw new RuntimeException(e);
    }
    return content;
  }
```

2. Render the chart image using `<p:graphicImage>`

```
<p:graphicImage value="#{chartController.jfreeChart}"/>
```

What just happened?

We have created a chart using the JFreeChart API as an image file on the server side. We have displayed the chart using the `<p:graphicImage>` component by using the `StreamedContent` adapter to stream image file content.

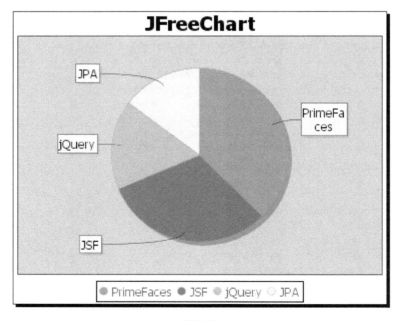

Creating interactive charts using the ItemSelect AJAX event

All of the PrimeFaces chart components support the `itemSelect` AJAX event which gets triggered when a series of charts are clicked on. The `itemSelect` event listener method receives an `org.primefaces.event.ItemSelectEvent` instance from which we can obtain an item index and a series index.

```
<p:growl id="growl" showDetail="true"/>

<p:pieChart value="#{chartController.pieChartModel}"
  style="width: 350px; height: 250px;"
  showDataLabels="true" legendPosition="ne">
  <p:ajax event="itemSelect" listener="#{chartController.itemSelect}"
    update="growl"/>
</p:pieChart>

public void itemSelect(ItemSelectEvent event)
{
  FacesMessage msg = new FacesMessage(FacesMessage.SEVERITY_INFO,
    "Item selected",
      "Item Index: " + event.getItemIndex()
        + ", Series Index:" + event.getSeriesIndex());
  FacesContext.getCurrentInstance().addMessage(null, msg);
}
```

We can use this `itemSelect` event listener to build drilldown charts. For example, when you click on a jQuery slice of a Pie chart, we can use the `itemSelect` listener and show a pop-up dialog with a Line chart displaying the count of jQuery posts over the years.

Summary

In this chapter, we have learned how to create various types of charts, such as Line, Area, Bar, and Donut. We also looked at exporting charts as images using the client-side API. In addition, we have looked into how to create dynamic images on the server side using the JFreeChart library and displaying them as a graphic image.

In the next chapter, we will look into how to use various built-in PrimeFaces themes, and how to build applications supporting multiple themes with the ability to switch themes dynamically.

13
Using PrimeFaces Themes

PrimeFaces components are built with theming support based on the ThemeRoller CSS framework. At the time of writing this book, PrimeFaces provides 38 pre-designed community themes which are ready to use for free. We can also create our own themes using the online ThemeRoller tool and integrate them with PrimeFaces.

Our TechBuzz application will be developed with multiple themes support, and users can select their favorite theme and change to other themes at anytime.

In this chapter we will cover the following topics:

- Configuring and using themes
- Using stateless ThemeSwitcher
- Using stateful ThemeSwitcher
- Creating and using custom theme

Configuring and using themes

The PrimeFaces components come with a default theme support called aristo and doesn't require any explicit configuration. If you want to use other themes you need to add those themes dependencies and configure them explicitly.

PrimeFaces themes are bundled as JAR files and we can download them from PrimeFaces Themes Repository `http://repository.primefaces.org/org/primefaces/themes/`.

Currently PrimeFaces provides the following list of community themes, which are free to use:

◆ afterdark	◆ humanity
◆ afternoon	◆ le-frog
◆ afterwork	◆ midnight
◆ aristo	◆ mint-choc
◆ black-tie	◆ overcast
◆ blitzer	◆ pepper-grinder
◆ bluesky	◆ redmond
◆ bootstrap	◆ rocket
◆ casablanca	◆ sam
◆ cruze	◆ smoothness
◆ cupertino	◆ south-street
◆ dark-hive	◆ start
◆ delta	◆ sunny
◆ dot-luv	◆ swanky-purse
◆ eggplant	◆ trontastic
◆ excite-bike	◆ ui-darkness
◆ flick	◆ ui-lightness
◆ glass-x	◆ vader
◆ home	
◆ hot-sneaks	

If you are using the Maven build tool you can add the `boostrap` theme jar as a Maven dependency as follows:

```
<dependency>
  <groupId>org.primefaces.themes</groupId>
  <artifactId>bootstrap</artifactId>
  <version>1.0.10</version>
</dependency>
```

In addition to these individual theme jars, PrimeFaces provides the `all-themes` jar, which includes all the themes support. In Maven `pom.xml` you can configure the `all-themes` jar dependency as follows:

```
<dependency>
  <groupId>org.primefaces.themes</groupId>
  <artifactId>all-themes</artifactId>
  <version>1.0.10</version>
</dependency>
```

Once the PrimeFaces theme jar(s) are added to classpath, we need to configure the `primefaces.THEME` context parameter in `web.xml`. The following configuration enables the `bootstrap` theme:

```
<context-param>
  <param-name>primefaces.THEME</param-name>
  <param-value>bootstrap</param-value>
</context-param>
```

With the preceding context parameter configuration all the PrimeFaces components will be rendered using bootstrap theme. If you want to switch to any other theme you just need to change the theme name and no other configuration change is required.

Using stateless ThemeSwitcher

The PrimeFaces ThemeSwitcher component provides the ability to change theme on the fly without page refresh. Usage of ThemeSwitcher is similar to the SelectOneMenu component.

Time for action – using the stateless ThemeSwitcher component

Let us see how we can change theme dynamically using the ThemeSwitcher component.

1. Create a `<p:themeSwitcher>` component by providing list of theme names as options:

   ```
   <p:themeSwitcher style="width:165px">
     <f:selectItem itemLabel="Choose Theme" itemValue="" />
     <f:selectItems value="#{userPreferences.themes}" />
   </p:themeSwitcher>
   ```

2. Implement a managed bean method to return the list of all Primefaces supporting theme names:

   ```
   @ManagedBean
   @SessionScoped
   public class UserPreferences implements Serializable
   {
     private List<String> themes;
     public UserPreferences()
     {
       themes = new ArrayList<String>();
       themes.add("afterdark");
   themes.add("afternoon");
   themes.add("afterwork");
   themes.add("aristo");
   ```

```
themes.add("black-tie");
themes.add("blitzer");
themes.add("bluesky");
themes.add("bootstrap");
    . . .
    . . .
themes.add("ui-darkness");
themes.add("ui-lightness");
themes.add("vader");
  }
  public List<String> getThemes()
  {
    return themes;
  }
}
```

What just happened?

The preceding ThemeSwitcher component renders a drop-down menu with a list of themes as follows:

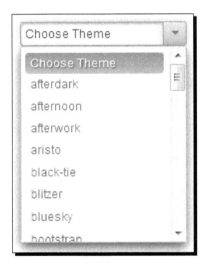

When you select a theme, the selected theme will be applied to the current page without refreshing the entire page.

However, when you navigate to a different screen the page will be rendered using the theme configured in `web.xml`. To keep track of the selected theme throughout the session we can use stateful ThemeSwitcher, which we are going to discuss next.

Using stateful ThemeSwitcher

We have seen how to configure a theme in `web.xml` using a context parameter. Instead of configuring a static theme name, we can bind it to an EL expression, which resolves to theme name.

Time for action – applying a user-specific theme using stateful ThemeSwitcher

In this section we will learn how to use the ThemeSwitcher component to apply theme for entire application based on user preference, and how a user can dynamically switch themes:

1. Configure Primefaces theme name in `web.xml` using EL expression:

```
<context-param>
  <param-name>primefaces.THEME</param-name>
  <param-value>#{userPreferences.selectedTheme}</param-value>
</context-param>
```

Here EL expression `#{userPreferences.selectedTheme}` resolves to a theme name.

2. Create ThemeSwitcher component using `<p:themeSwitcher>` with `value="#{userPreferences.selectedTheme}"` along with the AJAX event listener to update the user-preferred theme to the selected theme name on server side:

```
<p:themeSwitcher value="#{userPreferences.selectedTheme}"
style="width:165px">
  <f:selectItem itemLabel="Choose Theme" itemValue="" />
  <f:selectItems value="#{userPreferences.themes}" />
  <p:ajax listener="#{userPreferences.saveUserTheme}"/>
</p:themeSwitcher>


@ManagedBean
@SessionScoped
public class UserPreferences implements Serializable
{
  private List<String> themes;
  private String selectedTheme = "aristo";
  public UserPreferences()
  {
    themes = new ArrayList<String >();
    themes.add("afterdark");
    . . .
    . . .
```

```
        themes.add("vader");
    }
    public List<String> getThemes()
    {
        return themes;
    }
    public void setSelectedTheme(String selectedTheme)
    {
        this.selectedTheme = selectedTheme;
    }
    public String getSelectedTheme()
    {
        return selectedTheme;
    }
    public void saveUserTheme()
    {
        //logic to update the user preferred theme name in DB
    }
}
```

What just happened?

We have configured a Primefaces theme name using EL expression to apply a user preferred theme. Also we have created a ThemeSwitcher component, which provides the ability to change theme dynamically. When you change theme, the selected theme name will be stored in `userPreferences.selectedTheme` and invokes AJAX event listener method `saveUserTheme()` where you can write logic to persist the user-preferred theme in database. As theme name configuration in `web.xml` is referring to `#{userPreferences.selectedTheme}` the selected theme will be maintained across all pages.

Without AJAX event listener, ThemeSwitcher won't invoke `userPreferences.setSelectedTheme()` immediately when you change theme. Register the `<p:ajax>` event listener if you want to trigger immediate processing of this component as follows:

```
<p:themeSwitcher value="#{userPreferences.
selectedTheme}">
  <f:selectItem itemLabel="ChooseTheme" itemValue="" />
  <f:selectItems value="#{userPreferences.themes}" />
  <p:ajax/>
</p:themeSwitcher>
```

We can also create an advanced `ThemeSwitcher` component displaying a theme preview image along with theme name using the nested `<p:column>` elements:

```
@ManagedBean
@SessionScoped
public class UserPreferences implements Serializable
{
  private String selectedTheme = "aristo";
  private List<Theme> themePojos;

  public UserPreferences()
  {
    themePojos = new ArrayList<Theme>();
         themePojos.add(new Theme("afterdark","afterdark.png"));
         themePojos.add(new Theme("afternoon","afternoon.png"));
         themePojos.add(new Theme("afterwork","afterwork.png"));
    ...
    ...
  }
  public List<Theme> getThemePojos()
  {
    return themePojos;
  }
  public void setSelectedTheme(String selectedTheme)
  {
    this.selectedTheme = selectedTheme;
  }
  public String getSelectedTheme()
  {
    return selectedTheme;
  }
}
```

Here, `Theme` is a simple Java Bean with `name` and `image` properties:

```
<p:themeSwitcher value="#{userPreferences.selectedTheme}"
style="width:180px" var="theme">
  <f:selectItem itemLabel="Select Theme" itemValue="" />
  <f:selectItems value="#{userPreferences.themePojos}" var="t"
         itemLabel="#{t.name}" itemValue="#{t}"/>
    <p:ajax listener="#{userPreferences.saveUserTheme}"/>
  <p:column>
    #{theme.name}
  </p:column>
```

```
    <p:column>
      <p:graphicImage value="/resources/images/themes/#{theme.image}"/>
    </p:column>
  </p:themeSwitcher>
```

The preceding ThemeSwitcher component will be displayed along with theme preview image as follows:

Creating and using a custom theme

In addition to the predesigned themes provided by PrimeFaces, you can also create your own themes using ThemeRoller online tool http://jqueryui.com/themeroller/. To use your custom theme you need to update the generated theme CSS file to the suite PrimeFaces infrastructure and package it as a JAR file.

For creating a new theme go to http://jqueryui.com/themeroller/ and update various CSS styles to match your needs. There are various types of UI widgets on the same page using the theme styles that are currently applied on the ThemeRoller tool, so you can see what the components looks like as you update the styles.

Instead of starting from scratch you can choose one of the existing themes in the **Gallery** tab and edit it:

Let us see how we can create a new theme named **seablue**.

Time for action – creating a new theme

In this section we will look at how we can create custom theme using the online ThemeRoller tool, and convert it into PrimeFaces theme library.

1. Using online ThemeRoller tool update the styles, click on the **Download Theme** button which will take you to the **Download Builder** screen.

2. Uncheck component **Toggle All** checkbox, enter `primefaces-seablue` in the **Theme Folder Name** input box and click on **Download**.

3. Extract the downloaded ZIP file and go into the CSS folder. You can see the following folder structure:

```
primefaces-seablue
  - jquery-ui-{version}.custom.css
      -jquery-ui-{version}.custom.min.css
      -images/
```

4. Now rename `jquery-ui-{version}.custom.css` to `theme.css`.

5. Image references in the `theme.css` file must be converted to JSF resource loading expressions.

For example, `url(images/ui-bg_flat_75_ffffff_40x100.png)` needs to be changed to `url("#{resource['primefaces-seablue:images/ui-bg_flat_75_ffffff_40x100.png']}")`.

6. Package the theme files as JAR with the following structure:

```
seablue.jar
    -META-INF
      -resources
        -primefaces-seablue
          -theme.css
          -images/
```

What just happened?

We have created a new theme called embolden using the ThemeRoller online tool and packaged as JAR file confirming the PrimeFaces themes infrastructure. Now we can use this new theme same as predesigned themes.

 At any time, we can view and modify the customized theme using the URL at the top of the css file generated by ThemeRoller tool. When you go to that URL you can see the ThemeRoller online tool with all the customizations you have applied so far.

We have seen how to create custom theme using online ThemeRoller tool, and convert it into a PrimeFaces theme library JAR file to fit into the PrimeFaces theme infrastructure. However updating the CSS files generated by the ThemeRoller tool manually might be tedious process. There is an online ThemeRoller to PrimeFaces themes converter tool (`https://themeroller.osnode.com/`) to automate this process. You can upload the custom theme ZIP file generated by ThemeRoller tool and provide the desired custom theme name, and then it will automatically convert into PrimeFaces theme JAR file.

Now that you have been introduced to most of the PrimeFaces components that are commonly used in web applications, there are few more components that are very useful based on type of applications.

Drag-and-drop support

PrimeFaces provides drag-and-drop features with various customizations such as, horizontal-only or vertical-only dragging, cloning, revert and draggable within a container, and so on. We can use these drag-and-drop features to build user-friendly rich UIs.

Working with GoogleMaps using the GMap component

PrimeFaces provides GMap component to integrate with the GoogleMaps API with various features such as, Zooming, StreetView, InfoWindow, and so on; which is very useful if you are developing an application providing geolocation-based services.

Multimedia components

PrimeFaces provides various multimedia components to work with images or videos like ImageCropper to crop images by selecting a region, ImageCompare to compare two images, PhotCam to take photos from WebCam, and Galleria to display content gallery with various effects. PrimeFaces also provides a media component, which is a cross browser generic player to embed multimedia content like video and audio with various formats such as flash, Windows Media, RealPlayer, quicktime, and PDF.

PrimeFaces push

PrimeFaces push is based on atmosphere framework, providing support building real time asynchronous applications using transports such as, WebSocket, Server Side Events, Long Polling, Streaming, JSONP, and traditional AJAX techniques.

 For more information see `http://www.primefaces.org/showcase/push/index.jsf` and `https://github.com/Atmosphere/atmosphere`.

The PrimeFaces extensions

The PrimeFaces extensions is an open source component library, which is built on top of PrimeFaces, providing enhanced features along with various additional utilities such as ClientBehaviors, Converters, TagHandlers, and so on.

Time for action – installing and configuring PrimeFaces extensions

Let us see how we can install PrimeFaces extensions and configure it.

1. Configure a `primefaces-extensions.jar` dependency in `pom.xml`:

```
<dependency>
  <groupId>org.primefaces.extensions</groupId>
  <artifactId>primefaces-extensions</artifactId>
  <version>1.0.0</version>
</dependency>
```

2. Add a `primefaces-extensions` namespace and use any of its components. Let us use tooltip component's `autoShow` feature:

```
<!DOCTYPE html>
<html xmlns="http://www.w3c.org/1999/xhtml"
xmlns:h="http://java.sun.com/jsf/html"
xmlns:p="http://primefaces.org/ui"
xmlns:pe="http://primefaces.org/ui/extensions">
<h:head>
</h:head>
<h:body>
  <h:form style="width: 800px; margin: 0 auto;">
    <h:panelGrid column="3">
      <h:outputLabel value="Name:" />
      <p:inputText id="name" value="" title="Enter your Name"/>
      <pe:tooltip for="name" autoShow="true"/>
    </h:panelGrid>
  </h:form>
</h:body>
</html>
```

What just happened?

We have configured a `primefaces-extensions.jar` dependency in `pom.xml` and added its namespace `xmlns:pe="http://primefaces.org/ui/extensions"` in our facelets page. We have demonstrated how to use PrimeFaces extensions tooltip component's `autoShow` feature.

The following are some of the notable extension components:

◆ **DynaForm**: Normally we use static forms with fixed input fields. But in some cases we may need to build forms dynamically based on configurations. In those scenarios we can use DynaForm to build a dynamic form with labels, inputs, and any other input components by using DynaFormModel backing bean. DynaForm component supports expandable extended view area (grid), autoSubmit feature, open/close state saving, and so on.

◆ **MasterDetail**: Displaying MasterDetail form is a common requirement in many applications. The MasterDetail component provides flexible navigation system between master and detail forms with Breadcrumb, Wizard, and Drilldown style of navigation.

◆ **KeyFilter**: The KeyFilter component is similar to InputMask but provides many additional features such as regex based pattern matching, and easy to use predefined pattern aliases.

◆ **Exporter**: Exporter is extension of the dataExporter component with features such as, multiple tables, expandable tables, subtable, grouping, cell editing, customized format, and dynamic columns table. Exporter also supports exporting the DataList component data in addition to DataTable.

◆ **CKEditor**: CKEditor is a **WYSIWYG (What You See Is What You Get)** rich text editor, which provides plenty of formatting options like Microsoft Word and OpenOffice applications. This component is very useful for content posting scenarios such as blogging, forum posting ,and so on.

◆ **TriStateCheckbox/TriStateManyCheckbox**: TriStateCheckbox and TriStateManyCheckbox are enhanced versions of **SelectBooleanCheckbox** and **SelectManyBooleanCheckbox** with three states for undefined, checked, and unchecked mapping to 0, 1, 2 String values.

◆ **Tooltip**: The tooltip extension component enhances the PrimeFaces tooltip component by providing additional features like shared tooltip that can be applied for multiple components based on selector, `autoShow` mode to display tooltips automatically on page load and client-side API to show, hide, and destroy tooltips via JavaScript.

◆ **Timeline**: The Timeline is an interactive visualization chart to visualize events in time with automatic adjustment to timescale on the axis. Timeline events can span across multiple dates or on a single date. Timeline supports zooming and moving events in the timeline by dragging and scrolling.

PrimeFaces extensions provide many more features in addition to the mentioned components in the preceding bullet list. For more information on PrimeFaces extension project visit `http://primefaces-extensions.github.io/` and see a live showcase demo at `http://fractalsoft.net/primeext-showcase-mojarra/views/home.jsf`. If you face any issues you can file bugs at `https://github.com/primefaces-extensions/primefaces-extensions.github.com/issues`.

PrimeFaces mobile

PrimeFaces Mobile is a UI toolkit, powered by jQuery Mobile and PrimeFaces, to create JSF applications optimized for mobile devices. Mobile applications developed using PrimeFaces Mobile can be run on iPhone, Android, Palm, Blackberry, and Windows Mobile platforms. For more information see `http://www.primefaces.org/showcase/mobile/index.jsf`.

PrimeUI

PrimeUI is a JavaScript widget library based on jQueryUI. PrimeUI embraces the latest HTML5 and CSS3 features to build rich UI widgets. Similar to PrimeFaces, PrimeUI also integrated with ThemeRoller and supports multiple themes. At the time of writing this book, PrimeUI provided 35+ UI widgets including the commonly used **Datatable**, **Accordion**, **AutoComplete**, **Dialog**, **Menu**, **Paginator**, **TabView**, **Tree**, and so on. For more information see `http://www.primefaces.org/primeui/`.

As you might already know, no software is bug free. PrimeFaces has a vibrant community forum `http://forum.primefaces.org/` to post any PrimeFaces-related issues or bugs and get help from PrimeFaces experts and other PrimeFaces users. You can also use PrimeFaces issue tracker, `http://www.primefaces.org/issuetracker.html` to file bugs or create new feature requests and track them.

Summary

In this chapter, we have learned how to use PrimeFaces provided themes, and how to use ThemeSwitcher component to change themes dynamically. We have also learned how to create custom themes using ThemeRoller online tool and use it.

PrimeFaces is a rapidly growing open source JSF component suite, and providing more and more components for each release. So keep an eye on what is coming up next in the PrimeFaces ecosystem. For more information, visit `http://www.primefaces.org/`.

We wish you all the best and happy coding!

Index

R

Rating component
about 177
attributes 177
client-side API functions 179
used, for star-based rating input 177, 178
region
blocking, BlockUI component used 80, 81
registration form
dialog, creating with 66-70
RemoteCommand component
used, for invoking server-side methods 32, 34
used, for validating email 32, 34
RequestContext.addCallbackParam() method
used, for adding callback parameters 60, 61
RequestContext.execute() method
used, for executing JavaScript code 59, 60
requestContext.isAjaxRequest() method 58
RequestContext.scrollTo() method
used, for scrolling to component 62
RequestContext.update() method
used, for updating UI components 58, 59
RequestContext utility 58
resizable column feature, DataTable
component 219
row expansion feature, DataTable
component 211
rowspan feature, PanelGrid
component 255, 256

S

Schedule component
about 244
creating 244-246
used, for managing events 244
scrolling feature, DataTable component 218
ScrollPanel component
about 257
used, for displaying overflowed
content 257, 258
search expression framework
about 85
using 86
search users page
displaying, in dialog component 71, 72

SelectBooleanButton component
about 134
used, for creating toggle button 134, 135
using 134, 135
SelectBooleanCheckbox component
about 135
used, for creating Off option 135
used, for creating On option 135
using 136, 137
SelectCheckboxMenu component
about 153
used, for creating overlay menu 153, 154
select Event
used, for selecting tag in TagCloud 231, 232
SelectManyButton component
about 144
using 144
SelectManyCheckbox component
about 137
using 137, 139, 140
SelectManyMenu component
about 152
using 152, 153
SelectOneButton component
about 143
using 143
SelectOneListbox component 150
SelectOneMenu component
about 145
grouping options 148-150
used, for creating drop-down lists 145
using, with editable options 146
using, with filter options 146
using, with POJOs 147, 151
SelectOneRadio component
about 140
using 141, 142
selectors, PrimeFaces 82
server
partial data, submitting to 24
server-side methods
involking, from JavaScript 32, 34
SlideMenu component
about 296
creating 296
used, for creating nested menus 297

Thank you for buying
PrimeFaces Beginner's Guide

About Packt Publishing

Packt, pronounced 'packed', published its first book "*Mastering phpMyAdmin for Effective MySQL Management*" in April 2004 and subsequently continued to specialize in publishing highly focused books on specific technologies and solutions.

Our books and publications share the experiences of your fellow IT professionals in adapting and customizing today's systems, applications, and frameworks. Our solution based books give you the knowledge and power to customize the software and technologies you're using to get the job done. Packt books are more specific and less general than the IT books you have seen in the past. Our unique business model allows us to bring you more focused information, giving you more of what you need to know, and less of what you don't.

Packt is a modern, yet unique publishing company, which focuses on producing quality, cutting-edge books for communities of developers, administrators, and newbies alike. For more information, please visit our website: www.packtpub.com.

About Packt Open Source

In 2010, Packt launched two new brands, Packt Open Source and Packt Enterprise, in order to continue its focus on specialization. This book is part of the Packt Open Source brand, home to books published on software built around Open Source licences, and offering information to anybody from advanced developers to budding web designers. The Open Source brand also runs Packt's Open Source Royalty Scheme, by which Packt gives a royalty to each Open Source project about whose software a book is sold.

Writing for Packt

We welcome all inquiries from people who are interested in authoring. Book proposals should be sent to author@packtpub.com. If your book idea is still at an early stage and you would like to discuss it first before writing a formal book proposal, contact us; one of our commissioning editors will get in touch with you.

We're not just looking for published authors; if you have strong technical skills but no writing experience, our experienced editors can help you develop a writing career, or simply get some additional reward for your expertise.

PrimeFaces Cookbook

ISBN: 978-1-84951-928-1   Paperback: 328 pages

Over 90 practical recipes to learn PrimeFaces – the rapidly evolving, leading JSF component suite

1. The first PrimeFaces book that concentrates on practical approaches rather than the theoretical ones

2. Readers will gain all the PrimeFaces insights required to complete their JSF projects successfully

3. Written in a clear, comprehensible style and addresses a wide audience on modern, trend-setting Java/JEE web development

Instant PrimeFaces Starter

ISBN: 978-1-84951-990-8   Paperback: 90 pages

Design and develop awesome web user interfaces for desktop and mobile devices with PrimeFaces and JSF2 using practical, hands-on examples

1. Learn something new in an Instant! A short, fast, focused guide delivering immediate results

2. Integrate Google Maps in your web application to show search results with markers and overlays with the PrimeFaces gmap component

3. Develop a customizable dashboard for your users that displays charts with live data, news feeds, and draggable widgets

4. Implement a live chat system that uses Prime Push to send updates to desktop and mobile users simultaneously

Please check **www.PacktPub.com** for information on our titles

Java EE 7 Developer Handbook

ISBN: 978-1-84968-794-2   Paperback: 634 pages

Develop professional applications in Java EE 7 with this essential reference guide

1. Learn about local and remote service endpoints, containers, architecture, synchronous and asynchronous invocations, and remote communications in a concise reference

2. Understand the architecture of the Java EE platform and then apply the new Java EE 7 enhancements to benefit your own business-critical applications

3. Learn about integration test development on Java EE with Arquillian Framework and the Gradle build system

Learning JavaScriptMVC

ISBN: 978-1-78216-020-5   Paperback: 124 pages

Learn to build well-structured JavaScript web applications using JavaScriptMVC

1. Install JavaScriptMVC in three different ways, including installing using Vagrant and Chef

2. Document your JavaScript codebase and generate searchable API documentation

3. Test your codebase and application as well as learning how to integrate tests with the continuous integration tool, Jenkins

Please check **www.PacktPub.com** for information on our titles